ANDRÉ CHOURAQUI

A
MAN
IN
THREE
WORLDS

GW00694496

TRANSLATED BY KENTON KILMER

UNIVERSITY
PRESS OF
AMERICA

LANHAM • NEW YORK • LONDON

Translation Copyright © 1984 by

University Press of America,™ Inc.

4720 Boston Way
Lanham, MD 20706

3 Henrietta Street
London WC2E 8LU England

Originally published in French as
CE QUE JE CROIS © Copyright EDITIONS
GRASSET & FASQUELLE, 1979.

Library of Congress Cataloging in Publication Data

Chouraqui, André, 1917-
  A man in three worlds.

  Translation of: Ce que je crois.
  1. Chouraqui, André, 1917-   —Addresses, essays,
lectures. 2. Judaism—Addresses, essays, lectures.
3. Israel—Addresses, essays, lectures. I. Title.
DS126.6.C47A3313   1984   907'.2024   84-15338
ISBN 0-8191-4242-5 (alk. paper)
ISBN 0-8191-4243-3 (pbk. : alk. paper)

ACKNOWLEDGEMENTS

Scripture selections marked (NAB) are taken from the NEW AMERICAN BIBLE copyright (c) 1970, by the Confraternity of Christian Doctrine, Washington, D.C., and are used by permission of copyright owner. All rights reserved.

Scripture selections marked (AC) are translated from the French of André Chouraqui.

The poems, "Be fearless at the gate," "Each glance at you increases thirst for you," and "Seas tranquil for the host of ships well-armed" were published in the Jul-Aug 1982 issue of the NEW OXFORD REVIEW, copyright (c) 1982 New Oxford Review. Reprinted with permission from the New Oxford Review (1069 Kains Ave., Berkeley, CA 94706).

The poem, "I have heard the impassioned weeping of a Rachel," was published in the December 1982 issue of MIDSTREAM. Copyright (c) 1982 by The Theodore Herzl Foundation, Inc. Reprinted with permission from Midstream.

Koran selections are taken from J. M. Rodwell's translation, published in Everyman's Library by J. M. Dent & Sons Ltd, 1909 and subsequent printings. Reprinted with permission from J. M. Dent & Sons Ltd.

TABLE OF CONTENTS

BY WAY OF A PROLOGUE

	Page
A blood compact	1
Abraham among us	2
Of a name and of a destiny	4

I
THE ROOTS

THE ESTRANGEMENT OF THE EXILE
The refusal to die	10
In the lions' den	12
The handing down of the message	14
Magic and superstition	15
Votive offerings to the saints	16
It's he!	18
The mistresses of our destinies	19

THE HEBREW PERIOD
Learning the Bible	23
The hammam	26
The bride sabbath	28
Hitched to the stars	28
The sanctuary overwhelmed	32
The African exile	34
The victory of the Church	41
Under the sign of the Crescent	42

THE ROOTS OF A FAMILY
Natives of Israel	43
Sons of the East	44
Poet and mathematician	45
Statesman and martyr	47
The rejection of the world	49
Faces of my Algeria	51
Baba the Just	52

II
THE UPROOTING

PLUCKING OUT
Our forefathers the Gauls	66
El Cojo	69
The dream at an end	71
Son of the Commandment	72
The course of study for the bachelor's degree	75

The discovery of self   78
The baptism of the desert   79
To be from nowhere   85
The discovery of the West   86
Bisillusion   91
An insufferable violence   94
The pariahs of Europe   97

THE ROADS OF MY RETURN
God exists   98
To the study of Hebrew   100
Intolerance of limits   101
The Cabala   104
The power of prayer   105
Do you tremble?   107

BREAKING THE FURROW
To drink the bitter cup   109
In the Resistance   110
The frenzy of the dialogue   113
The lessons of the heart   113

III
THE RETURN

THE DECISION
Rebirth of Israel   122
Algeria is burning   125

CHANGES
Discovery of Israel   130
The revolution of the return   134
Brought back to life   137
The enthusiasm of the departure   142

GOD IS DEAD
We have killed him   147
The great schism   152
Landmarks   160
To liberate the word   166
The frenzy of the unnamed   175

EMBATTLED BROTHERS
A fratricidal conflict   176
Make ready for peace   182
Reasons for hope   188

EPILOGUE

FOR A NEW PROPHETIC VISION
If not now, when?   198
In deadly peril   200
To conquer hunger   203
Mastering the technique   204
To choose life   206
To come together   210
To conquer death   213
The call from Jerusalem   217
Utopia will come to pass   222

EPILOGUE FOR THE AMERICAN EDITION, 1984   230

Saadyah Chouraqui, the author's paternal grandfather, in Ain-Témouchent, Algeria, in 1913. P. 13.

Abraham Meyer (Baba), the author's maternal grandfather, with Rahmouna, his second wife, in Ain-Témouchent, Algeria. (Undated.)   P. 52.

The author with his family in Aïn-Témouchent in 1921. André is standing between his father's knees. P. 110.

The author at the Oasis of
Ouargla in 1940.   p. 123

The author on a blue donkey
at the Oasis of Ouargla in
1940.   p. 123

The author with David Ben Gurion, during his
tenure as Ben Gurion's Counsellor, 1963.   p. 269.

The author during his tenure as Deputy Mayor of Jerusalem, 1965-1973.   P. 188

BY WAY OF A PROLOGUE

A blood compact

On Saturday, the eighteenth of August, 1917, at the intersection of the Rue Pasteur and the Boulevard of the Revolution, in Aïn-Témouchent, toward noon, Rabbi Shelomoh Amar, clothed in his caftan of ocher silk, sliced with an expert knife-stroke the foreskin of my penis. I was eight days old. My cries, drowned out by the hallelujahs of my family and of our friends, announced to heaven and earth that a son of man had just concluded a blood compact with the God of Abraham. The treatment to which I had just submitted my reluctant body reproduced exactly the actions of the Bronze Age, when, thirty-eight centuries ago, Abraham, servant of the Most High, made with his God a covenant, for himself and for his posterity.

Rabbi Shelomoh had cauterized my wound by blowing on it, out of his toothless mouth, a spirt of an appropriate drug -- which, however, did not prevent hemorrhage. I barely escaped a premature death, thanks to the vigilance of my sister, who discovered in my cradle the bath of blood in which I was about to be extinguished. Such was the ceremony that marked my entry into the world, and my first lesson in religion. I had signed in my blood my witness to the faith of my ancestors.

A body of doctrine is valid to the extent that its witnesses are willing to give their lives for their faith. "To believe...!" "To have faith...!" Words to make one dream! Moreover, for the man that I am, for that ancestor from the Bronze Age who breathes in me, to believe is not only, as Robert's dictionary teaches, "to hold to the reality of a thing," or, as in Littré's definition, "to be convinced that a thing is true, real." To put belief at the level of things dumfounds me. What is the use of holding to the reality of a thing? A thing is or isn't, independently of what I think about it. For me, to believe is not an intellectual proceeding, separated from the realities of life -- of my life. In Hebrew, faith is called emunah, from a root which has given us the word amen. This word expresses the state of being of one who adheres, who assents to what he hears or what he sees. Faith is thus the act of adherence, of

1

assent, to a person or to an idea that becomes incarnate in the man as _amen_ -- as the saying of _amen_.

The point is much more than "to hold to the reality of a thing," or "to be convinced of it." The faith that is adherence engages not only the judgment, but the entire being of a man: his flesh, his thought, his action. Even that bleeding penis whose open wound had narrowly missed killing me!

Abraham among us

Blame Abraham, the patriarch, the knight of faith, as Kierkegaard calls him. Blame Abraham because he held to a God in whom no one had ever wanted to believe, the one God, a God of justice and of love, the God of the word of life, the biological Elohim who would give to him, for himself and for his posterity, the land of Canaan as their dwelling-place. Blame Abraham for my blood-stained penis, and my tormented childhood, and my exiles, and my wars, and even my Jewish search for justice. Blame Abraham for my natal Algeria, torn between Christians, Moslems, and Jews, all of whom claim to be his children; for western racism, that mortal illness; for my departure from France and my return to Jerusalem. Yes, blame Abraham for my deep-rooted Jewishness, my faithfulness to my people of Israel, my studies in Paris at the Rabbinic School of France -- and my departures, like him a big-tent nomad, constantly on the roads of more than twenty-four of the countries of our tiny and splendid planet.

Blame Abraham for what I believe and what I do, what I say and what I write.

"But how can one live as a fossil from the Bronze Age in our atomic era? To be Hebrew, that will do. But Jewish, is that permitted?"

"Hebrew, I am that, and Jewish: of the tribe of Juda, of the land of Juda, and of the religion of Juda, as was said by Jousse. What can I do about that? That comes about without either permission or explanation. Have you ever asked a horse why he is a horse?"

"Heine said it: 'Judaism is not a religion but an affliction.'"

2

"Perhaps, but in that case it can hardly be distinguished from the affliction of being man. If God created man, man invented Satan."

"And both have laid the Jews on our shoulders!"

"Hey then, you, the Jew, it's easy to say, 'Blame Abraham...' First of all, you are plagiarizing Gavroche, who said, 'It's Voltaire's fault...' And then, your Abraham was a man with a complex that made him put on the level of the phallus the sign of his relation with God! Phooey!"

"Since you ask me for an accounting, I will give it to you. And you may well expect it, with compound interest. I have read some ten or more of your recent proclamations of faith. You use high-sounding words; they are always above the level of reality -- who could deny it?"

"Doesn't a catechism have to make a good appearance?"

"I compare what you say, my equals, my brothers, with what you are, with what you live and create, with what you kill and destroy. And I tremble that I must declare, I also, what I believe; I tremble lest I also be a liar, a juggler of words torn apart from the realities of life, of my own life. Stay at the level of the soil. Respect the purity of the language, the chastity of words, the permanent virginity of the real..."

"You speak of virginity?"

"In Hebrew the word virginity, bethulim, exists only in the plural: virginities. There are in us a multitude of virginities, whose unveiling is permitted only to love. This is the truth symbolized by what the Koran says of the houris, forever virgins in Paradise. All love lived absolutely remains virginal."

"But who's talking about love? Tell us how what you believe is worth more than what we believe: we Christians, Catholic, Protestant, or Orthodox; we Marxists or atheistic scientists; or your Moslem brothers."

3

"Surely I won't do that. I hate all apologetics, all speeches in defense of race and family, and I have no denominational interest to defend. I am from 'elsewhere,' I have told you. Isn't that enough for you?"

"From elsewhere, from elsewhere... But from where, then?"

"From the East and from the West, which is the same thing as being neither from the East nor from the West.

"Like the desert palm trees that draw their sap from Quaternary pockets four thousand meters away from their branches, so my life draws its nourishment from the heritage of ages. By capillary attraction, I am an authentic contemporary of Abraham."

"A survival, a fossil! Then Toynbee was right!"

"One of those fossils that come back to life: my language, killed twenty-five centuries ago, has come to life in our day. When you hear it, think that you find in that a reality as astounding as would be a diplodocus or a dinosaur strolling on the Place de la Concorde."

"You arouse my curiosity, but will you know how to satisfy it?"

Of a name and of a destiny

To try to do that I'll speak of the man I am, of my Hebrew roots, of my exile from Africa, of my transplantation into France, of my harsh schooling in the Maquis of Haute-Loire, fighting against Hitler's persecution, then of my return to the Orient of my origin, at the moment of the rebirth of Jerusalem, awaited since the summer of 70, when Titus destroyed its Temple. What I believe rises out of the deep waters of the Bible, carried from generation to generation by my ancestors in their lives, cloistered in order to preserve the sources of their inspiration. The coloring of my belief comes through the prism of history, in French Algeria where I was born to assist at its last hours, in France where I pursued my studies in time to see all the values held by my teachers disappear under the Nazi rule. In Israel,

4

finally, to which I have returned to live in Jerusalem, whose memory my ancestors have treasured through two thousand years of exile, up to the threshold of its rebirth.

I live facing a view -- the Hill of the Temple, the Mount of Olives, Mount Zion, the Valley of Gehenna -- that one of my ancestors, Saadyah Chouraqui, poet, theologian and mathematician, celebrated in Hebrew at Tlemcen about 1680, without ever having seen it.

My time has plunged the world into the atomic age, and I have lived it on three continents:

> Africa, where I was born at the hour when it was preparing to win its independence, in the place where this independence was most dearly bought;

> Europe, where I made my studies in law and in oriental languages in Paris, from which I soon had to flee to take part in the battles of the Resistance;

> Asia, finally, where I have returned to take part in the rebirth of a country, my own, erased from the map twenty centuries ago by Roman imperialism. Counselor of Ben Gurion during the last years of his government, Deputy Mayor of Jerusalem at the hour of its unification in June, 1967, in my maturity I have changed not only my continent, but my language and my culture, stripping myself of the old man I had been in my lands of exile, to be reborn on the glistening rocks of my Judea.

"Nothing is nobler than a man who frees himself of a foreign culture in order to return to his own," wrote André Malraux. He also said to me: "For Jerusalem, there is no such thing as chance." This experience of returning to my spiritual wellsprings, my linguistic origins, my own land and my true culture I have chosen, at the age of forty, in full consciousness of what I was doing. I have deliberately changed my continent and my language; daily, from now on, speaking the Hebrew that I have had to relearn, and no longer the French and Arabic that were my native tongues. I have stopped writing from left to right, and must now draw my letters from right to left. A detail, you will think, but it is one that radically affects the inner equilibrium of a man. Gradually, this Jerusalem in which I have been living for twenty years has made of me another man. I had come here to put my life in accord with my thought and my beliefs. I shall say, then, what the new man I have become believes, speaking from my wellsprings in Jerusalem. What I am talking about is a change, a conversion, a return, which has renewed all my being and my thought, finally making possible, carried by the great currents of contemporary history, the sum total of a name and a destiny.

My identity strangely reflects the places and the cultures that polarize my existence. The registrar of the little town where I was born, Aïn-Témouchent, noted on his records, now kept at Nantes, that on Saturday, the eleventh of August, 1917, at noon, an infant of the masculine sex, named Nathan André, was born, the child of Isaac Chouraqui and of his wife Meleha Meyer. Names have their importance for everyone: each man keeps the name that identifies him, from his birth to, and even beyond, his death, and he suffers when it is badly pronounced or badly written. In those civilizations centered in the word, a person or an object is identified with the words that name it. A change of name, in the Bible, is the same as a change of personality. To identify me, the official record had recourse to the three languages of my cultural roots: Hebrew, Greek, and Arabic. This made of my identity a phrase filled with meaning: Nathan, dimunitive of Nathanaël, meaning in Hebrew God has given; André, in Greek, is man; Chouraqui is derived from the Arabic word that identifies the East, sharq. From this root comes the Greek name Sarakenos, which in English becomes Saracen, to identify men of the East, the Orientals. One branch of my family, that emigrated in the seventeenth century to England, and from there to the United States, simply translated its name into Spanish, and called itself de Levante.

God has given a man from the East. Having named myself, it seems to me that I have expressed the essence of my vocation and my beliefs, nourished by the cultures that have formed me: Hebraic, Greek, and Arab. Since my return to Jerusalem, the phrase that I have as a name, without my parents having wished it or

6

even understood it, has become, geographically speaking, more exact than when I lived in my natal Maghreb or in Paris. The Maghreb, I should perhaps explain, is Northwest Africa, usually understood to comprise Tunisia, Algeria, and Morocco. The stages of my life have carried out the order of my name in restoring me to that Orient from which my ancestors had been expelled, and of which they had not ceased to dream, through two thousand years, until it should be given back to me.

I
THE ROOTS

THE ESTRANGEMENT OF THE EXILE

The refusal to die

The madness of Don Quixote looks calm to me compared to the raging mania of my ancestors ever since they were driven out of Israel. They have never accepted their defeat and the victory of the Roman Empire. The Romans had invaded Judea in the year 63 before the Christian era. They were to occupy the land of the Hebrews through blood-bespattered centuries. The war culminated in the destruction of Jerusalem and of its Temple, the extermination of its people, and the condemnation of the survivors to slavery and exile. Upon this foundation of tragedy we have built our paradoxical existence: the Empire could not renounce the Hebrew territory, which strategically dominated the oriental possessions of Rome; and the Hebrews could not accept the Empire, which savagely repressed all who resisted it. The legions crucified, by the hundreds of thousands, the Jews who opposed the Roman power. For them, the pax Romana was primarily the peace of the cemeteries in which were buried, throughout the Empire, from Spain to Persia, the enemies of Rome. For the Hebrews, there was one circumstance that intensified the conflict; they believed in one sole God. Rome, in their eyes, was not only a detestable Empire, but an idolatrous power, not to be permitted on the land that a jealous God, their own, inhabited. Out of this fact arose the stern determination with which they fought this war that was destroying them. To put an end to this resistance, Rome had to ravage the land, dismantle their fortresses, and destroy even down to their foundations their towns and villages. Pompey had begun this work in 63. Two centuries later Hadrian completed it by plowing the ruins of Jerusalem and sowing the land with salt. Sure that he had destroyed forever the capital and the land of the Hebrews, he gave to the city the name of Aelia Capitolina, and to the land that of Palestine, meaning the land of the Philistines -- no longer of the Judeans, whose name he thought he had effaced. We were therefore exiles, who continued, in our Algerian ghettos, to resist the consequences for ourselves of this genocide. Logic would have dictated that we disappear in the turmoil, like the hundreds of other peoples crushed by the Roman legions, leaving no trace of our culture and no memory of our existence. My

ancestors refused to accept their defeat. The reason
for their resistance is clear: They did not for an
instant believe that the culture of Rome was superior
to their own. Strong in this certainty, they denied
the conclusiveness of their defeat. It was a question
of the honor of their God. Two driving ideas
sustained them in their struggle: the certainty of
the unique worth of their language and their spiritual
heritage, and the certainty of the ultimate triumph of
their God. This triumph was certain, since it was
foretold by the Book that never lies, and corroborated
by the vision of the prophets. The glory of Jerusalem
shone forth in the royal past of Israel. It will be
reborn at the end of the time of the nations, for the
salvation of the entire world, at the hour of the
return. To attain this harbor of salvation, it was
only necessary to repeat, to the point of
breathlessness: "Next year in Jerusalem," and to
believe it through two thousand years.

The glorious folly of the Hebrews of the exile --
who will ever know how to sing its praises? My father
would have been astounded if anyone had told him that
he "believed" something. There was no gap, for him,
between "believing" and "being." He was someone,
quite simply, and he took upon himself his spiritual
heritage as had a hundred and fifty generations of his
ancestors since Abraham, for the rhythms of his life
marched to the pulse of their history.

The practice of the Jewish way of life had become
somewhat more difficult after the destruction of the
Kingdom of Israel, in 720, by the Assyrians, and of
the Kingdom of Judah, in 586, by the Babylonians. The
defeat by the Romans, twenty centuries ago, had again
added to the difficulty of being Jewish, but at long
last there had been time for us to accommodate
ourselves to our situation, and to resolve most of the
problems that exile posed to the war refugees that we
never ceased to be.

"Don't you see that it is insane to set yourselves
up as war veterans, two thousand years after laying
down arms?"

"I see it clearly. Conquered, we were so
thoroughly disarmed that we are probably the only
people in history to have lived through twenty
centuries empty-handed, with neither javelins nor

11

guns, twenty centuries in which our condition, as an unassimilable minority, left us a ready victim of persecution."

"And you have never stopped being the victims of persecution...

"Killed, hunted, robbed, perpetually despised, often reduced to the condition of pariahs, condemned to an inferior status by Moslem law and barely tolerated by Christianity, without any secure rights, without either armed force or defined legal status. But what matter? We were following an indwelling dream so powerful that we were oblivious of the thorns along our road. We were living at two extremes at once: that of the creation of the world, which we never ceased to celebrate in our liturgies; and that of the end of time, in the glory of those final reconciliations for which we ardently hoped."

In the lions' den

The russet mustaches of my father, Isaac Chouraqui, his hair clipped very short, bare forehead, very white skin, and the stretcher-bearer's uniform that he wore on the front in Alsace, at the time when I was born, gave him a Celtic appearance. But King David, wasn't he also a redhead? There are many Tlemcen natives, Arab or Jewish, who stand out by their blondness against the Mediterranean type usual in the region. What struck me most in his appearance was the penetration of his gaze, the gravity of his voice; everything about him bespoke power, solidity, stability.

"He lives his life wisely who knows how to survive even if, like Daniel, he is thrown into a lions' den," he used to say. At that period, the entire earth had become truly a lions' den, and few indeed were the Daniels who could emerge unscathed. A concern for the public good was a tradition in my family. We have many written records attesting to this, even from as far back as the fifteenth century. My father, at the local level of his residence, was for forty years president of the Jewish community, and one of its representatives on the municipal council of the city of Aïn-Témouchent. I greatly enjoyed the talks he gave on great feast-days, in the beautiful synagogue over whose construction he had presided. Today it is

12

transformed into a mosque and Arab cultural center, since there are no Jews left in Aïn-Témouchent. His voice was well placed and his speech customarily slow, but he knew how to impart a sense of urgency and resolution.

My father was one in a family of eleven children: eight boys and three girls. His father, Saadyah, made his living from a farm, and then from a business, from which he could never have drawn much of an income. The sons, after earning the certificates for completion of their studies, had to leave the parental nest and fly on their own, since the most urgent family duty was to provide for the daughters. The choice of a husband was, indeed, the business of the whole family. Rabbis and sage old women would propose matches; but a marriage would be celebrated only when everyone agreed that the match in question was really a good one. The young lady had only to confirm the choice of her assembled kindred. My father, who had fixed his choice upon the eldest daughter of Abraham Meyer, had begun his career by working for a shoemaker, then for a butcher, before he established himself as a wholesale grain merchant. As soon as he could, he bought several hectares of vineyard. My brothers built him a winery in which they made good wines up to the collapse of French Algeria.

To be a son of Israel, for my father and the men of his generation, was to get up each morning before the sun, to go and welcome the day, phylacteries and leather thongs on the head and the left arm, praising the God of Israel for having created the world and chosen his people to serve him. It was to read and chant the Bible in its true language, Hebrew; to know the Psalms by heart, and enrich the daily prayer with them, from dawn to dark. He knew that he was made for this. It was his function on earth; for this he had been created, and this he was obliged to keep up, for himself as well as for his brothers of the exile whom he wished to serve. It was his duty, above all, to make sure of the succession of generations. As he had received his Jewish patrimony from his father, Saadyah, he had the mission of transmitting it intact to his own children. The secret of the permanence of Israel thus lay in the handing down of the message.

The handing down of the message

This transaction began early. As soon as a woman was pregnant she recited the Jewish prayers customary from the earliest times, to bless God, the universal father, for this life implanted in her womb. Some Christian commentators have conjectured that the Magnificat was an apocryphal text inserted, at a later date, into the Gospels. This critical attitude is based on a profound ignorance of the society in which the New Testament originated. In fact, every Jewish woman, as soon as she knows herself the bearer of a new life, says prayers similar to those attributed by the Gospels to Mary. Why should she alone not have pronounced them?

From the moment of his birth, a Jewish child is plunged into a veritable bath of Hebraism. At the head of the bed on which the mother who has just given birth to him is lying, his father, the rabbis, and the midwives pour fourth a torrent of prayers, of Psalms, of excerpts from the Fathers of the Synagogue or from the Cabala, intended to protect him from the "evil eye." By these means it is hoped that the infant will be snatched from the grasp of the demons, whose power over him is the more formidable in that the infant has not yet entered into the covenant of Abraham.

In some communities, strongly rooted in the Arab and Berber soil, and in the belief in the maleficent power of the djinns, each night from the child's birth to the time of his circumcision, there takes place the strange ceremony of the _tahdid_. The mother sits enthroned with her infant on her bed, on which are hung little bags containing a mixture of lavender flowers, thyme, benzoin, aromatic gums and sulphur. Gathered about her, the friends and neighbors partake of refreshments, chant traditional poems, Hebrew, Aramaic, or Arabic, and grow excited as they are captured by the cadence of the dances. As the emotion rises to a peak the father leaps forth from the group, armed with a saber. While the choir of guests chants the rhythmic exorcisms against the djinns, he aims great swings of the saber along the length of the walls, to kill or at least frighten away the evil spirits. The women give out strident cries while fumigating the surroundings with rue, thyme, and artemisia, trying to reach every nook and cranny of the house. The _tahdid_ completed, the saber is placed,

14

as a protective measure, under the mother's pillow, the djinns being thus warned that the child is well guarded.

We were living thus in an atmosphere pervaded with Biblical, cabalistic, or Spanish influences, and our surroundings imposed upon us numerous Arabic and Berber customs. Many among us had Arab surnames or first names. We were living among, and doing business with, the Moslems in an intimacy that permitted all kinds of cooperative association, and encouraged all kinds of syncretism. The superstitions associated with the different religious traditions overlapped and mingled, so that often it was impossible to unravel the tangled threads of their origins. The local magician had as his clients, quite indifferently, Moslems, Christians, and Jews. For almost everyone, life was hemmed in with risks and dangers from occult powers that must be rendered harmless. They believed in the evil eye, in the ^cain ha-ra^c, in djinns and even in the oubeyta, which were born of the mingling of blood from a brother and sister who had died a violent death. In defense, they had recourse to talismans and to all sorts of techniques of protection, ritual phrases, the figure five and its multiples, consecrated hands, and fishes endowed with magical powers to turn away the evil influences.

Magic and superstition

It is an easy slide from superstition down to magic. In grave cases, the magician dispensed his invocations and his potions: enchantments, disenchantments, divination, sacrifices and offerings to the djinns, invocation of the dead. All the ancient agonies of man were still troubling, all around me, the secret soul of the Maghreb. It was customary, even among the Jews, to take part in Negro-Berber magical rites. Most in vogue was the dance called the rabaybiya. The orchestra that played for this dance included a bagpipe, a drum, and a flageolet. When the music was Negro, the ceremony was called stambali, and the instruments were brass castanets, a big drum beaten with a club, and a tambourine.

When a woman was afflicted with some inexplicable illness, or consumption, or nervous or mental troubles, an evil spirit had entered into her and

15

possessed her. To exorcise it, the musicians squatted in a patio, leaning their backs against a wall, while relatives and friends crowded about them, always leaving clear the space in which the magic rite must be performed. The sufferer would take her place there, and the dance begin, accompanied by a slow, monotonous music, whose insistent rhythm gradually accelerated. It would quicken, become jerky and spasmodic, never calming until the dancer had reached a state of ecstatic exhaustion. Hands behind the back, hair flying in the wind, the woman would toss her head forward and back, spasmodically, brandishing in her hands the scarlet kerchief held out to her. At the first signs of fatigue, one of her companions would enter into the dance to inspire her to regain her high pitch of frenzy. The musicians were the only men admitted to the circle of women. When the crowd had reached a fever pitch of excitement, one of the women, in a voice raucous and strangled with emotion, would hurl forth fragments of a frantic chant, to which the choir of women would add a chorus of rhythmic yells. The dance would continue, persistent, overwhelming, all-conquering. Breasts shaking, the dancer would bend, straighten herself, shiver, exhaust herself in wild whirlings, and finish by flinging herself down, beaten, lifeless. This was the sign that the evil spirit that had possessed her had loosed its hold. In a <u>kanoun</u> the women would diffuse a smoke of aromatic herbs, and a sharp and penetrating vapor would enfold the bystanders, isolating them in a beyond, remote from the clamors of the present day. Dark powers were contending, and everyone stood frozen in place, to hear the oracular words of a <u>cera'a</u> in delirium.

The same intensity, drawn from the earliest dawn of the universe, was to be found in all the manifestations of our daily life, in the way in which we took upon ourselves our religious rites and our superstitions.

Votive offerings to the saints

It was easy to trace a Moslem influence in the kind of veneration we paid our saints, in our region, where "maraboutism" often took the place of religion. The Jews venerated some tens of saints in the area called the Maghreb, comprising Morocco, Algeria, and Tunisia. Generally these saints had been natives of

Judea. Other saints spread their influence over particular sections, while local santons, or little saints, were innumerable, each family claiming several of its own. I see myself again, as a child, with my parents, making a solemn pilgrimage to the tomb of Rabbi Ephraïm Enkaoua, on the road from Tlemcen to Bréa. This saint, fleeing from Spain after the expulsion of 1492, arrived at Tlemcen mounted on a lion, and with a serpent for bridle, as the legend tells us with obvious symbolic intent. After saying the ritual prayers, we lighted candles, and then, kneeling before his tombstone, we laid upon it a piece of sugar, sprinkled it with water, and, putting our lips to the stone, sucked up the sweetness.

These saints performed, it was said, ceaseless miracles: they cured the blind, the paralyzed, the mad. They made sterile women become fruitful, and were ready to help the men who appealed to them in all cases, no matter what the circumstances. Their powers were so generally recognized that their devotees were stopped by no sectarian or religious barriers. They were venerated without distinction by Moslems and by Jews, often, even, during the happier periods of the colonial regime, by Christian men and women. All brought offerings to the saints whose protection they wished to ask. In Marrakesh, I have taken part in strange liturgies. One Saturday evening, after nightfall, in an immense cemetery near the mellah, among the crowd of beggars calling out their complaints, I watched toothless old men conducting an impassioned auction, in which the winning bidder was to have the right to light a lamp in honor of the saint of his choice. The list of little saints thus honored at the close of each sabbath would run to dozens of names.

In the spring, we would go in crowds, gathered from all the far reaches of the Maghreb, to celebrate the hillula of Rabbi Shimon bar Yokhaï. The word hillula, in Aramaic, means a wedding. In commemorating the death of a saint, we were celebrating his nuptials with the God of Israel in Paradise, whence he continued, perhaps nineteen centuries later, to watch over his faithful ones. One week before this event, which took place thirty-three days after Passover, the communities that have the privilege of possessing a saint's tomb would prepare to receive thousands of pilgrims in tents especially

set up. Mystic exaltation, nourished by Biblical
chants and cabalistic prayers, swelled as the wave of
pilgrims rolled in, afoot, on muleback, camelback,
donkeyback, horseback, in carts or busses.

It's he!

Rich and poor were intermixed, thousands seized
with the same fervor. All were there to fulfill their
vows and to share in the holiness of the occasion. On
the night of the hillula, the exaltation reached its
peak of ecstasy in the middle of the night. The dense
crowd would intone the Psalms and Hebrew prayers by
the light of oil or acetylene lamps. The strange
light in which the cemetery was bathed accentuated the
emotion that agitated the feelings and the faces.
Each person felt rising in him unknown powers,
liberated by the incantatory influence of the prayers.
Suddenly, cries would break out, become more and more
frequent, and more and more piercing, announcing to
all the long awaited appearance: the saint invoked
had come to his wondering faithful. "There he is,
he's there, it's he!" "Ha houa ja," the crowd would
shout in the ecstatic transport that held them.
Braziers flared up, fed by whole chests of candles.
Pilgrims brought to a fever pitch of excitement would
leap over these flames, while the chants, the cries,
and the dances grew ever more impassioned. "The dumb
speak, the palsied walk, the blind recover their
sight!" The popular voice inflates the tales of
miraculous cures wrought by the apparition of the
saint. Some pilgrims would receive personal
instruction from the saint, others would drink from
the miraculous spring that they saw flowing from the
tomb. The rabbis would urge on the circles where the
Bible or the Zohar was being chanted, while the young
people disappeared into the neighboring woods.

We were trained, from the earliest age, to live in
a supernatural universe. In our ghettos, dispersed in
the immensities of the Maghreb, from Djerbe to Rabat
and Marrakesh, from the Atlas Mountains and the Sahara
Desert to the shores of the Atlantic Ocean and the
Mediterranean, the visitor was seized by some
indefinable perfume of the Biblical Orient, from the
moment he crossed the threshold of our mean dwellings,
at the ends of alleyways, often narrow, and clogged by
stalls where the vendor or the craftworker, squatting

on the ground, employed the same, or almost the same,
techniques as were used in the Biblical Orient.

The mistresses of our destinies

This impression was strengthened by observing the
clothes of those among our mothers and sisters who had
not been captured by western influences. My
grandmothers were dressed in blouses with puffed
sleeves, low, square-cut necks, decorated with a
profusion of little flounces of lace or embroidery,
and in ample sarawals pleated from top to bottom and
fastened with pins. They knew nothing, especially in
the South, of underclothing, except for the brassiere
made of many-colored thongs. In the street the young
women showed themselves wearing a piece of silk or
cotton cloth, the fouta, brilliantly striped, at once
concealing and outlining the rounding of their
haunches. A scarf of gold-embroidered silk covered
the face and completely concealed the hair, whose
exposure would be considered a kind of nudity. The
headdress for show was the splendid coffia,
embroidered with gold and embellished with beads of
gold and silver, gleaming like a crown. Delicate
high-heeled slippers or heavy wooden kab-kabs gave to
their gait a Biblical majesty. Cloaked in their
immense haïks of silk or cashmere, they often had the
appearance of classic madonnas.

In truth they were, in the intimacy of their
homes, the mistresses of our destinies. They held the
reins for a government in which the man was a sort of
minister of foreign affairs: he earned the family's
living, and brought home its food each morning. Even
the richest went every day to the market, immediately
after the prayer which had brought them together, at
dawn, in the synagogue. For the father had, among his
functions, that of representing his family before the
God of Israel in order to bring them the blessings of
Heaven, just as he brought them vegetables, fruits,
meat and fish.

The woman's domain was the home; there she was
all-powerful. Her primary duty was to provide for the
sexual needs of her husband. In consequence, she
would have children, often at the rate of one a year.
Sexual relations were considered by Hebrew law as
first among the rights of a woman in marriage.
Families of ten, twelve, fourteen children were not

19

rare, since deliberately induced abortion was debarred, and contraceptive methods generally unused. For everyone, the supreme value was life.

Our women were fruitful. They expected to spend, on the average, a dozen years or more in their capacity of breeder, entering so well into that role as to forget, or almost to forget, the rules. Biblical law forbids sexual intercourse for several days before, during, and after menstruation. Since the blood is the being, is life itself, the woman who is losing blood is forbidden to man. Any contact, even hand to hand, is forbidden to the married couple, who must sleep apart during these times.

The harshest suffering, for all, was to undergo so many miscarriages, and to see so many nurslings die. Such deaths were familiar in our families; of the ten children to whom my mother gave birth, only six reached maturity. I was her ninth child.

To have children was everyone's obsession. When I was six or seven years old, I was asked one day: "What will you do when you grow up?" And my answer was: "Have twelve children." Sons were evidently preferable; they assured the perpetuation of the "seed," of the succession and of the name, before the God of Israel. But if the child happened to be a girl, she was nevertheless welcome for the help she would bring to the household, in the care and rearing of the infants to come. The more the family increased, the more the mother, always aided by the grandmother and innumerable aunts, saw her task lightened. A family of two or three children was for her a heavier burden than a dozen, fourteen, or sixteen offspring. As in the beginning, procreation itself was of great value. It was a supreme achievement, applauded with admiration and envy by the men, and viewed with bitter shame and self-blame by the sterile woman. Such a woman would end by resolving to give her husband a second, perhaps even a third wife, since polygamy was legally permitted under Hebraic law, so long as it had not been replaced by the French code. The problems that arose in the polygamous household were, all in all, just more open than those that arise in our present-day arrangements of legal monogamy, rarely respected in actuality. Hypocrisy and lies become superfluous when a free woman who gives herself to a married man can officially take her place in his household and enrich it by her presence, her fruitfulness, and her labors.

The wife's rights were, however, no less guaranteed; if she were unwilling to share in this fashion, she could have her husband renounce polygamy by a particular clause included in the contract of marriage. Furthermore, the great ease of divorcing or repudiating a spouse gave to her, as well as to him, the right to succesive marriages. I have known women who have had legal weddings a score of times. These were extreme cases; for the great majority, the monogamous household held together solidly, the possibilities offered by law only strengthening the bond between the man and his covenanted bride.

The behavior of human beings, however we try to regulate it, remains the same in all kinds of social surroundings. Polygamous or polyandrous temperaments go their own way outside of marriage wherever strict monogamy is enforced, as no one denies; while men and women faithful by nature remain so without fail, even in societies where polygamy is legal or divorce to be had for the asking. In such societies, at least, there is no need of dissimulation to cover over the realities of the marital customs. Let us remember, in conclusion, that the Biblical law, like that of the Koran, permits polygamy. Its exercise has been prohibited since the eleventh century to Jews in Christian countries, but has remained in practice for Jews in Moslem countries, so long as they remain subject to Biblical law. Under Western influences, the State of Irael has decreed the strict monogamy of marriage. It allows polygamy only for Moslem citizens, or for Jewish immigrants coming from Moslem countries, and already possessed of two or more wives at the time of their arrival in the country. Insofar as it re-Orients itself, the new Israel, in the freedom of its Biblical roots, will be led to reconsider its rules of sexual morality. What it decrees today is the heritage of the medieval traditions of its western ghettos. As in Christian societies, this rule condemns too many men, women, and couples to dissimulation and hypocrisy. We must have the courage to reopen the dusty old code books, and to propose revisions that take into account the customs both common in the Bible and often existing today in our own territory.

The sexual life of the couple must be based on the ardor, the detachment, the unity and the light of love. This light must exclude all shadow of death, all abortion, all falsehood. Continence, freely undertaken, can maintain love, or it can destroy a conjugal life that does not, through its clear transparency, open itself to this light. The Biblical society practiced a legal polygamy that inclined toward a factual monogamy, and the legal monogamy of the west often degenerates into a clandestine polygamy. To free both the man and the woman in the life of the married couple, it remains true that nothing solid can be built on a foundation of pretense or falsehood -- least of all, love.

The desire to have children was exalted among us by the deliberate intention of perpetuating, not only the existence of the individual and of the family, but also, and even more urgently, the life of our people, Israel. We were a tiny minority, a dusting of individuals and communities scattered over the world, and we had taken upon ourselves the impossible mission of saving our language, our culture, and our Bible, until the hour of our return and our restoration in Israel, brought back to life around its capital, Jerusalem.

Through the ages of exile, each birth was an affirmation of our national existence, and gave us one more chance to persist and to conquer. Beyond that, each child had the possible vocation of being the Savior of Israel. The altar upon which we were circumcised was called the Throne of Elijah the prophet, because it was he who was to be the herald of the Messiah. After our overwhelming defeat by the Roman legions, we went on repeating, through two millenia, that a man was as important for our people as the Temple itself. We were thus literally haunted by the hope of salvation promised by the Bible, our own salvation, and that of all the world.

The education we received locked us into this obsession, the woman being the door-keeper. She it was who washed us, clothed us, fed us, taught us, and trained us in all the techniques of social life, and, most important to all, the art of being a son of Israel. The mother was the true sustainer of tradition, the priestess of the home, whose purity she protected in her bed, in her kitchen, at her table.

To bring up a child was for her to flood him with an inexhaustible torrent of love and attentions. Each one was, in her eyes, "a lion," "a genius," chosen for a most exalted destiny, and most certainly "the savior of his people." For each one of them she was ready to sacrifice herself, to let herself be cut into little bits from morning to night, and night to morning; and she did this with an untiring availability, a joy in every moment. She existed only for others, rejoicing ceaselessly in mothering them from the moment she received the semen in her womb until her very last breath. Having neither public life nor political power, normally fated to be the wife of one man only, resolved to be chaste before her marriage and faithful after it, she poured out about her, in her home, all her loving and creative power. Whenever the family came apart, usually on account of the weakness of the husband, the children received, alone, the full measure of her love.

THE HEBREW PERIOD

Learning the Bible

The father, and the rabbi, whose courses the child followed from the time he could stand, bestowed knowledge: how to read and chant the Bible, how to practise the commandments every day, how to understand the most obscure verses of the prophets, or to come to grips with a page of the Talmud or of the Cabala. It was the most important of our concerns; and first of all one must learn to read. The father and the rabbi taught us the letters, and, to make quite sure we would know how to recognize them, our mothers would make us twenty-two honey cakes in their shapes, and we would eat them with delight. Aleph, beth, gimel... The alphabet, and then each verse of the Bible, were thus going to become flesh in us; this custom echoed the gesture of Ezechiel in eating a scroll of the Scriptures. This was, indeed, a taking in of the word destined to make of us, the Children of Israel, living Bibles. Nobody escaped this. The rabbi gathered us in the synagogue and from daybreak on he taught us to read our earliest verses written on wooden tablets, indicating each syllable with a reed sharpened to a point. He made us repeat the verse twenty, thirty times, until we knew it by heart.

Discipline was ensured by corporal punishments. The most trifling of these was receiving on our little hands, held out, but shrinkingly, as many blows of the rod as we had made errors. The most severe was the _tahmela_, which consisted in applying to the soles of the feet of the culprit a shower of vigorous blows of a rod, sometimes enough to bring blood. The legitimacy of such educational methods might well be disputed, but not their efficacy, demonstrated through centuries. The class proceeded smoothly, and we zealously took in all that we were supposed to be taught. Through alternate strokes of honey cakes and _tahmela_, the whole Bible took possession of our minds, of our hearts, of our memories. Body and soul, we were embarked upon the adventure; praying, studying -- our entire being was involved in the performance. Even our bones had to sing the glory of YHWH, our God, along with our voices and our flesh. The rhythmic movement of our bodies helped in the memorization of the text. The best among us knew by heart, in Hebrew, the entire Bible. Ancestral and national tradition were thus enrolled in the biblical tradition which we all held to be divine. Since the Word was divine, its memorization had power to make it incarnate in us; we were lifted up by its divine breath and its sanctifying power. In the weakness of our exile, we were thus fortified to await the coming of the Messiah and the end of the world.

At home, our lives had for their sole center God, really present among us, in adherence to the religion of our ancestors. We lived essentially cut off from the rest of the world, focused on the rhythms of the Hebrew seasons, since, in defiance of all right reason, we were living in the time of Jerusalem, in the fifth millenium since the creation of the world. A day consisted of three prayers: that of dawn, under the guardianship of Abraham; that of noon, dedicated to the blind patriarch, Isaac; and that of the evening, devoted to the memory of Jacob, the lover of Rachel. Abraham, Isaac, Jacob, Moses, Aaron, David and Solomon were so close to us they seemed to be living in our house. Bibles in Hebrew were everywhere. Each meal was marked by a long prayer that put us in the presence of the creator of heaven and earth, the preserver, the redeemer. We were thus thrown back upon a fixed idea, that of the affliction that had been visited upon us, of the exile that weighed us down, of the hope for our return in glory, at the end of all exiles, to the land promised and given by God to our ancestors. Every time we ate a mouthful of bread, we prayed God to draw together our scattered people, to restore our country, to rebuild the city and the Temple of Jerusalem: "Build Jerusalem, the City of the Sanctuary, speedily and in our own time." And to be more sure of being heard, we thanked him in advance for doing it, by adding: "Blessed are you, Lord, builder, from its foundations, of Jerusalem. Amen."

We were exacting, insistent, unruly in requiring of our father in heaven, immediately and without delay, paradise, life, peace, and everything good -- that he reign over us forever and that he glorify himself finally in us, from eternity to eternity. Even Doudani, the itinerant hawker of books and papers, and Mouchi, the beggar, demanded of God, three times a day, not only that he sustain us well, but also that he break the yoke upon our necks, put an end to our exile, and finally bring us home to our own country. "We await," they said also, "Elijah, the herald-prophet of the Messiah, and his message of salvation and consolation." We were all awaiting, feverishly, the day of the Messiah and the life of the world to come. Fallen princes, in the humiliation of our ghettos, we remained the helmsmen of history, the stubborn guardians of a culture, the Hebrew, destroyed twenty-five centuries ago. We were the seed of its resurrection.

Nothing else counted for us; only this, to live and die in the light and according to the rule of the Bible. A week meant, in addition to the daily prayers, at the synagogue and at meals, the public reading of the Torah on Mondays and Thursdays; and it was, above all, the time that flowed from one sabbath to the next sabbath as a month did between two new moons. We were thus attuned to the cosmos as well as to its creator. For us, the sabbath commemorated the creation of the world. Since God had created the world in six days and rested on the seventh, we had to follow his example, working during the week, and abstaining from work on the sabbath.

25

The hammam

What delight, that day! We kept thinking of it all week long, and from Thursday evening on everyone got furiously busy in getting ready for it: houses cleaned and adorned, our clothes seen to by our mothers, hair and nails clipped for the entire community, and the men, women and children went to the hammam, the Moorish bath, to be as thoroughly clean as possible. We went in family groups, the men in the morning and the women in the afternoon, to take our steam baths in the hammam on the grounds of my grandfather's house. The Meyer bath had the reputation of having the best masseurs in the country. When they judged that we had worked up a sufficient sweat, they would spread us out on the burning hot slab and throw themselves upon us, on each muscle, bone, and joint; not a bit of our skin would escape the kneading of their expert fingers. We would feel our bodies becoming as supple as rubber in their hands. Our heads between our legs, our arms became handles from which we hung while they took off rolls of dirt from our skins as they peeled off the scurf. My black masseur, Bouali, had learned his skill from his father, for the office was hereditary. Techniques of massage reaching back to the Iron Age had thus been passed down through families. Bouali would not let go his hold at the end of his treatment until after he had soaped us from head to foot with a rough cord of yellow alfa-grass. He would rinse us by pouring out over us, in the semi-darkness of the bath, a bucket of ice water. One would be a son of Israel, all new and all pure, after being plunged three times in the water of the ritual bath, built in the dimensions demanded by the Talmud, in which God dissolved our impurities and freed us from our faults as Bouali had done with our dirt. Complete immersion was obligatory any time we knew ourselves to be in a state of ritual impurity, after any emission of sperm, any contact with a dead body, or, for women, after their menstruation. We, being thus rid of our impurities, physical and moral, stretched on the mattresses in the resting room, sipped with a knowing deliberation the green tea, flavored with fresh mint, that the master of the bath-house had prepared for us. We breathed in the brew, more than drank it, the better to appreciate its varied flavors as they reached our lips, our tongues, and our palates. It was fashionable to give a deep sigh of satisfaction after each mouthful. The glassful swallowed, the body relaxed and cooled, we were finally free to devote ourselves to the idle chatter of the weekend. It was here that the events, great and small, of the town were made known. Ritual, too, were those little round gilded loaves, intended, like our cleansed selves, to welcome and celebrate the completion of the creation of the world. My mother yielded to no one else the privilege of kneading the sabbath bread, which was called, in the colony, Jewish bread. She made it with her own hands, and the first to be taken from the oven was distributed to the poor. As children, we breathed deeply, filling our lungs with the smells that came from the kitchen where my mother, my three sisters, and the servants were busy from morning to evening in preparing the couscous for Friday evening and the _tafina_ for Saturday morning. This had to cook all night long so that it could be eaten, just done to a turn, after the prayers at the synagogue. There were also, of course, salads seasoned with oriental spices, meats, broiled fish with savory herbs, and a bewitching succession of cakes, made with almonds and with honey, masterpieces of generations of cloistered women, busied with making children and feeding them on the most delicate and exquisite confections of puff paste.

Dressed in fresh clothes, we presented ourselves before the God of heaven and earth to say to him, not without a suggestion of reproach: "You see, even in the terrible exile in which we live, we still stubbornly remain your witnesses. You seem to have forgotten us, your sons, your people. But we, we will never forget you."

Psalm 139 expressed perfectly our love for a God at once absent and present: wherever we went, we could not stray far from his spirit, nor could we escape his all-seeing eyes. Our days and our nights were filled with the interminable dialogue that we carried on with him, all of us: the old and the wise, of course, but also and especially the children, the women, and even Zouzou, the tuberculous carter, Touitou, the blind drunkard, and Nedjma, who was said to be a man of loose morals.

The bride sabbath

The liturgy of the sabbath began on Friday evening before sunset with the public chanting of the Song of Songs. This poem of passionate love, full of the most vivid images, apparently devoid of any reference to God, and whose narrative describes a naked couple, the birth of their love, their downfall, and finally their triumphant union, was chanted in full voice by our entire community, including women and children, without equivocation or the slightest constraint.

> He will kiss me with the kisses of his mouth.
> Yes, your caresses are better than wine...
> I belong to my lover and he belongs to me,
> The shepherd in the field of lilies. . .*

We declaimed the verses that described the thighs, the breasts, the belly of the Shulamite, her embraces, her delights in the arms of her shepherd with the same candor with which we chanted the Psalms of David. Small farmers, craftsmen, tradesmen, civil servants, teachers or doctors, old people or children, men and women, learned or ignorant, we were at one in seeing in this love poem the allegory of the eternal nuptials of God with his people. And since the love of mankind feeds upon the love of God, most children were conceived on that night on which the sabbath nuptials between God and Israel were celebrated.

Hitched to the stars

To preserve the survivors of the Roman massacre required a procedure perfected through twenty centuries by certain rabbis who undertook to snatch from annihilation the people and the culture of an Israel expelled from its land, deprived of its strength, and subjected to the law of Rome throughout the extent of the Empire. They set themselves to this task with such success that nothing could penetrate the shell under which, thanks to them, the Jews could live through twenty centuries of exile without losing their identity. In order to preserve both the men and the books, it was necessary that each man become a

---

*Song of Songs, 1,2;6,3.AC

28

book, each book a man. Time had to transform itself into the time of the Book, and the exiles, wherever they went, had to carry with them the land of Israel, without forgetting a bit of it, even for an instant. They had to live only for Jerusalem, in their mystic Jerusalem, which they must carry to the ends of the earth, and even to the end of time, in the deep-rooted and stubborn expectation of the return.

This was the pattern of our lives. From birth, our fathers and our rabbis made us swallow, willy-nilly, the Holy Scriptures in Hebrew. I have known children of ten who could recite by heart entire books of the Bible. There have been many men able to recite, hour after hour, whole chapters of the Torah, of the Prophetic Books, and of the biblical and rabbinic Writings. Each little community had its scholars, tirelessly devoted to the clarification of Mosaic jurisprudence, the rules of the Talmud, or the mysteries of the Cabala.

Time itself had turned Jewish for us. I have told what a day or a week meant in our family. Our calendar took no notice of the Christian measurement of time, nor of the very different Moslem measurement. Christians measured time chiefly by the sun, Moslems by the revolutions of the moon. We, the sons of Israel, marked our time by both sun and moon. Like the Moslems, we had a lunar month, but, in agreement with the Christian way, our year corresponded with the apparent annual revolutions of the sun. Periodically, therefore, we had to have an embolismic year, in which a thirteenth month allowed the lunar year to catch up with the solar year.

Thus hitched to the stars, our time kept faithfully to the shores of the Bible. On our New Year's Day, we celebrated the most universal of feasts, that of the Creation. Ten days later, it was the Day of Atonement, Yom Kippur, when we proclaimed the coming Last Judgment and the end of the world. These solemn festivals were accompanied by a month of extreme austerities. We were all in the synagogues, from three o'clock in the morning, praying for forgiveness for our faults. On Yom Kippur, we fasted from one sunset to the next. We would have let ourselves be cut to pieces rather than to drink a mouthful of water or eat a crumb of bread on that day, when God would decide on the life or death of everyone. The forgiveness for which we prayed reached out to the nations of the entire world. Between the two temporal poles of the Creation and the end of the world, there existed nothing but the penance of our earthly exile, illuminated by the gift of the Bible, which lived in every breath we took, in every hour of our existence.

After these cosmic and solemn observances, the rest of the year was marked for us by the commemoration of the three great Biblical feasts, Tabernacles, Passover, and Pentecost.

For the Feast of tabernacles my grandfather Abraham Meyer would abandon his big house to live in a tent built of reeds and decorated with tapestries, that he built each year on his terrace. This had been the period of the autumnal labors in the fields of Israel. At Aïn-Témouchent also, among our cactuses and our oleanders, we had to remember that, like our ancestors the Hebrews, we were nomads cast out forever into the deserts of history. So we were obliged, each year, to go out of our bourgeois homes and live in the discomfort of our flimsy tents. What a delight it was!

Passover, also, was the celebration of a departure, which our fathers imitated in rising from the table to go forth from the land of bondage. Each year they put an end to their exile, and set their feet on the road for the Kingdom of God and its capital, Jerusalem. This feast involved us once more in a departure, and a liberation. Jewish houses were thoroughly cleaned, to make sure of getting rid of the smallest crumb of leavened bread. The houses, like the hearts, must be cleared of all leaven. They were repainted, adorned, decorated in the joy of a springtime in which men and nature together sang the lively delights of the Song of Songs. The "bread of poverty" that we ate, the round flatbreads prepared at home, before industry started sending them to us from Oran, from Algiers, and later from Jerusalem, seemed to us delicious. Their taste was to us that of a decisive setting forth toward freedom, the taste of the marvelous, of the miraculous. We cried it out with all our strength in the liturgy of the passover meal; it was not our fathers only who were come forth from Egypt, but we ourselves like them, and with them. My father, at the beginning of the meal, would stand,

holding up in both hands the ritual platter of the
passover meal, with the sacrificial lamb, the bitter
herbs, and a sort of nougat that represented the
mortar of our ancient servitude. He would pass it
over our heads, walking around the table, chanting:
"Yesterday we were the slaves of Pharaoh. Today we
are here. Tomorrow we shall be free men in
Jerusalem!" In pronouncing the name of the Holy City,
Yerushalayim, he would hold the platter on my head for
a long time, because I was the youngest of the family,
and then everyone would answer in a loud voice:
"Amen, amen."

These gestures, and these words, we have been
repeating each year for two thousand years. But the
platter would surely have fallen from those fatherly
hands if anyone had then said to us that our prayer
was heard, that the road to Jerusalem would open
speedily and in our own time, before us -- that the
hour for return had at last struck, and that little
André, grown up, would really live in Jerusalem. For
him, Utopia would become history.

The last of our feasts, Pentecost, seven weeks
after Passover, denoted the gift of the Torah, the
entrance of the Bible into the course of our lives,
the instant when prehistory became history. We were
then brought forth out of Egypt, we wandered in the
desert after our miraculous deliverance when, before
our very eyes, Pharaoh's army had been swallowed up in
the waters of the Red Sea. Gathered together before
Mount Sinai, we received the Torah from the hands of
Moses. God was present among us to give us these
books, his word of life and truth.

The parchment scrolls, upon which the Five Books
of Moses were written, were our true, our only
fatherland. They were enthroned in the coffer of the
synagogue of Aïn-Témouchent at the true center of our
life. We brought them out of their cupboard to go
with them in procession up to the pulpit, where we
disrobed them as one might do with a bride, to drink
eagerly of the springs of wisdom. We danced with them
in our arms, intoxicated by our song:

The voice of the Lord on the waters,
The God of glory thunders,
The Lord on many waters,
The voice of the Lord in power,

The voice of the Lord in splendor,
The voice of the Lord breaks the cedars,
The Lord breaks the cedars of Lebanon...
The voice of the Lord carves the flames of fire,
The voice of the Lord makes the desert tremble.
He causes to tremble the desert of Kadesh.
The voice of the Lord makes the oaks tremble,
And he despoils the forests.
In his palace his all says: "Glory!"*

We were the many waters, the fiery flames, the
desert of Kadesh, the despoiled forest, the oaks and
the cedars of his palace. We trembled as we cried
out: "Glory!" as one cries out: "Have mercy!" Our
flesh and our bones sang and danced to the tune, harsh
as our solitude, of a triumphant march which I cannot
now evoke without trembling again.

The sanctuary overwhelmed

These feasts burned us inwardly, left in us acid
to eat away our indifference. They kept us constantly
on the watch, day and night, from the beginning to the
end of the year, in a sustained exaltation, that of
our deeply felt vision. When we commemorated the fall
of Jerusalem and the destruction of its Temple, in the
midst of the dog-days of August each year, the ninth
of Ab, our mourning was as intense as though, in each
household, we were bewailing the loss of a spouse, a
betrothed, or a mother. As a sign of this mourning,
we would cover the mirrors with great white cloths
that took on, in my childish imagination, the look of
ghosts. Before fasting, we took our last meal seated
on the ground, in the deepest sadness. At that time,
our reading from the Book of Lamentations would be
interspersed with our sobs, and mingled with the
strident cries of the mourners. It was a tragedy, so
actual for us that during thirty hours of the
strictest fast we were prostrated by it. The men
didn't shave throughout the month of Ab, as though
mourning the death of a father. They abstained from
every joy, from women, from music, from drinking, in
their unfeigned grief.

---

*Psalm 29: 3-5,7-9.AC

32

"But, after all, isn't it crazy of you to fast for 1908 years because Titus captured Jerusalem and destroyed a temple hardly any bigger than a village church? Nations have lost empires without regret or remorse. What would you do if you had lost, not a tiny kingdom subject for centuries to foreign conquerors, but a great empire?"

"No doubt we would fast four times a week -- and to the end of time!"

But we have lost no empire; it is the Empire that has lost us. This is what we have never been able to forget; that we shall never forget. Our Temple, in our eyes, was more than a place of worship. It was, for us, the sole point at which the eternal uncreated and the creation could come together. The victory of Titus sent us forth on the roads of our wanderings; but, along with us, our God himself was involved in the exile. His true name, YHWH, could be pronounced only in the Temple on the Day of Atonement, as the high priest offered the sacrifice for the salvation of the seventy nations of the earth. The Temple once destroyed, the ineffable name could never again be pronounced by anyone. We, a remembering people, who have forgotten nothing of our history or of our books over thousands of years, we are stricken with an amnesia concerning the essential: we no longer know how to pronounce the name of our God, to whom we consecrate all our existence. We must designate him by the four letters YHWH, unpronounceable, even by us. But his land, his Writings -- those we have hugged to ourselves so strongly that they have never ceased to stick to our skin. This phenomenon amounts to a veritable hallucination, which was condensed into a line of verse by Judah Halevi, a poet who lived in Spain in the twelfth century:

I live in the West, but my heart is native to the East."

"Classical schizophrenia. Just what I've always thought; schizophrenics, that's what you are, all you Jews of the exile."

"Maybe you're right. But what can we do about it? We can neither disown that elsewhere from which we come, nor go back to it. Hence our loss of contact, as it were, with reality."

33

The African exile

Since Roman times, or perhaps even further back
than that, Jews have taken refuge in the villages on
the peaks of the Grand Atlas, at an altitude of about
four thousand meters; and even after the passage of
twenty centuries they still call the Moroccan tribes
that surround them by the names of the peoples amongst
whom they lived in Judea before the exile: the
Jebusites, the Canaanites, the Moabites, the
Ammonites, etc. They have thus carried along with
them, not only their language, which they continue to
speak, their religion and their culture, which still
constitute their way of life, but even their
geography. The places to which they have been exiled,
and the peoples among whom they now live, remain to
their minds those places and peoples that they left
two millennia ago. Upon everything we look at, we
project the aspect of Jerusalem, of the "elsewhere"
which that City, our haven on the shores of eternity,
has never ceased to be for us.

The complexity of the universe in which I was
living was built out of those Hebraic loyalties that
had resisted the successive pressures of the different
empires that, in the Maghreb, served as the scale by
which we could measure our own continuity. Carthage,
Rome, the Vandals, Constantinople, the Arabs, and the
Turks encountered on their African route a scattering
of disorganized and powerless exiles, who,
paradoxically, were to survive the collapse of all
those imperial powers. Even before the country from
which we came, the land of Israel, had fallen victim
to the blows of the Roman invader, and up to the
resurrection of that land in the atomic age, through
more than two millennia, the Jews knew, in Barbary,
times of flowering marked by the expansion of their
religious ideas among the Berbers, and of defensive
withdrawal, following their national annihilation and
the triumph of Christianity in the Roman Empire, and
then the secluded life throughout the twelve centuries
of the rule of Islam.

The after-effects of this long history were as
evident in us and around us as the different levels of
an archaeological site. We carry family names and
forenames that disclose in us traces of the oldest
Berber past of the Maghreb. Whole communities of
Judaized Berbers, or Berberized Jews, use in their

daily conversation that Indo-European language that has persisted through almost three thousand years of Semitic influence. Even in our own time, some Jews celebrate in Berber the Passover liturgies, which we continue to chant, as Jesus did, in Aramaic and in Hebrew. In many of our rites, customs, and superstitions, it is possible to detect the survivals of the Maghreb's pre-history, grafted upon our ancient Hebraic trunk.

The conquest of North Africa by Carthage, beginning in the year 813 before the Christian era, marks the entry of the Maghreb into history. From that time on, it was never out of the orbit of the Semitic world. The Phoenicians introduced their language, a sister tongue to Hebrew, their culture, and their religious traditions. The rabbis profited by this profound Semitization of North Africa to spread their religious propaganda throughout the region: this effort succeeded in converting the Berbers, or Judaizing them, to such effect that the Middle Ages circulated the legend that the Berbers had originated in Canaan. Another tradition declared that the original home of the Jews was neither in Mesopotamia nor in Egypt, but in the Maghreb, whence they had emigrated into Judea. According to this tradition, Joshua, the successor of Moses, set forth from North Africa for the conquest of the Holy Land; and it is in North Africa, at Nedroma, that his tomb is, even to our own day, the object of devotion among both Moslems and Jews. Among the swirling mists of these legends are the tales that David defeated a Berber Goliath; that Joab ben Zeruiah is famous for having pursued the Philistines all the way to the border of North Africa; that Jonah traveled toward the Maghreb; that the Jews of Djerba had built their great synagogue at the time of King Solomon, three thousand years ago, upon a stone taken from the Temple of Jerusalem.

Thus the Carthaginian rule planted deep in North Africa Semitic and Oriental influences, opening the way for propagandists, Jewish, Christian, and later Moslem, of the three religions that owe their existence to the divine calling of Abraham. After the overthrow of Carthage in 146 before the Christian era, the Roman occupation put an end to the autonomy of Ifrikya (a region comprising what are now Tunisia and eastern Algeria), and brought it into full union with

35

the rest of the Roman Empire. The Pax Romana permitted freer communication among the numerous Jewish communities of the Mediterranean basin. These communities were reinforced by the arrival of great numbers of refugees from the genocide being perpetrated by the Roman legions in Judea and in Galilee. They took advantage of the general discontent among the peoples of the lands occupied by Rome -- the Gauls, the Greeks, the Orientals, and the Berbers of North Africa -- to convert them to the faith of the Bible, to the hope of justice and brotherhood that it held out to them. The legions slaughtered all who resisted the conquest, then reduced the survivors to slavery, or to the demi-slavery of payers of taxes, periodic levies, and fines, into the Roman treasury. First Judaism, and then Christianity, constituted the sole organized resistance to the savagery of the Roman Empire. It was not by chance that the infant Church chose as its emblem the cross upon which Rome crucified its slaves; the symbol was that of the revolt of the conquered peoples against their merciless and idolatrous invaders. Hence the rapid diffusion of the religions of the Bible in the Empire, in which, at the time of Christ, there were no fewer than eight million Jews and Judaizers.

The struggle carried on in Judea and in Galilee by the people of Israel, united in opposition to the Roman invader, developed into an implacable warfare that lasted more than a century. This war had broad repercussions in the two great African provinces, Caesarian Mauretania and Proconsular Africa. More than a million Jews were to be found at that period, according to Philo, in North Africa, including Cyrenaica and Egypt. They had brought with them the bitterness of their defeat, ready to show itself in sullen hatred, and, whenever possible, in armed revolt. The North African journeys of the most powerful Jewish personalities, notably the most unyielding adversary of Rome, Akiba, who was killed in 134, included contacts with representatives of these revolutionary movements. The most violent revolt took place in Cyrenaica, the last province in the Roman world in which we find an Israelite army victorious. "It was the Jewish sword that put an end to Hellenized Cyrenaica at the beginning of the second century after Christ," says Gauthier. Such military successes are evidence of a powerful organization, and of a

36

significant Jewish penetration in the depths of the Berber population. As it turned out, this desperate effort constituted the last spasm of Israel in opposition to the idolatrous Empire. Trajan, involved in the war against the Parthians and their Jewish allies, appointed Marcius Purbo to put down the revolt. The repression was pitiless, and marked the end of the ascendancy of Judaism in Cyrenaica, where Luknas, known as Messiah, and as King of Israel, had dreamed of reconquering the Holy Land, or, at least, of establishing an autonomous Jewish kingdom in North Africa.

Throughout this period, Jews and Christians had the same enemy, the idolatrous and merciless Roman Empire. The Berbers of the Maghreb must not have distinguished keenly between the followers of Luknas, King and Messiah of Israel, of Rabbi Akiba, who flourished the banner of Bar Kochba, King and Messiah of Israel, or of the successors of Paul, who preached the Gospel of Jesus, King and Messiah of Israel. They understood at first sight that all of these were in revolt against the Empire of Caesar; and in this they were all in agreement.

From this epoch dates the first deep division between the Judaism of North Africa and that of the Hellenized or Latinized communities of the Diaspora. This division penetrated the Berber environment. Two of the chief nomadic tribes, the Botr and the Beranese, whose wanderings extended through Tunisia and Tripolitania, were affected by Jewish influences. According to Ibn Khaldun, Jews were to be found among the Berbers of the Atlantic coast of Morocco, and also among those of the Mediterranian coast. Arab historians tell of the existence of a Jewish kingdom (in the Touat at the Gourara, between Tamentit and Sba Guerrara), where the language and the race of the Zenata Berbers have been kept intact down to our own times. This "kingdom" must have survived the Islamic domination well into the fifteenth century, and the wave of intolerance that swept through Islam after the expulsion of the Moors from Spain must have put an end to it, after 1492, by a general massacre. The existence of these nomadic Jews, whose importance was emphasized by Gauthier, would explain the diffusion of Semitic ideas and techniques beyond the Carthaginian and Roman spheres of influence, and as far as the

Judaized tribes of the Maghreb el Aksa mentioned by Ibn Khaldun, and even into black Africa.

Thus inhabited by autonomous Jewish communities, Souss, Draa, Tafilalet, and Touat, centers of Biblical culture on the caravan routes that furrow Africa from north to south, constituted gates of access for the Semitic East into the Western Sudan. Along these routes, and through these gateways, passed not only merchandise, but also techniques and ideas. They followed the "Golden Road" that ran from the Maghreb down to Mali, across Sudanese Mauritania.

In the twelfth century, a Moslem, Idrissi, author of _Description de l'Afrique et de l'Espagne_, said that he had heard, in the land of Kamnouiria, of men who proclaimed themselves Jewish, living in the auriferous region of Mali, near "the great mountains of gold of the Qartas d'Enon." The principal zone of the expansion of Judaism in black Africa would thus be located in the region of the Taillan or of the Gangara. This hypothesis would bring together logically all the collection of isolated facts and popular traditions: the existence of a Jewish kingdom in Africa, the tales of Eldad the Danite, the vestiges of Jewish civilization in the Adrar region of Mauritania, and the Jewish nomads, traveling in armed groups in the Gourara region of Algeria. It would also explain how Judaized black Africans happened to turn up in the wake of the campaign of General About Bakr ben Omar, in the eleventh century, in the Sudan. At that time, the general was attempting to put down a Sudanese revolt against the Berber dynasty of the Almoravides, then ruling a vast empire stretching from Spain into the Western Sudan. And it throws light on Idrissi's account of the tribe of Judaized black Africans, the Baffors, dispersed in consequence of that campaign in Mauritania, where they had been living on both banks of the Lower Senegal as farmers and fishermen.

To the problems raised by the Jewish influences evident among the Baffors, we might well add those, more hypothetical and more complex, raised by Charles Monteil, in his _Problèmes du Soudan occidental: Juifs et Judaïsés_, in discussing the Sebebaores. We should take note also of the existence of Jews assimilated into Arab, Berber, and Touareg populations, such as the Jewish nomad tribe, the Dagouton, whose existence

38

in the Sahara at the end of the nineteenth century was
noted by Mardochée Séror. In the eighteenth century,
Mungo Park, in his Travels in the Interior of Africa,
tells of finding Hebrew books deep in Mandé-speaking
territory. This fact, however, is less significant
than the problems raised by the presence of blacksmiths in the Western Sudan. The Koran emphasizes the
part played by the Hebrews in the discovery and
development of the iron-working trade:

>   And we taught David the art of making mail
> for you, to defend you from each other's violence:
> will ye therefore be thankful?*

>   Of old bestowed we on David a gift, our
> special boon:-- "Ye mountains and ye birds echo
> his songs of praise." And we made the iron soft
> for him:-- "Make coats of mail, and arrange its
> plates..."**

Let us take note that in North Africa all work
with iron was concentrated in the hands of Jewish
blacksmiths. The Sudanese traditions hold that these
artisans are descended from the patriarch Abraham,
called Nabout Nabihama in their language. The Jewish
blacksmiths would have come into the Sudan by way of
Egypt. They made farm implements and weapons. The
Senegalese Chronique de Fouta, based on the traditions
of the mountain region of Fouta-Djalon, in Guinea,
echoes this account, telling how the men of Diaogodon,
Semites, introduced the techniques of the extraction
of iron (and probably of copper) into Senegal. We
find, also, that the trade of blacksmith is despised
by the Berbers and by the Touaregs. The Oliminden
Touaregs of the present day still avoid pronouncing
the word "blacksmith," for fear of the evil eye. When
they speak of a blacksmith they use the term "the
other."

Here again it is possible to infer a foreign, and
probably Jewish, origin for these techniques,
confirming the passages from the Koran, and the recent
archaeological discoveries that associate King David
and his people, the Hebrews, with the dissemination of

---

*Sura 21.80.
**Sura 34. 10-11.

39

the knowledge of iron-working. It is less remarkable
that other African traditions credit the Jews with the
origin of the profession of singer. A Jewish
penetration of black Africa in still another
profession, that of market-gardener, is traced in the
Taarikh el Fatha, where it is related that, in the
sixteenth century, a Jewish colony was established at
Fassi, on the Niger, that grew fresh vegetables to
supply the caravans. The traditions of technical
cooperation between black Africa and Israel (whose
fruits have been many since the creation of the State
of Israel) go back, it is evident, to a far distant
past, confirming the antiquity of the Biblical and
Jewish penetration of Africa, and reflecting vividly
the presence of black Africa in the Bible.

The Berbers, Semitized by centuries of
Carthaginian influence, reacted favorably to the Jews,
and, before the fourth century, to the Christians who
came to appeal to them against the Empire, with no
power but the immaterial weapons of preaching. The
idea of one sole God, the ideals of universal
brotherhood, of justice, of love, of hope for a
Messianic future and for a paradisal "above" attracted
the adherence of vast numbers of Berbers to the God of
Abraham, of Isaac, and of Jacob. They abandoned their
fetishes and abjured the gods of Rome, joining the
numbers of faithful in the synagogues and churches.
Tertullian, in the third century, described Berbers
who observed the Sabbath, the days of feasting and
fasting, and even the dietary laws of Judaism.
Commodian, around the same time, castigated the
undecided pagans who wavered between Judaism and
Christianity, giving full adherence to neither. For,
since the end of the second century, Jews and
Christians, once united against the savagery and
idolatry of Rome, had now entered into a merciless
combat in rivalry, seeking to conquer the Gentile
nations for their respective faiths. They shared this
revolutionary zeal so obviously that, for a long time,
they were combined in restrictive legislation by pagan
lawgivers. Septimius Severus forbade at that time all
Jewish proselytizing, and, with no less vigor, all
Christian propaganda.

The victory of the Church

The conversion of Constantine in 311 and the Council of Nice in 325 mark the first triumphs of Christianity, now promoted to the dignity of official religion of the Empire. Little by little, the Jews found themselves excluded from the life of the city, and subjected to a discriminatory statute that barely permitted them to survive. The Christian emperors took away from them the right to proselytize, to convert pagans, to own or use Christian slaves, and to send their offerings and their tithes to Jerusalem. These measures were accompanied by a violent anti-Jewish propaganda, preached most virulently by Tertullian, Cyprian, Ambrose, Augustine, and John Chrysostom. From this period on, the triumphant Church set herself in implacable opposition to her humiliated sister, whom she represented in the outer courts of the cathedrals with a blindfold covering her blinded eyes, and a broken lance in her powerless hand. Jews were expelled from all public employment, and weighed down with taxes paid directly into the Imperial treasury. There was an effort to baptize them. The first recorded example of enforced conversion of Jews to Christianity turns up at Borion, in North Africa. This abuse strengthened the spiritual resistance of the Jews to the appeals of Christianity; for them the Church had identified itself with the enemy, the Roman Empire that was responsible for all the calamities that had befallen their fatherland.

From 431 to 533, throughout one century, the Jews pursued their obscure occupations under the domination, first of the Vandals, and then of the Byzantines. In 535, the Council of Carthage condemned the "errors" that these two powers had permitted to spread in the land: Donatism, Arianism, paganism, and, of course, Judaism, which Justinian outlawed in North Africa.

Throughout the Empire, the war between the Church and the Synagogue was entering its fiercest stage. Palestinian Judaism was destroyed, and everywhere open warfare was being carried on against the Jews; yet at the same time the Jews, trying to escape from persecution, took refuge in those countries that were themselves escaping from the power of the Empire, and among the nomadic tribes, which were favorably disposed toward these Hebrews, at odds with and persecuted by their common enemy. The ancient Biblical spirit, all that was unconquerable and quixotically desperate in the resistance of the Jews to the cruelty of the pagan world, grew stronger and gained new ardor as it awaited its encounter, in the seventh century, with a new manifestation of the fruitfulness of the Bible: Islam. The weakening of Byzantine power, the natural aversion of the Berber spirit to Romanism and then to the decadent Byzantinism, attracted once more to the Maghreb a conqueror -- this time the Arab, with his triumphant cry: "La Allah illa Allah wa Muhammad rasul Allah!" "There is no God but Allah. Mohammed is the prophet of Allah!"

Under the sign of the Crescent

The fantastic progress of the followers of Mohammed, flowing out from Medina, spread over Africa from 642 on. In 647, twenty thousand soldiers of Islam defeated Byzantium at the battle of Sbeitla, in Tripolitania, ridding the land of Africa of all Christian domination for more than a thousand years.

The Arab armies then clashed with the indigenous populations of the Maghreb, particularly the largely Judaized nomadic tribes. One among these, the Djerawa tribe, gave to the Maghreb the heroine and symbol of its resistance, Kahena, a Jewish woman who became the leader of this struggle of the Berber people against the Arab invader. Kahena succeeded Koceila, a Christian, who had been the first leader of this revolt. This strange story, more gripping than a novel, has been told us by Ibn Khaldun. The Berber defeat marked the beginning of the reign of Islam, which was to last twelve centuries in the Maghreb.

The Jews then had to adapt to this new power, which had not known how to persuade them to renounce their dream of the restoration of their own past greatness. The Koran, like the Church in its beginnings, censured them for their refusal to embrace the new faith. We, however, had a rendezvous with history, and nothing could have made us renounce it. Moslem law made a distinction between Believers and Infidels. By this law, Infidels must be expelled from each city, lest they contaminate it. But, between the Believers and the Infidels, Mohammed reserved a place

for a third classification, _Ahl el Kitab_, the People
of the Book, Christians and Jews, who, because they
believed in the Scriptures that had inspired Mohammed,
were entitled to a special legal status, that of
dhimmi, or "protected," endowed with certain rights
and duties. Their lives, their property, and the
independent exercise of their religion were protected
in the humbled condition that they were obliged to
maintain in relation to the Moslems. The statute
ensuring this relative freedom for Christians and
Jews, called the Charter of Omar, marked a notable
advance over the rule of Christian theocracy, which
recognized, as holders of rights, only those who
benefit from the mediation of Christ. The Jews, in
fact, were the only infidels to be tolerated in the
medieval Christian city, with such good and bad
fortune as might come to them. The Charter of Omar
gave a legitimate standing and a legal status to their
existence throughout all the extent of Islamic rule.

Though the Christian communities disappeared from
the Maghreb early in the twelfth century, the Jews
maintained themselves there until the end of World War
II. They found there so sure a refuge that through
twelve centuries, up to the rebirth of the State of
Israel, they had found no need to seek for another.

THE ROOTS OF A FAMILY

Natives of Israel

My family roots drive deep into the soil of
Israel. The Chouraqui and Meyer families, coming from
the land of Israel, had probably wandered around the
shores of the Mediterranean before establishing
themselves in Spain, where they remained until their
expulsion in the fourteenth and fifteenth centuries.
Choosing to leave, abandoning all their belongings,
rather than submit to the forced conversion offered to
them by the Catholic rulers, they took their way into
the Maghreb, and settled, first at Tlemcen, and later
at Aïn-Témouchent, where they lived until the new
exile of the nineteen-sixties, after the downfall of
French Algeria. Then they scattered -- toward France,
toward America, toward Israel.

Through twenty centuries of exile, my relations had forgotten nothing of their Judean or Galilean origins. I felt this, as a child, watching my grandfather, my father, and their friends, forever immersed in their strange Hebraic books, which seemed utterly foreign to Aïn-Témouchent -- Berber, Arab, and, for the moment, French. While I was still very young I hoped to solve the paradox of our having taken root in Algeria. I could see very well that my father, in the depths of his being, belonged to the mystery of the Hebraic tradition. He frequented the synagogue, as the bee its hive. There he made his honey, feeding upon the liturgies, upon the feasts, the accented times of the year, and upon the Psalms, which he recited tirelessly, day and night, at every free moment. All this troubled him no more than it troubles a bee to collect and pour out its nectar. I witnessed the same fervor in his brothers, my uncles, and in our neighbors, sometimes tending toward grandiloquence, which was moderated, in some cases, by a real nobility in the countenances, the attitudes, and the essential characters of the individuals.

Sons of the East

"The Chouraquis are proud," people used to murmur around me. On the whole, I saw nothing, in studying them, that could in the least justify that pride. I was put on the right track by Rabbi Isaac Rouche, who told me about the first bearers of our name who had left a mark in the history of Israel in North Africa. I undertook some researches, and followed the peregrinations of my exiled ancestors, first to the Balearic Islands, and then to Spain, probably in the province of Valladolid, where there is a place called Suraka -- which, like the the name Chouraqui, is derived from the Arabic root, Sharq, the East. Since returning to Israel, I have found not only the name Chouraqui, but also other forms -- Chouraki, Seki, Suraki, Chrki, Chèriki, Sherki, and Chergui -- borne by Jewish families coming, not only from North Africa, but from Syria, Iraq, and Kurdistan. I still hear the voice of my father, evoking our ancient family traditions, calling us the Oulad Chraka, the Sons of the East. The branch to which I belong did not wait for 1492 and the great expulsion from Spain to emigrate to Tlemcen. Our family had had to flee from Spain after the first persecutions of 1391. At that time, there were living at Gibraltar and then at

44

Tlemcen Scriptural scholars bearing this name, apt at interpreting texts and basing decisions upon them. In the seventeenth century there arose at Tlemcen the two best-known members of the dynasty of theologians, jurists, poets, and mathematicians, Eliyahu and his son Saadyah. The first of these is known for his liturgical poems in Hebrew, which are still chanted in the synagogues of the Maghrebian rite. He died at the age of one hundred, on the ninth of Ab in the year 1706. For his contemporaries and for his many disciples he was an incomparable master, a "great manna-giving tamarisk."

Poet and mathematician

More remarkable, and even more deserving of remembrance was his son Saadyah, poet, theologian, and mathematician, of whom one of his contemporaries wrote: "This is the tree of life planted in the center of the garden... proficient in all the sciences... an ocean of wisdom." When I first came upon these lines I saw in them no more than pious exaggerations, since those of his poems that I found published in a collection called Shibhei Elohim, the praises of God, seemed to me interesting, but nothing more. I tracked down unpublished manuscripts, however, going from door to door, from Algeria to Morocco, from Morocco to France, and then to Israel, before I found his two principal works, one in New York, in the vaults of the Jewish Theological Seminary, and the other in London, in the archives of the Jews' College. From these works emerges the portrait of a humanist whose vision, mutatis mutandis, resembles that which his contemporaries, Descartes and Pascal, had of the world.

The work that gives Saadyah Chouraqui a unique place in the history of Hebrew literature is his mathematical treatise, Moné Mispar, the numerical calculator, the first composition of the kind ever written in Hebrew. This came about in 1691, at Tlemcen: a man, two hundred and fifty-seven years before the resurrection of the State of Israel, taught, in a Hebrew astoundingly modern, the principles of the four arithmetical operations, their proofs, the concept of fractions, the rule of three, equations, the extraction of square and cube roots, arithmetical and geometrical progression, tables of squares, the determination of the value of pi. He concluded his work with a collection of mathematical diversions, inventing a new method of addition and of multiplying fractions, and teaching how to extract square and cube roots by the aid of a series of odd numbers. The discovery of this manuscript, published in 1973 in Jerusalem by Professor Gad B. Sarfatti, overturned all that had been taught about the revival of the Hebrew language. This revival had been placed historically in the context of the intellectual renaissance called the Haskalah, or Enlightenment, that developed in eastern Europe in the nineteenth century. To the general astonishment, it was now established that a teacher, in Moslem Algeria about two centuries earlier, in 1691, had been giving the kind of course in mathematics that was offered in the same year in the University of Heidelberg, and that he found around him a sufficient number of disciples to understand and transmit to others his teachings, given in Hebrew.

The poetic and theological work of Saadyah is surprising in the quality of its language, which combines the great tradition of Biblical poetry with the renovating influence of the Jewish cantors of Moslem Spain. But Saadyah was more than a fine poet. His flowing eloquence carried a content of theological learning. His extensive commentary on Psalm 119 is not without historical interest. Saadyah was the contemporary of Sabbatai Zevi, whose messianic venture was to collapse miserably. Immense crowds gathered in response to his appeal, and marched with him toward the Holy Land, in which they were to establish themselves. Sabbatai had, in 1648, proclaimed himself Messiah and Savior of Israel, arousing the mystical hopes of the dwellers in the ghettos by his promise that, as the long-awaited Messiah, he would lead them to the deliverance of their fatherland. His conversion to Islam, and then his death in 1676, put a tragic end to this messianic movement, one of the most powerful that had ever affected the Jewish people since the beginning of the Christian era. It was to the grief born of this bitter disappointment that Saadyah tried to address himself. For him, the tragedy of the exile had only grown more profound. The salvation of Israel would come from her return to her own land. To promote deliverance, it was necessary to heed the word of God, live according to the Bible and in harmony with its demands, but also to master the secular sciences and techniques; hence his treatise on mathematics. To the question of whether Saadyah insisted that the return of Israel to the Holy Land could be facilitated only by a technological revolution, one can only reply that his certainty was absolute. Jerusalem was going to be rebuilt; the exile of the people would come to an end in the joy of ultimate reconciliations. Jerusalem lay at the heart of the thought and the hope of Saadyah. Did he know that, three centuries later, one of his descendants would dwell in the center of Jerusalem?

Note especially this point: in all his works, Saadyah never uses the word Jew. He always speaks, as does the Bible, of the Sons of Israel. Nowhere does he use the word Judaism. He engages in no religious controversy, never claims that we are the holders of some undefined superiority, nor that our religion is better than those of others. He doesn't intoxicate himself with hollow words like "the lasting values of Judaism," or "the Jewish mission," words which so well concealed, in the nineteenth and twentieth centuries, for publicists of all parties, the profound realities of the thought of Israel, and hid the massive contradictions that set the Jews at odds with one another, until smooth phrases, contentious opinions, and the people themselves came close to disappearing in the gulf they had not been able to foresee. It would have been better to follow the example of Herzl, and be more lucid. This is what Saadyah did. He never pretended the tragedy of exile was something to celebrate. Instead of indulging in hollow oratory, he chose to teach to his brothers a rigorous method of Bible reading... and mathematics.

Statesman and martyr

The career of Mordecai Chouraqui or Shriqui also throws light on our history in the Maghreb. Probably a descendant of Eliyahu and of Saadyah, he left Tlemcen to become, under the name of Hazan Bacha, the principal confidant of the Sultan of Morocco, Sidi Mohammed ben Abdallah, who reigned from 1757 to 1790. By his side, Hazan Bacha participated in the promulgation of liberal policy and political and administrative reforms that brought about, along with other benefits, the re-establishment of peace in the southern region of Morocco. Sidi Mohammed ben Abdallah signed commercial treaties with Denmark, Great Britain, Sweden, France, and Venice. He sent diplomatic missions to France, Spain, and Turkey. He chose a Frenchman, Coralo, to build the city of Mogador, especially conceived as a city in which Moslems, Christians, and Jews might dwell together. Mordecai, or Hazan Bacha, so fully gained the confidence of Sidi Mohammed ben Abdallah that, as one Jewish chronicle assures us, he became not only his counselor, but his Finance Minister. In this office, he participated in the reorganization of the tax system, and of the currency, thus increasing the revenue of the kingdom.

Sidi Mohammed died on the ninth of April, 1790, near Rabat. His son, Moulay Yazid, had repeatedly rebelled against him. Recalled by his followers from the mountain where he had taken refuge, he seized power, and, in the anarchy that ensued upon his accession to the throne, he gave free reign to the persecution of Jews and Christians. Their properties were sacked and pillaged, while bandits took advantage of the general turmoil to seize for ransom and to kill everywhere in the kingdom. The Jews in the Sultan's circle were the first to suffer on account of Moulay Yazid's tenuous hold on his power. Many, like Messaoud Benzecri, were hung by the feet at the gate of the city of Meknès, where, for about two weeks, the crowd could watch their dying agonies, or their dead bodies. Moulay Yazid may have had an account to settle with Mordecai -- or perhaps he begrudged him his wealth. Having him arrested at Meknès, he promised to spare his life if he would apostasize and convert to Islam. According to the chronicle, Mordecai preferred martyrdom to apostasy, and died at the stake. The community of Meknès, suspected of having appropriated his estate, was persecuted, as was also that of Marrakesh, where Moulay Yazid, having laid waste his land with fire and sword, died a violent death in February, 1792. In later years, the Chouraquis swarmed in the chief Jewish communities of North Africa, while some representatives of the family finally managed to return to Galilee, where, in the second half of the nineteenth century, several members of the Chouraqui family held the highly honorable elective post of Grand Rabbi of Safed.

The rejection of the world

The death of Mordecai excited our childish imaginations. Yes, we felt, the only true witness is the one who signs with his blood the declaration of his love and his faith. We were growing up in a world apart from the realities of our time, a world in which our collective memory never ceased to keep alive the message of the Bible and the recollections of our family and national history.

Each year, Saturday after Saturday, we read in our synagogues the whole of the Pentateuch, and over and over again the complete book of Psalms, and a great part of the other books of the Bible. We also read many of the treatises of the Talmud and of the Cabala. We paid no attention to the fact that the Hebrew and Aramaic that we were using were vestiges of abolished cultures. In his little glass bowl, does the fish bother about whether he has been taken out of the sea or a river? What was essential to us was that we hold on to the chance of our resurrection, through an intransigent faithfulness to our origins. In truth, the world outside had been created only to demonstrate to us how right we were to persist in our refusal to be assimilated. Of that world, we could hold only gloomy memories, luridly illuminated by the incessant persecutions of which our ancestors were the victims in all the regions and all the centuries of their wanderings. There was no hope, either for us or for our wretched persecutors, but in the coming of an all-powerful savior, the Messiah, who would be able to gather us back into our own country and put order into the affairs of the nations.

For, black as we generally painted our enemies, we did not go so far as to hate them. We felt vaguely that the strange picture we must present to their eyes had been designed to arouse their hostility. How could people admit into their city such a stranger, armed with unreadable and suspicious-looking books, given to absurd taboos, and insisting on carrying with him through the centuries a mad dream of utopias, first among them being that of the restoration of his overwhelmed kingdom? Not to speak of his other fantasies, universal justice and peace, the resurrection of the dead, and the birth of a new free man on a new earth, and under new skies. We were attached to our fantasies more firmly than Don Quixote

49

to his Dulcinea. With our leather thongs on head and arm, with our prayer shawls that made us look like ghosts, we put ourselves in a situation in which we were bound to be either ridiculed or persecuted. Occasionally, these things happened to us. Being mocked, spat upon, and struck only confirmed us in our certitudes.

We were living our dream in the midst of the beautiful countryside of the Maghreb. Tlemcen, the cradle of my family, resembles the city of David in altitude, climate, fauna, and flora, to such an extent that we called it the Jerusalem of the Maghreb. Aïn-Témouchent, at the tip of the coastal plateau about Oran, was at the confluence of the valleys of the wadis Senane and Tèmouchent, where we loved to go and play among the oleanders and hawthorns.

The French colonists, to build their new city, half-way between Tlemcen and Oran, instinctively hit upon a site already chosen before them by the Arabs. And this site had been similarly chosen earlier, by Byzantines, Vandals, Romans, Phoenicians, and the indigenous Berbers. In the shady gardens of my native town, and in its verdant fields, I dreamed, as a child, of the village that the Phoenician colonists, come from the same shores as my ancestors, had founded there, at the center of Safar, giving it, at the dawn of history, the Semitic name of Sufat. There the Berbers venerated the jinn who haunt the Djebel Dokma and the grottoes, springs, sacred trees, stars, and certain animals, such as the ram, that determine the fortune or misfortune of men.

Aïn-Témouchent, whose name means in Berber the spring of the jackals, lost its Semitic name in the year 146 before the Christian era, when Rome had destroyed Carthage, and named their new Roman town Albulae. My town had been Berber and then Punic; it became Roman and Christian until the revolution that brought to it, in the year 700, the Arab troops that conquered and Islamized it. Under the rule of Islam, "the spring of the jackals" has deservedly become renowned for its wheat, its honey, its fruits, its oil and delicious wines, as well as for its fierce warriors, descendants of the Beni Amir, and of the Hilalians, and of the Beni Zorba. In 1517, these three tribes resisted, long and victoriously, the conquering march of the Turks under the command of Bab

Arouj, known to Western history as Barbarossa, while all other tribes of the region were yielding.

Faces of my Algeria

I dearly loved my natal Algeria, and Aïn-Témouchent, with its burning sky, its vineyards, its fertile red clay soil, its cactuses and its azure, its olive trees and the calling of jackals at night, its nearby sea, my Mediterranean, ever-present, my foster-mother. Hour after hour I swam in its waters or offered myself on its beaches to the broiling of its sun. Its shores, the clumps of broom on its hillsides, the variety of its plants and animals, its dawns and twilights never ceased to inspire and exalt my spirit as I grew to maturity. I have never tired of its landscapes, its culture and its traditions -- the traditions of its occupiers, whose history I have read in the stones of our fields.

I hated the racism of those who could never see the Algerians as anything other than "donkeys," blind to the nobility of their living traditions. The great misery of the masses never obliterated a spiritual depth which I kept discovering and admiring as I went my ways, in my ever-rewarding conversations with these strong and humble people, true and sorrowful witnesses of the transcendent realities in the life of man. Yes, more than hate, I feel contempt for the business attitudes of a certain Algerian bourgeoisie, such as I am here mentioning -- a class that shamelessly displays its vices, its faults, its boorishness, and, above all, its immoderate, and often exclusive, pursuit of money and sexual satisfaction.

My own Algeria was different from that of the Arabs, and even more different from that of the colonists. It was placed in an ageless elsewhere, with no profound connection with the surroundings with which it was veneered. It was a little like an island where finance and economics might be relegated to the lowest position. My essential Algeria was centered in the life of the spirit, present and palpable in the parchments of our Bible.

Baba the Just

My maternal grandfather, Abraham Meyer, was to my eyes the incarnation of all the fighting spirit and all the wisdom of that Hebraic Maghreb whose saga I have just sketched. He, too, was the descendant of a family that had left Spain, later, indeed, than the tumultuous Chouraquis, but surely soon after the expulsion of 1492, and probably in company with a miracle-working rabbi of Tlemcen, Rabbi Ephraim Enkawa. I knew very well this grandfather, who died at the age of eighty-four, on the seventeenth of February, 1929. I was eleven and a half when he breathed his last breath in my presence. His final anxiety, just a few seconds before his death, had been to find out from his wife, Rahmouna, whether she had provided enough food for the hundreds of relatives and friends who had hurried to his bedside from all corners of the country. Abraham, Baba as we called him, had been the provider all his life. The passion of his God and of his people was his; and as his goal he had the impossible mission of keeping alive the language, the culture, and the seed of Israel, in the expectation of their rebirth.

Baba limped as the result of osteomyelitis, which he had had at the age of five; his right knee was stiff, and his right leg five centimeters shorter than his left. At that time, his parents had vowed to clothe him in the traditional dress of Jews of the Maghreb who had emigrated from Spain, a costume which he wore until the time of his death: an ample, baggy sarawal, drawn in at the waist by a broad band, a short Spanish jacket or bolero, cut in a curve, and a vest of brilliantly dyed and richly embroidered materials. At thirty, he had been married to a girl of fiteen, by whom he had eight children. After her death, he remarried, and had three children by the second marriage. He was seventy-one years old at the birth of the final two children, twins, Edmond and Edmèe. There were then grandsons and sons-in-law who found his reproductive zeal excessive. The old man was rich, but, after all, eleven parts made a considerable diminution in his estate. And at the age of seventy-one! Having got wind of these murmurs, Baba called his family together and gave them an impressive speech, ending with the proclamation: "So you want to castrate me! Next time, you mark my words, I'll make three at once!" And next year his

52

second wife, thirty-one years his junior, became pregnant again. To his disappointment, however, instead of the awaited triplets, there was but one child, who, moreover, was not to survive.

He brimmed over with vitality, constantly on horseback on the roads and across his fields. He was a pioneer in buying fallow land to plant vines. He had a love of the soil, and personally directed the work in the fields. At vintage times, he would crush with his own feet, in the vat, his finest grapes, to produce the Meyer wines, his boast. Think of it! He exported his wines for sale in the Franch markets, and they took prizes at the International Fair of Marseille, beginning with the end of the nineteenth century.

He took upon himself, to the best of his ability, the religion and the destiny of his people. Keeping closely associated with his Arab surroundings, and free from all racism, he found it hard to bear the anti-semitism that raged in Algeria at the time of the Dreyfus affair. The movement had taken over the Oran region. Synagogues had been profaned, stores pillaged, and there had even been several dead, killed by gangs crying, "Death to the Jews!" or a popular slogan, "The suitcase to the station, Jews to the slaughterhouse!" Elias Benfredj, a giant in a purple shirt, armed with an axe, had spat in the face of the virulent leader of the anti-semites, Max Rêgis. The situation grew dangerous. Baba was uneasy about the fate of his Jews of Aïn-Témouchent, where hatred was beginning to inflame hotheads. It was then that he invented an unpublished method of combating anti-semitism. Gathering together his numerous household, carrying pitchforks, spades, pickaxes, sticks, and brooms, he had them march through the streets of the town, with him at their head, chanting parodies of the hate slogans:

"Down with the Jews, down with the Jews,
We have to hang them by the nose!"

The anti-Jewish ringleaders saw that their own noses were being pulled, in this unexpected manifestation at once of force and of humor. Once the shock of surprise had passed, the laughers began to laugh on the right side, and the storm passed over without breaking.

To say that Abraham Meyer was a man of faith would insufficiently express his solid and clear attachment, unfailing and unwavering, with all his heart, with all his being, with all his intensity, to the God of his fathers. He was a man of prayer: every morning, before his regular devotions, he would improvise, in Judeo-Arab, songs of praise, accompanying them on his mandolin. He loved music. His love songs were inspired by the folksongs and malagueñas of his ancestral Spain, whose traditions he was perpetuating and illustrating. He venerated his father, Ba Nathan, a true colossus of a man, who had such a reputation for sanctity that at his death, at the age of ninety-two, his body was taken into the synagogue to the accompaniment of singing by all the assembled community. Everyone felt that he was being accompanied, not to the cemetery, but directly to paradise, where his place was reserved near the Almighty and his prophets, Abraham, Isaac, Jacob, Moses, Aaron, David, and Solomon.

The world in which we lived was peopled with ineffable presences, whose secret we alone knew. Thus it was that Elijah the Prophet was seriously expected at each Passover meal, in every home. His place was set, his chair ready. Was he not the forerunner of the Messiah who was to come to rescue Israel from the slavery of her exile?

Closer to us, there were two devoted intercessors that each of us invoked regularly on every occasion, good or bad. Rabbi Meir, the miracle-worker, and Rabbi Simeon bar Yohaï were intimately involved in our family life. As a child, I saw in them two powerful cousins to whom one appealed when the least difficulty occurred -- when a child fell, or became ill; when anyone went on a trip; when anyone undertook some serious task, or incurred a risk. To open oneself to them was enough -- they would give a favorable hearing. In Jewish memory, they had never disappointed anyone. Later, I came to know that these two admirable protectors were mystical and miraculous rabbis, the forefathers of the Cabala. They lived in Galilee nineteen centuries ago. Baba gave to them a limitless devotion. He took up collections in their names on every occasion, and sent sums of money regularly to foundations in Tiberias, where Rabbi Meir, the miracle-worker, is buried.

We lived in a perpetual miracle in which everything that happened had reason and meaning because it all came from the will of God. The Bible held the central place in our lives, and was ever-present in each of our thoughts, in each of our actions. During the war of 1914 to 1918 Baba saw his four sons and two sons-in-law go off to the front, which was then devouring a great many human lives, especially of Algerians. To whom could one entrust their precious lives if not to the protector of the family, Rabbi Meir, master of the miracle? The technique prescribed to ensure this protection was detailed, but simple. Baba would put into the collection that he sent regularly to Tiberias eighteen sous-or (worth a tenth of a franc apiece) for each day, and for each soldier whose protection was particularly asked for. When one of them went on furlough, and must cross the Mediterranean, infested with German submarines, while "the reality of cold was covering the entire world," Baba would advise him to take these measures: at the port of departure he must set aside three sums of eighteen sous-or each, for insurance, one for the ship, one for the passengers, and one for himself. The sums of money always had to be counted in multiples of eighteen, that figure being, in Hebrew, the number of life and of the living. Upon his landing, when he returned, Baba would be there to receive these insurance premiums and send them at once to the pious foundation of Tiberias. Never, I must say, has any scheme of insurance been more efficacious. Our six heroes, after a hard-fought war, all returned to their homes safe and sound, without a scratch.

Baba spent himself without stint in good works. In his business, nobody asked for his signature -- his word was the best and surest of guarantees. The Arabs of the region honored him as a saint, asking his advice in matters of business and also in their family problems. On market days, each Thursday, they would entrust to his keeping the sums, often considerable, that they were carrying. Nobody ever counted the bundles of papers deposited or withdrawn, and there was never any dispute.

This is how he himself described the marriage of an orphan girl in a letter to one of his soldiers: "On Wednesday, March 14, 1917, Esther, the daughter of Hadâne, married a young man of Bou Hadjar. Long ago,

I had promised to give him a woolen mattress. In spite of the present scarcity, I have succeeded in getting fifty kilos of wool at a price of two hundred gold francs a hundredweight. Rachel and her mother asked me to go with them to the town hall. Since she has no father, it fell to me to perform a father's part. Although my mind is preoccupied, I have decided to take her to the town hall in my auto, while her mother rides with the groom in Siboni's auto. Then we will bless the couple in the synagogue. I will fulfill the commandment of God because she is an orphan. God is the father of orphans. I fulfill God's commandments so that you will be saved -- you and your brothers. Yes, you will all come back home unharmed, untouched, well in every way, and I will rejoice at your marriage... Put everything in the hands of God, blessed be he. He himself will show you your way. He will save you through the merits of the teacher, our Rabbi Meir, the master of the miracle, whose merit is our shield. Amen. He will always be with you. Amen, so be it."

The insurance taken out through Rabbi Meir, the master of the miracle, is much more effective than one could imagine. Witness a note dated February 16, 1917: "On Sunday I wrote you nothing about the freight train that was derailed during the night of Friday, the eighth of February. It was heading from Oran toward Témouchent with twenty-six carloads of merchandise. At the point where the Rio-Salado bridge crosses the river, it was derailed on a curve at 7:35 o'clock. Twenty-three cars were smashed, one on top of another. Of the twenty passengers and crew, sixteen were killed and four injured. Benattar lost twenty-five sheep, killed in the accident. The financial loss is estimated at a million gold francs..." The "miracle" of the train and the "miracle" of the sugar grew out of this event.

Baba had succeeded in finding, at a period of great scarcity, twenty-five hundredweight of granulated sugar for his customers. But let us read further. "Thursday, before the derailment of the train, I was told that my sugar had been consigned to that train, and Saturday that it had been loaded. The station at Oran advised me officially that it had been lost in the accident."

Baba testified that when he had bought that sugar he had arranged with Rabbi Meir, the master of the miracle, to insure it so that it would be brought to him in good condition at Témouchent. This time, it seemed that the insurance had not worked, or at least not completely; but that was to view the matter superficially. In fact, two survivors of the accident had been able to give a warning, in the nick of time, to a train that was coming in the opposite direction, from Témouchent, thus saving the lives of four hundred men on military leave. Console yourselves, therefore, for the loss of twenty-five hundredweight of granulated sugar, and place all confidence in the miraculous powers of Rabbi Meir. In spite of the loss of the sugar, a lack that kept the good citizens of Témouchent, until the coming of better times, from drinking coffee or tea, the insurance had paid off handsomely.

But it would not do justice to the perfect effectiveness of the saint to admit that there could be the slightest defect in his performance. While Baba was rejoicing in telling his son Makhlouf about the miracle of the four hundred furloughed men saved from death by Rabbi Meir, he received a new message from the station-master at Oran, telling him that, by an error, his sugar had not been loaded on the train that was derailed, and that it was expected to arrive in good condition the next day. The mystical insurance had thus spared him a loss of five thousand five hundred gold francs. "You see plainly," Baba concluded, "that God, blessed be he, and Rabbi Meir, the master of the miracle, are with us. Call upon them, and fear nothing, my son."

This massive faith, this devotion to a God of motherly love, who gave to him, himself, to his household, and to the entire universe, the precise portion that was due to each, never forsook him. It was of the very essence of his being. He worshiped a living God, the life God who was also for him the love God. At the beginning of January, 1917, he lost his twelfth child, little Charles, and it was in these words that he gave the news to his son Makhlouf in Northern France. "To the friend of my soul, my breath, my beloved, the light of my eyes, Señor Makhlouf Meyer, may his Rock guard him and give him life, from me, the undersigned. I greet you warmly. The reason for these lines is that I have not been able to write you for the past two weeks to let you know of the disaster that has struck us. My dear one, Charles, has died of pleurisy. I did not want to give you this bad news. When Joseph, your brother, told me that he had written to you, I spared him no reproach. But, after all, this is what God, blessed be he, has given to us. Charles had lived up to the age of four. We dressed him up and played so happily with him! He had learned to speak French as well as Arabic. He had become extraordinary. All day he would show his clothes to all who came into the house and say: "Today, I am a man!" But God, blessed be he, willed otherwise. We have accepted the decree of God, blessed be he. We did everything possible to us, and even more than the possible, to save him. But God, blessed be he, who had given him life, has taken it back. God gave it, God took it away. May the name of God be blessed, now and forever. Behold what he has given us, our God, blessed be he. So, my son, take care of yourself. Don't be sorrowful. All this comes from God."

When his four sons and his two sons-in-law had returned from the front, and his third daughter, Diamantée, was married, he decided to make a solemn offering to the God of heaven and earth. What to offer? Why, the Bible, of course, the Scrolls of the Torah. The Torah of Moses -- that was the letter that came from heaven, teaching us to know, love, and serve the Creator of all life. He, Abraham Meyer, would employ the best of scribes to transcribe the book of God on the finest of parchments, and it would be kept and read forever in the synagogue that he had founded, on the upper floor of one of his buildings in Ain-Témouchent.

He bred especially, on one of his farms, a flock of sheep, meticulously cared for, to furnish the parchment for the Scriptures. Wasn't that, for those animals, as great a privilege as, in former times, to go up to heaven in the smoke of holocausts, on the altar of the Temple? Rabbi Shelomoh Amar, the same one who had circumcised me, was chosen to be the nimble-stylused scribe who would perform his masterpiece of calligraphy. He installed himself in the vast house belonging to my grandfather, whose wings stretched along the Boulevard de la Rèvolution from one cross street to another. Rabbi Shelomoh occupied a room just above the Moorish bath of the

family, since he had to make his ablutions in the
ritual bath each time he had to write the Name of God,
the ineffable Tetragram, the sacred mantra of the God
of Israel, YHWH. Rabbi Shelomoh was lodged, fed,
paid, and honored in proportion to his task, the
highest to which a son of man can aspire: to write
the word of God. Each letter was a foundation stone
of the mysteries of the faith, and the slightest
error, from which God preserve us, risked loosing the
worst catastrophes, not only upon Aïn-Témouchent, but
perhaps upon the entire universe, since it had been
created in the image of the Torah. The fate of the
world was directly linked to the calligraphy of the
letters of the Bible.

Baba came to suspect that Rabbi Shelomoh might be,
to some extent, making a good thing of his commission,
since he took no less than three years to finish his
masterpiece. But at last there was the masterpiece,
plain for all to see. The Hebrew characters sparkled
with the black of India ink on parchment of immaculate
whiteness, pliant as velvet. Never had anyone seen a
more beautiful book. Its consecration was the
occasion for a feast that was long talked of in the
whole Département. The whole region had been invited.
Everybody was praying, chanting, eating, for three
days. The principal ceremony preceding the
introduction of the sacred parchment into its ark, in
the synagogue, was this: Rabbi Shelomoh, at the end
of the scroll, had left some hundreds of letters
faintly outlined, that were to be religiously
completed and made solid with that indelible ink whose
receipt had been transmitted from father to son, in
our exile, through thousands of years. This was in
order to offer to the greatest possible number of Sons
of Israel the privilege of having written a Torah.
They came from everywhere, artisans and peasants, the
rich and the beggars, to gain, in heaven and on earth,
this notable merit. To me, last-born of the
descendants of Abraham Meyer, was reserved the best
part, the final letters of Deuteronomy. At the age of
six, I applied myself to making the Hebrew letters
well. This was the first Bible to whose production I
contributed effectively.

Of Abraham Meyer, the fiery-eyed, the man of
indomitable energy, there remains to us an irrefutable
testimony, the eighty-one letters that he wrote to his
favorite son, Makhlouf, while he was fighting for

Alsace and Lorraine in the trenches of the Argonne. In corresponding with his son, he wrote his letters in a handwriting handed down from the Middle Ages, in the Hebrew cursive called Rashi script. His language itself makes this collection of letters a unique literary document: it was Arabic, mixed with Hebrew and Aramaic words. Baba had mastered those three languages. But to be sure of being understood by his son, who had been educated in French schools, and daily encountered the Spaniards of the Oran region, he interlarded his missives with words, and sometimes phrases, in French and in Spanish. Five languages, used by a single letter-writer, whose script arose out of the bronze age of Israel! Who can top that? In substance, his letters constitute a steadfast profession of faith, not that of a catechism, but the heartfelt cry of a father, solicitous for the life of his children. One day I shall publish this life-breathing document, precious not only for what it reveals of Baba and his faith and family affection, but also for the information it gives about life in Algeria during the First World War. Baba always had the right word; he could see clearly and tell a story vividly. His religious understanding had more stability than that of many theologians. Witness these few lines, taken from a letter of December.

"Be open-minded and calm; this war comes from God, and is universal. The age is in a state of insurrection, and God will reward his servants. Look at Rumania; it was keeping quiet, and then, all of a sudden, it plunged into the dance, bidding defiance to the whole world. It has been laid waste, and its inhabitants have been wanderers on the face of the earth for the past month and a half.

"In this situation I urgently exhort you to pray to God unceasingly. He is our own God, the God of the Jews; he will answer you. To be sure, he has punished us. He is punishing us now on account of our misdeeds. But he has pity on those who call upon him. In the Bible, God calls us his Sons, and the nations of the world his servants. Here is the reason: a son, even if he is the wickedest in the world, would never disown his father; and a father always continues to love his children, even if they behave badly toward him.

"If the son appeals to his father, the father will pardon and uphold his son to the very end. He will give up his own life and all that he possesses for his children. This is how we, the Sons of Israel, stand in relation to God. He it is who, out of his own mouth, calls us his sons. He has told us: 'You yourselves are sons to the Lord your God. Banim attem l'Adonai Elohekhem.'

"I am preaching you this sermon because I want you always to pray to God. It is he who is your true Father. As for me, I am only your foster-father, and I pray for you, night and day, to God, my own true Father. I know the world and its ways; yes, God owes it to himself to listen to me. You all will be saved. You will come back unharmed, safe and sound. You will come home without a scratch, with the help of God, our Father."

For him, to pray to God meant also to do his will, and to help others to do so. He implored his sons to observe the traditions of Israel at the front. He sent them unleavened bread for Passover, for themselves and for their friends; and he sent them kilos of kosher food, begging them not to deprive themselves of anything on account of the expense -- "not to spare him in matters of money."

Baba was, in the fullest sense of the term, a man of the Bible. He knew it by heart in Hebrew, and could read, in Aramaic and in Hebrew, the most erudite Biblical commentaries. He was a man of the Bible in virtue of the solid fullness of his faith; to live meant for him to place himself in full view of God and his saints. The existence of evil and death, and the vexations caused by the colonial administration, posed no problem for him, though he saw himself as the administration's chosen victim. He spoke no word of protest against his sons, who, when they had come back from the war, risked his ruination by their daring financial speculations or by their extravagance. He was a patriarch, serene, joyful, incredibly full of life even on his deathbed. His wife remarked candidly: "At eighty, Baba is as vigorous as on our wedding day." We, his grandchildren, had no better playmate than he. He held us spellbound by his stories, his magic tricks, his pranks, and, above all, by the epic story of our people, which he never wearied of telling us, often accompanying himself on

61

his beloved mandolin. Sometimes he spoke in prophetic accents, for example in his letter of September 15, 1918, one of his last letters to his son:

"May you be sealed in the Book of Life and of Well-being for many years, with the help of God. Amen. So be it.

"To the friend of my soul, my breath, my son, my beloved, the light of my eyes, Señor Makhlouf Meyer, may his Rock guard him and give him life, from me, the undersigned. I greet you warmly. The reason for these lines:

"... Today, Sunday, we have reached the eve of Yom Kippur. We are sorry you and your brothers are not with us. Next year will be better than this one. Peace will be re-established over the whole world. You will return unscratched, whole in your body and in all your being. With the help of God, your wife will be with you. Your brothers will come back whole, unharmed in their bodies and in all their being. You will be at home, in your houses, all brought together around me. As for me, I shall be living, whole, unharmed, vigorous; I shall be at your side, and you all will be reunited around me, with the help of God; by the merits of my ancestors, the holy Abraham, Isaac and Jacob, Moses and Aaron, David and Solomon; by the merits of the Teacher, our holy Rabbi Judah; by the merits of the holy Rabbis of the Maghreb, Rashbas, Ribash, and Ephraim Enkawa; by the merits of the Sages of the Bible; by the merits of the Prophets, the Teachers, the Preachers, the Just, the Worshipers, the Upright; the Rabbis who have passed through the world; and, finally, by the merit of the Teacher, our holy Rabbi Meir, the miracle-worker, he whose merit is our shield, he through whom you are insured, you and your brothers. He will intercede for you with God. Inscribed in the Book of Life, you will all be saved. So be it." And so it was.

Abraham Meyer was of another world and of another time. His "elsewhere," his course in life, were clearly defined! But the world was in rebellion; God rewarded his servants, the nations of the world, and, contrary to Baba's hopes, "he did not let that furnace cool again." The rising generation had come down from the magic mountain on which burned, though under the ashes, the fire of Jerusalem. The young men had

62

fought in the ranks of the French army, and studied in the schools and universities of France. For this generation, it was the time of those uprootings whose anguish I have described. Baba, as one incident demonstrates, was to suffer in this way even through his own children. The youngest of them no longer understood either his character or the depth of his thought, or even his language. With his limping, his crooked legs, and his clothing, which, while magnificent, seemed, in western surroundings, to be a kind of fancy dress, he looked like a caricature to modern eyes, even those of the youngest among his own children. He had, furthermore, a gift of eloquence that often expressed itself in Arabic or in Hebrew, languages forgotten by the young, who were now devoted exclusively to the language of Voltaire.

On the thirty-first of January, 1917, Baba mentioned in a letter the following facts: on the preceding Sunday, his son Mordecai telephoned him from Algiers at eleven o'clock in the morning, asking for one hundred and fifty gold francs. The next day, he claimed, he had to take ship for France. Baba scolded Mordecai for being so late in letting him know of the need. It would have given him so much pleasure to go himself, to take that money to him, and to have the joy of bidding him an affectionate farewell. In fact, Mordecai, as we read between the lines of his letter, did indeed want the money (during that very month he had drawn eight hundred gold francs from the paternal treasury) but not that old father, hobbling along in his eighteenth century Spanish costume. He would rather have the pretty girls who were, throughout his life, his most constant need. A handsome lad, fascinating and self-assured, he had definitively burned his bridges behind him in abandoning all that his father represented of true nobility, and of authenticity. Baba writes down the fact, while masking the true cause: "I have passed a painful night. Yes, if Mordecai had told me his departure was set for Wednesday, I could have left on Sunday evening and been at Algiers with him, on Tuesday. But he, my darling, lied to me because he didn't want to give me trouble, knowing that we were having bad weather here."

This is how he departed for France, your Mordecai, and along with him everyone sprung from your loins, heroic and laughable Baba. I see you, Baba, stuck

63

there in your fantastic planet, now buffeted night and day by the storms of the new age, that are tearing it to pieces, even to the foundations.

Baba must bide his time. He is to wait, as he waited patiently until the day of his death. He will wait until the Last Judgment and until the Resurrection of the Dead, witness to an unquenchable hope.

The uprooting and the departure -- it was God who ordained it for millions of people. God alone, therefore, could permit the returns, the ultimate reconciliations, the salvation promised to Israel and to the nations of the whole world. Speedily. Amen. So be it, since death is on the prowl and the world is burning.

II

THE UPROOTING

Our Forefathers, the Gauls

"Our forefathers, the Gauls, were big, brave, strong, and quarrelsome. Their priests were called the druids...!" With these words, which we chanted in class at the top of our voices, the West invaded my life to crush in it the seed which a resistance lasting two thousand years had permitted my ancestors to plant in me. This first sentence of our history textbook, Lavisse, had to be learned by all the pupils in French schools. Since "Algeria is France," it became a truth for all of us, Jews, Spaniards, Arabs, and even Negroes, all sitting together on the benches in the same school.

At a stroke my East was wiped out. My ancestors were no longer Abraham, Isaac, and Jacob, but the Gauls. Their priests were not those of Jerusalem, the Cohens and the Levys, but the druids under their noble oak forests, in Gaul.

The marvelous thing about this is that not a single one among us even winced at the ponderous assertion with which the nuns of the kindergarten on the Rue Pasteur, and then the lay teachers of the public school of Aïn-Témouchent, came down upon us. Our forefathers, then, were the Gauls; this was the official truth, nonsectarian and government endorsed, over all the expanse of the French Empire. This was manifestly intended to be a display of generosity. France had done us the high honor of adopting us. From now on we belonged, body and soul, to the French family; so much so that the forefathers of the French had to become, on account of that adoption, our own forefathers. We had embarked, and our true ancestors stood on the shore, with the books of the Torah, the whole Bible, the Talmud in Aramaic, the Cabala, which teaches the mysteries of God and the secrets of creation. They watched us recede into the distance on the ship in which France, and through her the West, was taking us away with no hope of return. Baba, his legs still more crooked, his beautiful mandolin useless and silent, was becoming antiquated, even ridiculous, in the brilliant society that was welcoming us, that of Encyclopedists, Revolutionaries, and Technicians. He stood on the shore surrounded by

66

his kin: Abraham, Isaac, Jacob, Moses, Aaron, David and Solomon, the Prophets and the Saints.   Upon suddenly discovering that his universe was doomed to disappear, he must have thought: "Even Rabbi Meir, with his miracles, has been powerless to prevent this departure, to bring back to me my precious seed, Mordecai, the first of the family to enter a university, and all the rest of my descendants."   In hopelessness, or rather with a secret hope beyond all hope, our old people made no effort to hold us back. They even encouraged us to take our departure, and to merge, as quickly as possible, into that French fellowship, so generous and brilliant in France itself, so powerful and so rich in Algeria.   In this way the vivisection was made without too great pain.

Baba and our parents continued to pray for us, and to butcher a cock, each feast of Yom Kippur, for the expiation of our sins, which must be many.   For us, too, they would solemnly read from the Torah, in its parchment scrolls, and chant the Psalms through entire nights, to music more intoxicating than alcohol.   No more did we belong to the same world as they, even though we were still of the same race.   On account of this fact, the bonds between us were never completely broken.   An umbilical cord still held us attached to the island of our origin.   Even the most completely assimilated of us never paraded our turning away from the world out of which we came.   Modesty, delicacy, the traditional politeness of the Maghreb, almost as subtle as that of the Chinese, avoided any confrontation.   The young people came back from their schools and universities for the religious feasts. They lent themselves, with more or less good grace, to the tribal rites.   After all, even if they had lost their souls, they remained "Jews," since the West declared itself unable to assimilate them.

Baba, on the shore, kept up his dialogue with his true father in heaven.   There he was, waiting, always ready to welcome his darlings, and refusing to recognize the fact that some of them were getting farther and farther away from him, estranged from his religion and culture, ignoring God and his Bible, and thinking nothing of Rabbi Meir and his miracles.

The mothers had one source of consolation: those of their children who had become the most downright atheists, who preached Marx and knew nothing of

Isaiah, kept on greedily devouring their cooking. About that, there could be no dispute. Nobody, absolutely nobody, questioned the supremacy of couscous over beefsteak and french-fried potatoes. The feasts, emptied of their spiritual meaning, continued to bring us together around generously loaded tables. Isn't the Jewish cookery of the Maghreb among the finest in the world?

The break was complete. The schools acted as though the world out of which we came had never existed, leaving us to conclude for ourselves that it was worth nothing. Not that the majority of us were in any hurry to cross over. From kindergarten to university, the emphasis was placed exclusively on French culture, purged, through the French heritage of radical laicism, of its Biblical element, so that our ignorance of our origins became abysmal. It was not only Baba's turban, bolero, and baggy trousers that were anachronistic in our eyes, but his faith, his language, his culture, his books, his songs, his way of being and expressing himself, his way of living and hoping. The Empire was not satisfied with having our bodies, it wanted our souls, so that our loyalty might be perfect -- our souls, Jewish, Moslem, or even African. For the Republic to be indivisible, wasn't it necessary that it be _one_? The distinct languages and cultures of the French provinces having been wiped out, it was necessary to reduce those of the whole Empire to one common denominator. And wasn't it also in the interest of the colonized peoples to free them from the darkness out of which they were emerging, and to adopt them without reserve, by giving them, as their sole culture, the secular and republican culture of France?

In vain did Baba, on the shore, thrash out the problem with his customary protectors, the Patriarchs and Prophets, invoking, in this cause, even the angels and archangels, and God himself. He understood very well that nothing more could be done. The Hebrews had been able to survive the empires of Egypt, of Assyria, and of Babylon; they had risen up against the Roman legions and barred their road to the East; they had victoriously resisted the temptation to succumb to Christianity or to Islam, preserving their identity through twenty centuries of exile. Now, with one little sentence, the French Empire had succeeded where all the others had failed: "Our forefathers, the

68

Gauls, were big, brave, strong, and quarrelsome..."
All of a sudden, oblivious of our past, we embraced
the belief that we were, every one of us, authentic
descendants of Vercingetorix.

El Cojo

The French school separated me from my origins,
cut my roots. Illness was, after that, to take from
me the wholeness of my body. The incident that
preceded my being felled by an acute attack of
infantile paralysis was significant. I was going to
discover in my interior life a new dimension, that of
suffering -- and, with the suffering, a perception of
the meaning of suffering.

It was a summer day, one of those days on which
the sirocco bathed Aïn-Témouchent in a grey light, the
color of the Sahara, and immersed us in an atmosphere
sparkling with sand particles suspended in the air.
The school was almost the only place where Christians,
Moslems, and Jews mingled, all still hampered by the
prejudice and bigotry of their birth and upbringing.
"Dirty Arab!" was shouted at a Moslem, and he would
reply, according to circumstances, "Dirty Jews!" or
"Dirty Dago!" since most of the French around Oran
were of Spanish descent.

I no longer remember just how all this started.
Fierce disputes between groups of children belonging
to the different clans were not rare. Sometimes they
developed into real battles that spread out among the
oleanders by the river-bed or in the pine grove next
to the school, which we pompously named "the Sea." It
was near noon, and we were leaving the school to have
lunch at home with our families... In the street I
was chased with shouts of "Dirty Jew!" by a pack of
children, who were emphasizing their remarks by
hitting my head with their book-bags. I was six years
old, and alone. I ran, pursued to the door of our
house by the cries and blows of my schoolfellows. In
my mother's arms I trembled all over, my teeth
chattering with fever. I had to be put to bed. Our
family doctor, Dr. Léon Achard, diagnosed my illness
too late to mitigate its consequences. When I was
completely paralyzed, immobile, head to foot, he
realized that I had had an acute attack of polio. I
had become a poor little thing, suffering and
motionless, at the bottom of a bed, where only my

eyes, made enormous by my thinness, bore witness to the fact that I still lived. For a long time, despite all the care that was lavished upon me, I could not hold myself up on my legs. Like the "Beggar" of Murillo, I dragged myself along the floor from room to room of our house, using my hands. My studies were naturally interrupted for months, and I devoted this time, with the help of a rabbi, to improving my knowledge of Hebrew. Slowly, the use of my right leg and of my left arm came back to me. My parents did everything they could to put me on my feet again. They consulted the best doctors, and had me take treatments and cures that finally succeeded in giving me back the use of my body.

That no possible remedy might be left untried, they took my case also to faith healers and wise men. They put me to the test with their concoctions, and loaded me with medals, such as those of the holy Moslem priest of Nedromah, and those of rabbis thought to be miracle-workers. Bone-setters, in order to reawake my sleeping muscles, advised that I be plunged into the steaming stomachs of oxen just that moment slaughtered. My parents took me to the slaughterhouse, and I floundered, naked, in the belly, filled with still hot chyme, of ox after ox, butchered before my horrified eyes. My extreme sensibility became morbid. I took my refuge in reading, becoming addicted to it, night and day, as to a drug. I read everything that came into my hands, the best and the worst, trembling with emotion as I discovered the interior world. The exterior world was to me a wound. My Jewish origin told me plainly, in the brutally anti-Semitic atmosphere of colonial Algeria, that I was from <u>elsewhere</u>.

My crippling was severe. At that time I could hold myself up on my left leg only by pressing my hand down on the knee to keep it straight. My disability quickly convinced me that I was no longer just from elsewhere, but rather from <u>nowhere</u>. Childhood is cruel. "El Cojo," "Limpy," was a nickname that pierced me to the quick every time I heard it called out by my little companions. The term "invalid" seemed to freeze me through and through; for months I hid in my room a novel by Estaunié that I dared not open, <u>The Invalid with Hands of Light</u>! I made wide detours in order to avoid making a spectacle of myself in passing by a sidewalk café. Sometimes, at night, I lay sobbing in my bed. What would I ever be able to do? Who could ever bring herself to love me? The cruelty of the world became as familiar to me as the jerky dance that, for me, took the place of walking. I did have, at any rate, a refuge in my family, in which my mother and my three big sisters hovered over me tenderly, supporting me with their attentive warmth: my mother, loving, sad, sensitive and often irritable; and the young girls, Marie the blonde, and Lucie and Alice with hair black as jet, their faces illuminated by eyes of endless depth and fire.

My brothers, Albert, and especially Charles, a giant, served as my bodyguards. No one could touch a hair of their little André. And all the while my father kept up his unflagging effort to keep alive the bond that held me to our interior Jerusalem, and made me a resident of the Hebraic Empire of the Bible.

The dream at an end

When I was snatched from the family nest and put in the boarding school for boys at Oran, things almost turned out very badly. The long hours of being cherished in the arms of my pretty sisters, lying stretched out against their breasts on the rocking-chair in our parlor, were over. Over, too, were my mother's stories about the marvels of our family, of our ancestors, and of our people. Over, the long hours of prayer between the knees of my father at the synagogue, and at the ecstatic night services, in which the chanting of the Psalms snatched us out of our heaviness, our gloom, our fears, and placed us in the light of a glory that embraced and uplifted us. The Hebrew words were spoken by the praying assembly like so many projectiles directed against our lethargy. Yes, we were Sons of Israel, Hebrews, the last survivors of a people that refused to die, the authentic custodians of the Bible, and almost the only ones to know how to read it in its original tongue. In order to preserve it, we had accomplished the extraordinary feat of traversing twenty centuries of exile, dreaming, all the while, of nothing but our return to Jerusalem, the coming of the Messiah, and of universal peace and justice, forgetting nothing and falsifying nothing, in the infatuation of a mad love.

71

End of the dream: in the Oran school I was transformed, at the age of ten, into a robot that waked, walked, ate, studied, and went back to sleep at the beat of a drum. Its rollings put us in motion from dawn to dark. From hour to hour, keeping in step, we went to the dormitory, to the refectory, and from class to class, goaded and punished by our overseers and ushers. Out of this experience I have retained an accurate sense of time, an exactitude that can stand no tardiness, in myself or in others.

Suddenly, I was living in surroundings exclusively masculine. Gone were my mother's skirts, my sisters' caresses. I was let loose in the midst of a horde of rampant boys, who could hardly stand being held in leash, having, to turn against me, the facts that I was the youngest, the weakest, and even crippled. I kept from being utterly crushed by turning inward, by seeking my life-giving oxygen on the other planet where lived my loves and my books. One day, when one of my companions had made himself far too offensive, I got him by the throat. I have always had, in my hands and arms, the strength that I no longer had in my legs. Lucien was the muscle man of the gang. When they managed to get us apart, he was half conscious. This exploit earned me the respect of the experts. I had earned the right to a little tranquillity.

Son of the Commandment

The sight of my father, praying, blessing the wine and the bread; and of my mother, blessing the sabbath candles, were among the memories that most securely bound me to my Jewish religious traditions. Along with these, there come back to me the smiling presence of Abraham Meyer, the fascinating odors that arose from dishes that could be had nowhere but at our house, the memory of our songs brought out of Israel and Spain, and the strangeness of our customs. All this, which recalled me to that "elsewhere" out of which I had come, and from which I was withdrawing more and more as I grew older, seemed to be a kind of folklore.

As I approached thirteen, we had to think of the celebration of my religious coming of age, when I was to become a _bar mitzvah_, a son of the commandment, a man grown, fit to perform fully all his duties toward God and man. This affair was of importance under several aspects: I was the youngest child of my family, the third of the three boys to celebrate this occasion, which had to be invested with all the more splendor because my father was the chief Jew of his community, and president of the consistory. It was also the first feast celebrated in our family since the death of my grandfather, Abraham Meyer. I must, therefore, be prepared meticulously for all the rites of initiation which were to make of me a true son of Israel. I was set again to the intensive study of Hebrew. Every day, during my vacation, Rabbi Journo came to give me lessons. The decisive test was to recite in Hebrew a section from the Torah and one from the Prophets before the whole community, brought together to judge the merits of the candidate, and to welcome him.

The text I had to read from the Pentateuch, my parashah, was from the story of Noah and the Deluge, telling of the rebirth of humanity and its new covenant with God, its saviour. We were, ourselves, also the generation of the deluge, born during the Great War of 1914-1918, and grown to maturity in time to take part in the Second World War, witnesses of the immolation of our brothers, vanished in waves of flame in the crematory ovens. But we were the men who were going to reconquer the Land of Israel, ha'aretz, the Land, as we call it in Hebrew, coming forth from our ark of salvation, miraculously preserved as were Noah and his sons, we were destined to become the first men of the return, renewed, purified, and ready to ratify the new covenant of our reawakening and restoration. The text from the Prophets, my haphtarah, which I had to chant in our traditional recitative style, so close to Gregorian chant, was even more significant. I read, from Chapter 54 of Isaiah, in a voice choked with emotion, sentences whose full meaning I only now comprehend:

"Raise a glad cry, you barren one who did not bear, break forth in jubilant song, you who were not in labor,
For more numerous are the children of the deserted wife than the children of her who has a husband, says the Lord.
Enlarge the space for your tent, spread out your tent cloths unsparingly; lengthen your ropes and make firm your stakes.

For you shall spread abroad to the right and to the left; your descendants shall dispossess the nations and shall people the desolate cities..."*

Almost a half-century has rolled by since I, a child, chanted these words from the pulpit of carved wood in the synagogue of Aïn-Témouchent. I am deeply conscious today, as I write these lines in a Jerusalem rebuilt from its ruins, that they were prophetic for me and for my generation. We have been plucked out of the sterility of our ghettos and gathered together on our land, where we can at last "enlarge the space for out tent," rebuild and repeople our desolate cities. This passage was constantly in my mind when, at the head of the city of Jerusalem from 1965 to 1973, I took part in the great leap that snatched her out of the desolation of her ruins and her partition.

The celebration was splendid. On the terrace of our house the old people gathered around the traditional orchestra of Btaïna, the greatest expert on Jewish songs in Spain and in the Maghreb. The young people preferred to dance in the yard, to the waltzes and tangos of a modern orchestra. The festivities went on all night on these two levels, without anyone noticing their evident contradiction. At dawn, young and old reunited to lead me, in solemn procession, to the synagogue. Sunrise at Aïn-Témouchent is particularly splendid. The colors, the odors, and the music of Africa there blend with those of the Mediterranean. On this eighth of September, 1930, I had solemnly put on my prayer shawl and my phylacteries. After my public proclamation of those truly prophetic texts, I was to become a man, a son of Israel, a disciple of Moses. This rite of initiation, that, in principle, should have meant my complete identification with my tribe, marked, in fact, my leaving its maternal breast. The public school of Oran snatched me into its anonymity. A boarder, seventy kilometers away from Aïn-Témouchent, from Baba, from my family, from our religious ceremonies and from our graves, I was delivered over completely to the influence of my new masters, whose duty it was to make me succeed in passing those different but

_____

*Isaiah 54, 1-3.NAB

74

equally formidable examinations that constituted the secular and republican _bar mitzvah_ known as the baccalauréat.

At fifteen, my full growth being attained, I underwent an operation, a muscle transplant that gave me back the use of my legs. I still limped, but it no longer seemed as though I had no feet. With my body thus given back to me, I could take part in all the sports, including walking. I got really good at swimming and gymnastics; no longer was I "an invalid with hands of light!" My lameness bothered me less, and I could give myself the luxury of living _as if_ it didn't exist.

The course of study for the bachelor's degree

It was intellectually that I now began to limp. The bond that held me strongly to my family seemed broken, at least insofar as it pertained to ideas, culture, and attitudes toward life and toward God. The public school of Oran was justly esteemed for the quality of its teachers, most of whom were graduates of universities or of "normal schools." Their teaching purely and simply disregarded the world out of which I came. I can't say they scorned it, because they didn't even suspect its existence. The Bible, the Mishnah, the Talmud, the Cabala, the Jewish people, religion, God??? Dunno! I aligned myself, naturally, with the new verities, and proclaimed myself an atheist, a socialist, and a friend of the USSR. Politically, Lèon Blum became my idol. It must be said here that the brutal anti-Semitism of Algerian rightists, who joined in the unbridled fury of the Latin Union, left us little choice. It took, later on, the shock of my discovery of God, through my encounter with Christian and Moslem spirituality, and the trauma of the Hitlerian persecution, to pull me back to my Jewish well-springs. Since Hitler wanted to take my life because I was Jewish, at least I wanted to die with my eyes open, knowing what it means to be Jewish. Since the proselytizers, secular or religious, on all sides, seemed to bear a grudge against my soul, I wanted at least to know what it was they wanted me to renounce, before deciding whether I should follow them. The operation to which we schoolboys submitted was somewhat reminiscent of the old Chinese tale: a headsman was charged by the emperor with the task of beheading one of his best friends. "Don't worry," he said, "I won't hurt you a bit." His head on the block, the victim muttered, "Well, when are you going to do it?" "It's already done, my friend. Just move your head, and it will fall!" For us, the surgery had been so radical, the uprooting so complete, that it seemed to have left no scars or other traces. I did not experience the battle of the generations because all of a sudden I lived in a different world from the one I had been born in, and in which my parents, surrounded by their strange black books, kept their vigilant watch. They expected from God the salvation of Israel, the building of Jerusalem, and the coming of the Messiah. Their mental attitudes, their notions, which had provided me with poetry and dreams throughout my childhood, seemed to me utterly stranded in the past. Taking into account the dry bones of official Judaism, I was not far from agreeing with Toynbee's opinion that the Jew was an archeological survival, a fossil. As for me, I had become, thanks to the secular and republican culture, a modern, a man of the Age of Enlightenment, a son of the French Revolution, a free citizen of a country whose motto, which had become mine, was Liberty, Equality, and Fraternity. If there was anything worth while in the disordered heap of my ancestral traditions, it was the seed of the edifying realities of the era of progress. Science and revolution would bring to the world, at last freed from the obscurantism of religion, what God had been unable to give it.

You don't lay blame upon a fossil. That which constituted the heart, the flesh, the blood and the soul of life for my family and friends was, in this light, a folklore, feeble enough, and evidently destined to disappear, but never failing to rouse in me the warm feeling that I had always had for it. My nature granted me the grace of never putting myself in open conflict with the tribe out of which I had come. I was broken-hearted to learn that Baba, coming to see us at the school, a little while before his death, had waited in vain for one of his sons. The wretch was hiding at the bottom of an areaway from which it was impossible to extricate him. He was ashamed to show himself before his schoolmates in the company of his too-picturesque ancestor, Baba, his bow legs arched under his immense cloak, his turban in battle array, and his fiery eye. Baba, fading from this world, last of the giants of his line, those who guided us up to

76

the Promised Land, the ultimate goal of their heroic and bloody Odyssey. Like Moses on Nebo, he was destined to die before crossing its threshold.

I still wonder today at the efficiency of the system that molded our minds during the years through which I hastened, from morning to night, along the immense corridors of that school, built like a Napoleonic barracks. The task of our teachers was not easy. They had before them the offspring of a heterogeneous population, Christians of French, Spanish, or Italian descent, Moslem descendants of Berbers, Arabs, or Turks, and finally, Jews, more or less recently escaped from their ghettos. Within a single class, the differences in age exaggerated our diversity still further. In the sixth grade, when I was ten, some of my fellow pupils were sixteen, and had come down from the mountains, where they had still been living in the iron age.

The courses that led to a bachelor's certificate were designed to level off our differences, smooth over our diversities, in order to make of us pure products of the French school system. To this end, our masters achieved true miracles. I have seen a Moslem come down from his mountain hamlet to enter the third grade, and, from his first year of study in the school, carry off all the first places and the prize for general excellence, of which no one was ever able to rob him afterward.

Our training, more intensive, perhaps, than anywhere else, gave us the taste and method of good workmanship,. In all my life, I have never seen anyone work as much as we did in the year of our first certificate. From the second story, where our dormitories were, we would climb on the roof, at the risk of breaking our bones, to get our books at four o'clock in the morning, and never put them back until well after the official lights out.

In these Mediterranean latitudes, sexuality engrossed our attention all the more because it was strictly forbidden to talk about it with our parents or with our teachers, and because our classes were made up of boys only. To see a girl was for all of us a notable event, an event which the biggest boys soon learned to bring about, often beginning at the onset of puberty, by going to visit them on the free

Thursdays and Sundays, in the whorehouses of the Rue des Jardins. Some tall gawky fellows were pederasts, and satisfied their cravings by taking advantage of the "blues," generally boys newly arrived from France. Masturbation was done in plain view -- it was the principal occupation, during French lessons, of one of our schoolmates, who, a short time afterwards, was put in prison for having shot his father, a caïd of the region of Sig.

From the moment we entered the doors of the school, our past detached itself from us like the sloughed skin of a snake. It would have been more shocking to bring to light any of the realities of that past than to describe the exploits, real or imagined, of the alcoves in the Rue des Jardins. I never heard any one of the teachers refer, even in a single word, to our origins, religious, national, ethnic, or cultural. Algeria was French, and we, therefore, were all little Frenchmen, and must all be educated like our fellow-pupils of the Ile-de-France. We were so educated, so efficiently that our ancient roots died away before any new roots could take hold. We were transplanted, and were left no possibility of becoming cultural mongrels. Moslems, Jews, Christians, Spaniards, Italians, Berbers, Arabs, or black Africans, we must all become authentic Gauls. And so we did, to the pride and wonderment of the new world that had adopted us.

The discovery of self

This world, even before I had made the circuit of it, did not seem to me sufficiently vast for me to seal myself into it hermetically. I had undertaken the discovery of the world in which I lived. Of the Hebraic world, certainly. I kept wondering about its origins, its meanings, the reasons for its survival, and for the hostility it never ceased to stir up.

I looked at our religious rites, our customs, our nature and way of life, with a fresh eye. In what way were we not "like the others?" What caused our inability to conform ourselves? I endlessly questioned all those who might help me to find an answer, but without much success, I must admit. On one side were the "ancients," of so strict and intransigent an authenticity that they didn't ask themselves any of the questions that were troubling me, and on the other, the "moderns," for whom the past from which they had been liberated held no interest whatever. I was thus put on my own.

At the synagogue, to which I continued to accompany my father, I learned more about it than I did from the books. I loved our traditional chants, in which rang the echoes of our places of origin, Spain and the East. All our ceremonies were structured about the reading of the Bible, whose scrolls, written in Hebrew, were venerated equally with the God whose word they contained. Their being taken out of the Ark, and the procession with them to the tribune from which we proclaimed the Scripture, the living Word, in its original tongue, constituted the high point of our worship. We were standing erect, wearing our prayer shawls, to sing exalted hymns with all our might. In vain had I crossed the border -- what was happening there never ceased to impress me and to raise questions in me. Plunged into that Hebraic universe, I studied it intensely, trying to translate it, and, first of all, to find its meaning for myself.

The Arab world puzzled me just as much. Why did our teachers tell us so little about it? Why that universal scorn of the "donkey?" Why did our Arab companions seem still more ill at ease about the world out of which they had come than we about our own? Pedaling on my bike, I went from hamlet to hamlet, from farm to farm, trying to understand that world with which I felt we were engaged in a drawn match. It was impossible to act as though it didn't exist. Baba and my parents were an integral part of the Arab world. Arabic was their mother tongue, and it was in their house and in their office that I learned it, and that I formed my first friendship with Moslems, whose nobility and generosity of character have never failed me. They were great gentlemen, even when clothed in rags, and I was fascinated by their culture, and by the manner in which, in their daily lives, they took upon themselves the eternity of Allah.

The baptism of the desert

It was then that I discovered the desert. One spring, taking advantage of the Easter vacation, which I regularly passed at home with my family at Aïn-Témouchent, I made my first Saharan escapade,

79

adventuring into the southern part of Algeria. Leaving my green and subtly-shaded countryside, I discovered in the Sahara a reflection of my interior landscape. The burning sands and rocks, stretching out to infinity, without hedges, without trees, without human beings, a ridgeless universe in which no separate life was possible, evoked the absolute, which weighed upon me, rose up before me, flinging at me the fires of its skies. There an eagle would sometimes launch itself from its mountains, to fly over our caravan as it made its way along the straight line of the road. After hours of solitude on the tracks, life took up once more in the neighborhood of the oases. The ruminations of camels were swallowed up in the shade of palm trees and gardens as they threaded their way, at Bou-Saada, Biskra, or Ouargla, between the oleanders of the dry river-beds that I explored.

Under the arcades of the village of Temacine, near Touggourt, passing by Arabs, impassive under their white or brown burnooses, I squatted at a corner in a lane, and wrote in a copybook held on my knee: "I am going through a land where at last the dream coincides with the reality." The dream, even at this early period of my life, was, for me, vibrant with the all-powerful presence of love. I came upon that reality, and, dazzled, I knew nothing to say of it except that it "was." It rolled in upon me, extremely similar to my own self, wave upon wave of sand, with the sharp and violent contrast of the oasis, luxuriant with greenery, mysterious shadows, women, flowers, fruits. The presence of love was there, a promise stretched along the very ground, a cry flung out against all that could deny life. Whenever I could, I went out again to the discovery of my Saharan horizons.

One day in spring, the season in which Ouargla solemnized its multiple weddings, under the shade of numberless palms, the whole town was buzzing with talk. Twelve couples were celebrating their union on the same day. From early morning, the procession of men was winding its way in pilgrimage to the local marabout. At its head, an orchestra of drums and flutes riveted my attention. Its pulsing rhythms, untiringly repeated, incited the piercing cries of the women. The bridal couples were surrounded by an unimaginable Cour des Miracles (beggars' quarter) of toothless old women, some of them blind, shrilling up to the heavens their incantatory cries, throbbing with faith and with magical powers. These were the same women who would mourn, the next day, the dead of the oasis. The cries of joy and grief here mingled in a paroxysm of emotion that seemed somehow an echo to the silence of the surrounding sands. Like the chanting women, taking off in pursuit of the throbbing rhythms of their orchestra of flutes and drums, in their multicolored robes in shaded gardens, I had to take up my quest for love, separating myself from all that was not that quest itself. One image seems to express best my experience of the desert, my immersions in the infinity of dunes and rocks -- I was like a man who, hanging in the air, is falling endlessly without finding a point of support. This was my situation as I journeyed from oasis to oasis. In the emptiness of the desert, I had given up hope of finding any solid ground to receive me, but that of my tomb in exile. Unless...

A stranger to myself in the ghetto where I was born, come from elsewhere and transplanted into French soil, I could never be, in the eyes of my Arab friends, anything but a dhimmi, a member of a tolerated and protected class, who was struggling to explore and understand the city of Islam, on whose borders I had grown up. In our towns, built in western style, the presence of Islam was hardly perceptible. It was impossible to detect it in Oran or even Témouchent. It was in the Sahara that I looked, face to face, upon its true countenance.

I rose before daybreak. Seated in eastern fashion, like the rabbis of the oases where I lived, singing my Hebrew Psalms on the terrace of the house where I was staying, in the shadow of the palm trees, I was a prayerful assistant at the ceremony of sunrise. My days included from ten to twelve hours of work, struggling with the Hebrew text of the Bible, which I was trying, by translating it, to understand more deeply. At twilight, in the conflagration of the sunset, piercing the noise of chain-pumps and of their falling waters, I listened to the Symphony of the minarets, from which sounded the voice of Islam. I was living then in the oasis of Ouargla. The venerable cadi of the place gave me lessons in Arabic with an enthusiasm all the greater because he had hopes of turning me into a good Moslem. This would have been beneficial for both of us: Islam guarantees to the convert, as well as to the one who converts him, a place in Allah's paradise. Thus he interlarded his course in Arabic with recurrent arguments in favor of his religion, in which he believed with all his soul. He had conceived for me, as I tried in exchange to teach him French, a sincere friendship. "You are better than a key that serves to open doors; you are a tree upon whose fruits the whole man may feed himself." On the day I arrived in Ouargla, where he was waiting for me, he had found a spring in a garden that he had owned for some years. The coincidence had convinced him that I was the cause of his precious discovery. A spring in an oasis guarantees a considerable increase in income. Not being an ingrate, my man at once offered me a share of his possessions, and could never understand the reason for my refusal. It was still harder for me to repulse his missionary zeal. One day, when he ws at his most insistent, I found the decisive argument, to which he could find no answer.

"What about Moses? Who is he for Moslems? I asked him.

"The first of believers, the confidant and beloved of Allah, the prophet chosen and favored beyond all men, the author of numberless miracles..."

"And for Christians?"

"They are with us in seeing in him one of the greatest, if not the greatest, of the prophets."

"But you yourselves, you Moslems, what do you think about the divinity of Jesus?"

"One thing is certain in our eyes: Jesus, the Messiah, son of Mary, is neither God nor son of God. The Christians blaspheme."

"Indeed. Tell me further, what do the Christians think of Mohammed?"

"Those sons of bitches make fun of him, shamelessly accuse him of being a sick man, a liar, a forger. They accuse him, the prophet of Allah, of being possessed, or a sorcerer!"

My friend was crimson with indignation. His eyes, habitually squinting, intensified their squint until it seemed as though they were going to combine in the middle of his face into a sort of Cyclops eye. But I cut short his fury by declaring:

"Now look, you acknowledge all the message of Moses, which I have received from my ancestors. For what comes from Mohammed and Jesus, have patience. I'll wait until you come to an agreement before deciding about it. Try, in the meanwhile, to be less unfaithful to Moses, to Jesus... and to Mohammed, won't you?" I concluded, resuming my lesson in Arabic.

Of course, this was only a casually uttered pleasantry, but it proved so convincing that he spoke to me no more of conversion.

The Sahara was my constant refuge, my reservoir of power. I kept going over it, in all senses, passing whole days in contemplation of the play of light on its translucent dunes. There, between sunrise and sunset, my solitude was disturbed only by the visit of a swallow, or of a long-beaked bee-eater with crest erect, flying around me, astonished to see a human being in these arid wastes, where they were searching for some sort of unlikely food. In the Arab house I was living in, at the heart of the oasis, the old black who was looking after me came now and then to make sure I was still alive. Each dawn, the palm trees, held up like bouquets of light, raised to the skies the cry of the muezzins, from the tops of their minarets: "Allah akbar!" "God is great!"

Twenty minutes of rain, brought to us by a storm, had made a feast-day for the oasis. The palms glistened, the gardens sang in celebration of the baraka fallen from the heavens, faces and relaxed bodies quivered with a new energy in the troubling tumult of music. I had come upon a group of youths making a game of tormenting a shining, multicolored bird. The storm had made it fall into their hands. I bought it from them for seven sous. It could no longer fly. I tried to get it to drink some water. It shuddered all over, waved its wings wildly as if in a final goodbye to life, then, with a flash of light in the eyes set in its hawk-like head, it was dead without a cry.

83

Thus, a man died in me in the demi-ecstasy of my Saharan paradise, where I became aware of the true scope of the spirit. I could no longer satisfy myself with the André Gide-like fervors that summoned up to my mind the lascivious contours of the Ouled-Naïl girls, with their stirring beauty, roses of the sands, dancing their joy in light robes of green and red. The blind alley of Marxism became laughable in the boundlessness of what I saw, its aspirations naive and obsolete in the urgency of the dangers I anticipated. Under the little cupola that rose above my very bare room, I learned from my Bible to find another grammar: fasting and meditation had become a constant in my life. One day, when I was standing on the threshold of my door, an Arab appeared and took hold of me. His eye glowed with fervor. He was a disciple of the Sufi mystics of the Zaouia of Mostaganem. "I was waiting for you," he said, by way of salutation. Then he said: "My place is no place, my footstep no footstep. Whoever does not come forth from the palace of nature can never attain the city of truth. Love is the annihilation of self will, the destruction of desires. He is come; he has freed me from all that is not he; he has molded me, after having felled me and melted me into himself like sugar in water."

The man glowed with inherent power. After asking my permission, he foretold my future. I listened to it all without believing in it: everything was there, the publication of numerous works, then, when not one had been planned, travels and missions to the four quarters of the globe, my establishment in Paris, and then in Jerusalem, when no notion of these things had yet sprouted, and even the rôle that "a Jew, bearded and wearing a sword," would play in my life. When this was said, I knew no one who could fit that description. Some months later, I was to meet René Cassin, on the very day on which his academician's sword was given back to him. Now that this vision, forgotten as soon as heard, has been realized with such precision, how are we to explain the possibility of foreseeing the future? My Sufi friend, clearly free of any sectarian limitation, taught me far more of the profound realities of the God of Islam than did the worthy cadi of Ouargla. When I went off to Paris, where I was to pursue my studies, my atheistic convictions, that my teachers in the boarding school at Oran had tried so hard to implant in me, were shaken. The Bible no longer seemed to me a useless

84

accessory, and God a waning moon. Along the way I had discovered Spinoza, to whom, for a time, I clung, as a midpoint between the atheism of my professors and that new universe, that of the God of the Bible, to whose intoxication I was soon to surrender.

To be from nowhere

I had been, ever since I crossed the threshold of the French school in the Rue Pasteur of Aïn-Témouchent, a colonial subject who, in the eyes of the educators, became the material for a fascinating experiment: how to make this little barbarian into a veritable descendant of Vercingetorix? In order for the operation to succeed, it was necessary that it be unnoticeable to the subject. Nothing must be said to him about it, but every trace, every vestige that could recall his past must be made to disappear, and there must gleam before him his extraordinary happiness in having been snatched out of the darkness of his origins to be reborn in the glory of the greatest, the most beautiful, the most generous of languages, of cultures, of civilizations in the world -- those of France.

The product turned out by this process, furnished with his bachelor's certificate, was in fact a strange mixture of East and West. I was a stranger everywhere. Nowhere did I feel at home. My East itself was not pure; it was no longer the flawless diamond whose sparkle made the bearded countenance of Baba glow with joy; it was no longer the Islam of my cadi; and still less the fervent inspiration of my Saharan mystic. As for my West... The label of France had been put on a bachelor package, as on a colony, on the supposition that this would be, not only profitable, but even sufficient to effect the transubstantiation of our Arabian, Jewish, or Spanish deserts into neat little French parks. Moreover, our masters, devoted and efficient as they were, found themselves handicapped by the requirements of the program laid out for them, and, still more, by their own abysmal ignorance of what we really were. In fact, the colonial situation, the relation between colonized and colonist, had alienated us. All of us had become strangers even to ourselves. My discomfort in feeling this was the more profound in that, colonized equally with my Moslem friends, I was no longer, in fact, on their side. Jews were among the privileged beneficiaries of the colonial rule. France needed dependable men for the administration of the colony, and to serve as buffers between them and the Arabs. The Crèmieux Decree, like a magic potion concocted at Tours on the banks of the Loire, made of us, the Jews of Algeria, authentic French citizens, all in one day, October 24, 1970.

The discovery of the West

I had, all of a sudden, the feeling of living on the other side of the looking-glass. The orchestras, the choruses of the Opera had stopped playing out of tune. The snow, the autumn colors, the moss of the underwoods, the long twilights -- all had come forth out of the literary domain to become palpable realities. Still more: that famous French civilization, about which our masters had battered our ears fruitlessly in Algeria, was demonstrating its own existence, and had become incredibly real.

In company with my brother Charles, I arrived in Paris, where my uncle Maurice had studied medicine, to enter law school. It was October, 1935, and France had bandaged the wounds inflicted by World War I, and was not yet thinking of the still more severe trial that was soon to be inflicted upon her. The technological revolution was just taking its first steps. I was able to dash around on my bike, academic cape flapping in the wind, between the University City, where I lived, and the Latin Quarter. The streets still had their antediluvian look. We were no longer in the age of stage-coaches, but the age of jets and three-wheeled cars had not yet begun.

In the intoxication of my discovery of the true France, the events through which we were living slipped over me as though they were never to concern me. The invasion of Ethiopia by Mussolini, the war in Spain, Germany falling under the power of Hitler and the Nazis, and the rise of the Popular Front -- all these were disquieting facts, to be sure, but hardly dulled my enthusiasm about my discoveries. Everything was new for me in the marvelous universe that was offering me, at last, the unqualified adoption for which I longed -- so much so that I saw nothing any more but lights. Enough, in truth, to dazzle my thought upon its awakening. At Oran, closeted among

86

my literary enthusiasms, I led a life captive to my dreams. The moment I stuck my nose outside, I met the slap in the face of anti-Semitism, swastikas daubed in tar on the walls of our houses. The racism that fell upon the Arabs was even worse. The "donkey" was less than a man, less than an animal -- at best, a machine under the orders of the colonist. The colonial bourgeoisie was subject to the supreme master of its Pantheon, Mammon, the Money-God; a God so jealous that even Dagon, the God of sexual debauchery, had a hard time worming his way into the lives of his slaves. As for the Christians, even the militant Christians, they also were victims of that concentration camp universe; a universe that found the assurance of its stability in the fact that each person, hermetically sealed behind the closed doors of his ghetto, obeyed the rules of the colonial game. The consciousness of freedom that I experienced in France, nourished by so many friendships, finally shattered my atavistic barriers and opened me at last to the great winds of the life of the spirit.

And this was my astonished discovery of the West! Generally on my bike, alone or with friends, I set myself to making an inventory of a civilization, the European, whose essential wellsprings and highest realities had been hidden from me by the bookish education I had been given. Paris became the center from which I went forth on my expeditions. Every week-end, at Christmas, at Easter, and still more during the long vacations, eager and light-hearted on my steel wheels, I went from country to country, from town to town, to satisfy my craving for the treasures of their humanity, their museums, their places of prayer. Spain, where I rediscovered a violence that is a part of my own heritage; the Italy of Fra Angelico and of St. Peter's in Rome; the midnight sun of the Scandinavian countries; Belgium and Holland; Switzerland, a country made to the measure of man, whose high mountains I loved to climb; Great Britain, with such calm nerves, such stinging wit, such perfect music under the vaults of Oxford or Cambridge, with souls so well attuned, with the sober elegance of readings from the King James Bible. More thrilling still was the pilgrimage I made in France, from book to book, from high point to high point, on the roads of Ile de France, Normandy and Brittany, the Massif Central and the Pyrenees, Provence and Alsace. There I discovered, to my amazement, the secret that my

87

secular teachers had so completely hidden: that
France is a Christian land, whose language I could
better understand -- even the language of its atheists
-- under the arches of Notre-Dame, Vezelay, Moissac,
or Chartres.

More essential for me was the warm participation
and fellow-feeling of Paris. With what wonder I
experienced the sense of togetherness that unfolded in
a trip on the Metro, a concert at the Pleyel Hall, or
an hour at a cafe. Our student evening parties in the
Latin Quarter or the University City snatched us out
of our tiredness and lethargy. We had ceased to be
prisoners of the ghetto, and become true world
citizens. The authority of our professors, their
human worth, and even their contradictions permitted
us to unfurl our sails to the winds that could send us
forth on the high seas. They gave us more than mere
knowledge, in forging our minds into instruments fit
to penetrate what was going on within us and around
us. Conscious of my own limits, I prayed one day at
Notre Dame, near that pillar at which Paul Claudel was
converted, that I might have the clear-sighted
fortitude never to sacrifice to idols. "To live in
truth" had become the motto to which I strove to be
faithful.

I was held in the orbit of the French language and
culture, under the spell of their power over men,
hailing from all corners of the world, whom France
gathered into that Religion of Equals described by
Hugo, the religion of free citizens of the world. We
felt ourselves at home in Paris, at the University,
among our teachers or with our fellow students. Gone,
or almost gone, was the obsessive fear of being
rejected on account of being Jewish. Everything
seemed open before us: the nation, the government,
the people, and even the churches. All boundaries
seemed to have been wiped out; we were going to
rediscover our liberty as men, our origins and our
aspirations were going to be understood and respected.

What a delight it was to read and reread,
endlessly, Pascal and Racine, Voltaire and Rousseau,
Chateaubriand and Verlaine, Rimbaud, Lautréamont, and
breathlessly, Claudel and Valéry! The Greek classics,
and Dante, Shakespeare, and Dostoyevsky, as well as
Bach, Mozart, and Beethoven, lived again in our
evening gatherings, and dwelt in our memories. We

thought we had finally come upon our chosen land; had become totally French, in every sense of the word. All this seemed natural to us: the French civilization, the generosity of our friends, the love offered to us, because we were young and full of life. Nothing was ever refused to us on account of our race or religion. We no longer understood the reserve of those Jews, from Central or Eastern Europe, who retained the seclusions and the sensitivities of their ghettos. To them, all this brotherhood, free as life, free as love, was a snare and a delusion, that might well bring us to our deaths. The cry of the survivors of the great Roman massacres of the first century haunted their memories: "Put no trust in the goyim, even forty years after their deaths!" We complained of their being so unyieldingly distrustful, those Jews from the ghettos. We had opted for the universalism of France. France was so generous that she allowed us even to respect, if we wished to, the beliefs and traditions of our ancestors, since she accepted all, and explained all. Rather than waste away our time behind the sealed walls of a ghetto, however Jewish it might be, we wanted to cultivate a garden in the French style, in which we might discover, even to rapture, the joy of living as free men.

Christianity itself took on, in my view, an altogether different aspect. In Algeria, I had never set foot in a church, and had never had any contact, even the most superficial, with any true Christians. Those whom I came across seemed to me to be corroded with prejudices, contempt, and sometimes hate for "the Christ-killers," which was what we were in their eyes. I had an aunt who lived behind the church of Aïn-Témouchent. When, as a child, I went by myself to see her, I would make a detour that doubled the distance, in order to keep away from the threshold of the church. I was quite simply scared by its symbols and by its adherents, who were identified in our eyes with the rightists of the colony, reactionary and thoroughly anti-Semitic. When a priest, or, more probably, a minister, took an interest in us, it was with the acknowledged intention of converting us. He had no more success in achieving it among us than among the Moslems. Racism had separated us by walls so thick that they were known to be inpenetrable. We must die as we had been born, in the prisons of our respective ghettos.

All of a sudden even this seemed changed. I admired the cathedrals that served as landmarks along my roads, the sacred music and the liturgies; I loved the Gregorian chant, whose origin stemmed from the Temple of Jerusalem, like the chants of our Eastern synagogues. I came to know Christians who had nothing in common with the racists or with the medieval persecutors of my Jewish brothers in Europe. At the Clinique de la Montagne, at Courbevoie, where I had been operated on at the age of fifteen, I had known young and pretty Protestant nurses who were preparing to go, for the love of God, to care for the lepers in Africa or in Oceania. One of them, Yvonne Jean, inspired my return to the Bible, my discovery of God, and my meeting with the minister, Louis Dallière, one of the Christian prophets of the rebirth of Israel.

On the Catholic side, I then witnessed the flowering of several religious vocations which have not been without effect on the religious history of our times. A gentle pharmacist of Neuville-sur-Saône, Marie-Thérèse Prost, sold all her possessions to go and offer her services to the lepers of Cameroon, where she died. Jules Monchanin, one of the most profound thinkers of our time, left Lyon at the age of forty-three to found, at Kulitalai, an ashram where he devoted his life to the understanding of India. It was he who put me in touch with Renè Voillaume, whose foundations I followed, along with those of Sister Magdeleine de Jèsus, in Africa, in Asia, in Europe, and in America, maintaining with them a fraternal affection that was never betrayed. No more than Claudel or Maritain did these Christians ever think of demanding that I renounce my Jewish faith. On the contrary, I had the feeling that they hoped, themselves, to learn more of Israel and Judaism. The Judeo-Christian movement was then just beginning. I then attended Monchanin's conferences on the religion of my ancestors. They were of an extraordinary profundity. No modern rabbi, no Jewish publicist, could have expressed the essence of Judaism with more penetration than he did. "Faith predominates in Islam, hope in Judaism, love in Christianity; no one of these virtues is possible without the others..." Monchanin hoped for a reconciliation between Judaism, Christianity, and Islam, on a journey toward the Promised Land where God will be all in all. We all believed, together, in the reign of universal brotherhood, in a new man, living in a land without frontiers, and under new skies.

Politically, we aspired to go beyond the blind nationalism of governments by working for the federalism of which Arnaud Dandieu, Alexandre Marc, and Robert Aron were the European pioneers.

Disillusion

My adoption by France, my entry into the West, hadn't been just an illusion, had they? Hadn't they been a childish dream that came just at the stage of life at which I was making the great discoveries of life, wonderings and enthusiasms, first loves and great friendships? While I was exulting in the discovery of France and of Europe, Hitler was forging the arms of his war, and beginning his descent into the abyss. Since I had left my father's house, everything seemed to have conspired to make me forget that I was a Jew; but Hitler kept reminding me of it. In the anguished atmosphere of the eve of war, the harassing presence of anti-Semitism, both that of Germany and that of the French disciples of Hitler, had an effect on me like that of a drug. I regularly read two or three newspapers that existed only to express hatred for the Jew, for the masochistic pleasure of knowing what our enemies were thinking. I was sick with humiliation, powerlessness, and revived fury before such hateful, such deadly absurdities.

My years in the boarding school, and still more my Parisian schooling, had put a distance between me and my tribe, whose ways now seemed to me more and more to belong to the field of folklore. Jews, indeed, were persecuted -- but didn't they put themselves in a state to provoke persecution, with their passion for keeping apart, their beards, their phylacteries, their strange books and their odd customs? All this, that smelled of dissension, was obvious; why be astonished at it? There was also our atavistic mania for wishing to live among Jews, in ghettos, and our determination to marry only within the tribe. Didn't this also smack of racism? And wasn't there a similar taint to the contempt, or even fear, that some of us felt for the goy? What was the use of our way of reading and understanding the Bible, whose purest ideals had been in the public domain for two thousand years? I saw

91

clearly that official Judaism, especially in the West, had lost the consciousness of its profound meanings. Instead of taking upon itself the mystery of its origins, and the hope of its destination, it did no more than perpetuate congealed rituals, led by rabbis dressed like priests, and subordinated to committees of businessmen. Everywhere else, war was threatening; there, the business of the religious rites was still being carried on.

Wasn't truth to be found in the assimilation that the secular universities of France offered to us? That building wasn't slow in showing me its cracks, and soon almost crushed us, crashing down upon us in the disaster of the Second World War. Anti-Semitism had suddenly ceased to be an archaic survival of an abolished past. We were no longer exposed to the vulgar abuse of the Petit Oranais, which had engineered the election as mayor of Doctor Molle, with his militant followers, the members of the Neo-Anti-Semitic Party. The doctrine of Drumont, at the end of the last century, had, by its impassioned tone, intensified the animosity of the ethnic groups that coexisted in Algeria. Europeans, Arabs, and Jews lived in a segregation that became more and more hostile -- a hostility that a voracious gang exploited to its own profit: hate campaigns in the press, prohibitions applying to the Jewish population, systematic exploitation of the Arabs, demonstrations in the streets, racist provocations, riots, profanations of synagogues, pillaging of stores, false accusations, assassinations; our fathers had known all that and much more. Since we were now living in the age of enlightenment, we thought that these manias of another time, worthy of the Middle Ages, or, strictly speaking, of the time of the Dreyfus affair, would never happen again.

And now, behold, a great country, the most cultivated and the most powerful in Europe, was changing the disused apparatus of traditional anti-Semitism into a terrifying war machine. Persecutions were multiplying in Germany, where the Nazis, faithful to the program of Mein Kampf, were preparing the extermination of an entire people, the Jewish people.

The resources of a powerful government supported the Nazi propaganda. It enlisted in France an intellectual elite, quickly followed by a mob of gangsters, to howl with the wolves. No one seemed to foresee the dangers into which this was leading us. Christians like Jacques Madaule, and Jews like René Cassin and Edmond Fleg, uttered cries of alarm, but these were unheard in the general indifference.

Among the Jewish intellectuals, the blindness, except for a very few, was total. The reawakening of anti-Semitism and the open persecution in Germany had only impelled them to wall themselves into their defensive positions. For them, argument was the only possible reply to concentration camps and crematory ovens. What was needed was to enumerate all the good reasons we had for being Jews, and to boast of "the lasting values of Judaism," without recognizing the fact that these values, like the Bible itself, belonged to all. To tell the truth, nobody could foresee the catastrophe that was to claim fifty million victims in Europe. Nor, it seemed to me, could anyone comprehend the real dimensions of the spiritual drama that we were living, nor the resolution of it that could be given by the Bible. Herzl in politics, Buber in philosophy, and especially Rosenzweig in theology -- were these the sole Jewish thinkers of our time? In our desert, I found only publicists or official spokesmen for a particular creed, confronting the apocalypse rolling in upon the world.

My double uprooting left me defenseless before the griefs and dangers that were coming. The French school had eclipsed the world, the culture, and the faith of my fathers, wiped out God and his saints, and held up before my eyes the whole Jewish life as no more than a troublesome archeological survival. But nothing that I could accept was offered me in exchange. The brilliance of the secular culture disclosed to me could not conceal its emptiness. The ideals of liberty, equality, and fraternity, and the belief in the onward march of socialism, had been enough to arouse my enthusiasm at fourteen. They gave way under the hammer blows of Italian and Spanish fascism. To the Hitlerian hysteria, France had the brilliant idea of rallying the opposition behind an eminent aesthete, and a Jewish one, at that, Léon Blum! All the revolutionary phraseology, so feebly handled by the French left, with which, for lack of a better choice, I had to sympathize, sounded hollow to

me. How could we feed on such fooleries, and find in
them a source of inspiration, while there blew over
Europe a wind of madness that was to lay it in ruins?

Of the fervors of Gide, whose portrait once
adorned my student room at the University City of
Paris, I have retained his command to have "a life of
empathy, not of tranquillity." I wished to seek "no
other repose than that of the sleep of death." For
the rest, I had followed the final Gidean counsel:
"And now, Nathanaël, toss away my book, think of
yourself, more than of it, and of others, more than of
yourself."

I grew up, thus, leaning on any support that might
help me escape from despair. The study of law, which
I took very seriously, even passionately, gave me more
than a technique of thinking. It initiated me in an
understanding of the social structure, and of the laws
that govern the functioning of society. But my
strongest feelings were involved more and more in
other matters: in Ethiopia, where the legions of
Mussolini had driven Haile Selassie; in France, where
the Popular Front had just seized power; and in Spain,
where Franco was murdering the Republic. I shall
never forget the look on the face of André Malraux,
whom I then met for the first time, calling for a
revolt against the fate decreed for Republican Spain.
My deepest and most hidden wound, however, and the one
which was to determine my destiny, was that which came
from Germany. The yells of hate that formed the Nazi
propaganda humiliated and maddened my adolescence, and
ended by driving me down into my well of solitude,
where, freed from the crushing weight of anguish, I
tried to fend off the clutch of madness.

An insufferable violence

Yes, I was filled with an insufferable violence as
I contemplated the condition of the world at that
time. It sometimes seemed to me that I was balancing
along the brink of the precipice of lunacy, and that,
at the slightest misstep, I might pitch headlong into
that abyss. To get rid of the visions of my breast
pierced by a dagger, or my bleeding head smashed
against a wall, I had to climb laboriously, one by
one, the steps of my internal upheaval, finishing with
the most devastating of all, the open wound of my
solitude and of my liberty. I called to mind my

recent scaling of a rocky wall that rose abruptly from a beach to a peak. I had to take each step with the precise step of a goat, and proceed with the patience of a termite, the ample crowning of my task being a glance at the dancing wavelights on the sea, my heart quieted by its fingers of light. I thought seriously of the postscript of a letter from Dostoyevsky to his brother: "I have a project: to go mad."

Since my arrival in Paris, on October 11, 1935, I had never ceased to feel a premonition of the collapse of the West into fire, brimstone, and death. Neither Germany nor Russia nor an Anglo-Saxon domination, improbable in the long run, seemed to me able to fill the void that would be left in the aftermath of the coming deluge. In my notes I described the unprecedented devastation whose approach haunted me. I had the compelling certainty that the world was witnessing the lifting of the curtain on a tragedy whose magnitude no one could yet suspect. Afterward, men must be found to build the new world in which I still believed. "We must have men," I wrote. "Ourselves, in the first place. Everything is going to ruin for lack of inspired leaders." I imagined the welcome that might be accorded to a sufficiently powerful appeal to the fatherhood of Abraham among the peoples of the earth. What was needed was to found an order that would plunge its roots into the still living depths of Israel, of Christianity, and of Islam. The vocation of this order would be to act as the secular arm of a revolutionary movement redirecting the course of history, by returning it to the springs of justice and of peace. I foresaw the gathering forces of a universal crusade of denunciation of all the crimes and hatreds, a crusade that would bring down our idols, whose names, perhaps, had changed through the centuries, but which were even more murderous in our days than those that were long ago condemned by the Prophets of the Bible. From such an effort there might emerge, in the aftermath of the deluge, salvation. I didn't know whether I myself would be there to take part in this development, but I was sure it was necessary to lay its foundations. I foresaw the bursting forth of Marxism, its renewal on the basis of a metaphysics that escaped the bounds within which its critics had confined it. The idea of building a bridge between the Cross and the Crescent obsessed me. Who but Israel could achieve this? For me, this was not a matter of an ideology or

95

abstraction; in my life and in my identity, I myself was such a bridge. I could see clearly that the future of humanity had to pass by the frail footbridge of a reconciliation of the monotheistic peoples, returning to the springs of their beginnings, and so refreshed by them that they could work effectively toward the salvation of the world. We were separated from that future by the veil of our own blindness. At this thought I was seized by a strange vertigo. I remembered -- we didn't exist! All our effort must thrust us forward, bring us together in vigor, profundity, and truth, to make of ourselves an offering for the joy of the world. Toward this, I had one primary efficacious instrument, which I began to discover: the most foolish and absurd prayer, in which wishes are dependent upon an invincible sword. What a great work on the brink of the abyss in which we were about to be swallowed! Instead of sharing the sufferings of the people, bleeding all around me, I must needs thrust into the midst of their sufferings the muzzle of love! but it was already quite clear in my mind that the message that met the needs of the world was that of the Bible, and that it must take flesh in a living community established in Israel. Only be returning to its sources could this community live and be true to itself. A new life had to be grafted onto our ancient roots, in the hope of fruits that could feed the hunger and thirst of the world. In Paris, another man had come into being -- neither the old man who was dead in me, nor the man to whose birth French culture had contributed. Another self was born in me, more drunken, more avid for absolute certainties, on the threshold of the developments of adolescence. The stresses of travel and of successive settlings in different lands encouraged this change in me. Equipped with burning brands, I could soon commence my mad career. I learned to know, or, more precisely, to foreknow, just what was meant by renunciation. I sometimes felt the wish not to go out of myself any more -- to sew myself into myself, as it were, so strong was my joy and inner drunkenness. I knew, from here on, what powers could be unleashed by a message of love incarnate. How beautiful, then, will be our going up to Jerusalem, to bring into being that which must be, that which is written...

The pariahs of Europe

I knew that I had to investigate, not the easiest matters, but the most difficult; not the shining and pleasurable, but the unattractive; not the highest and most precious, but the lowest and most despised. This, I am sure, is why the Hitlerian persecution and the anti-Semitism of which it was the savage expression resulted in separating me from that Europe in which I had become a pariah, harassed by the racial laws. The year 1933, when I was sixteen, marked for the Jews a harsh awakening from a long slumber. Up to that date, Israel could identify itself with the nations in which it lived in exile. It sought to forget its origins by losing itself in the hope, now perceived to be mythical, of an impossible assimilation. I was struck by the airy manner in which anti-Semites and Jews alike discussed anti-Semitism. In the Diaspora, the scattering of the Jews in their lands of exile, Hitler ought to have understood, Judaism was dying a natural death -- there was no need, for that, of the help of concentration camps and crematory ovens. The synagogues were deserted by all but a few old men, the Hebrew language all but forgotten, along with the Bible and Jewish traditions. There was a general rejection of all that could attach the Jew to the people who had inhabited the ghettos for thousands of years, and rejection, above all, of the God given to the world by Israel, the God of Abraham, Isaac, and Jacob, he who overcomes the ancient idolatries, and seemed to me our last refuge against the savagery of the modern idols: those called, in our times, Race, Sex, Money, Nation, Empire, and War. Yes, these were certainly more formidable idols than those of antiquity.

I had not yet come to know the youth of Israel. But facing what I saw: the gates of war wide open in the universal abdication of the forces of life, I decided only folly could tempt the man of thought. The frenzy of the prophets, of Jesus and Paul of Tarsus, of Nietzsche and Van Gogh -- the frenzy of those living hinges on which the world turns. Anyone who sees the universe through two civilizations, two cultures, or two divinities, is close to the split personality that is called schizophrenia. Thus it was necessary to grub up and throw down, to destroy and despoil, before building and planting.

My sensibilities were put on edge by the contradiction offered by the world to all that I thought and believed. I was obsessed by the despair and emptiness of that world in which I found, horrified, that I must live. I saw the anxiety, the aberrations of the Jewish world to which I was beginning to be reconciled. There, also, ritual was the formalized repetition of a mechanical act, lifeless and soulless. I suddenly discovered the vast extent of evil and its universal sway, as well as the all-powerful freewill of man, capable of causing irreparable damage to the harmony of the world. I learned for the first time to perceive the evil in myself, in contrast to the objective perfection that I recognized in the world about me. I was sometimes shaken by sobs of despair before the power of the forces of evil, intent upon destroying instead of building, despoiling instead of planting. Why? And, since things were in such a state, what direction should I give to my life? Since I had rejected forever the temptation to settle for mediocrity, what other road remained for me that would preserve my integrity, and my yearning for love? Only the hard choice: to pass through the narrow door, to enter upon a life of heroic struggle. I was twenty. I took an oath never to surrender to evil, never to consent to the second-best, and to die rather than betray the truth that lived in me.

THE ROADS OF MY RETURN

God exists

In order to be stripped of all preconceptions and outside influences, I wanted, first of all, in my new nakedness, to find once more my first roots; to be attached to reality as an oak to its earth. My rock, ever since I had first encountered him, had been the God of Israel. It was on the tenth of February, 1937, after passing a meditative vacation among the snows of Briançon, that I received an illumination that has never since left me: that God exists, that he is in everything and outside of everything, though everything exists in him. I could no longer conceive the possibility of living without the consciousness of my dependence upon him, since he is the unique source of all life. Without him, the absolute Existence who reveals himself directly to man, it would not be

98

possible to arrive at more than fragmentary truths. I was lifted up by a breath of enthusiasm, rising out of the depth of ages in which my roots were plunged. It intensified my keen awareness of the tragedy which was about to overwhelm Europe. We had no choice but to confront that tragedy, drawing from meditation the energy for the struggle.

I wrote:

> Each glance at you increases thirst for you,
> My joy, my longing, are for all in you,
> This gift of fire in me has come from you,
> The blazing of your immanence in me.
> O you, who are not anything of me,
> My all is nothing that is not from you.
> Naught without you, I come from nothingness,
> And go toward nothingness.
> All that lights up my life is but the joy
> Of you within me.
> Your smile, a sun beyond the heavens,
> Your presence, more than all that is created,
> Reality that wipes out all appearance.
> Your look can penetrate and pierce my eyes,
> It wounds me with the discords of the world.
> My strength dies at the sign which I see in
>   my night --
> Your hand pulls me out of the earth,
> Makes me a stranger to myself.
> Take to yourself the little that I am,
> And free me from the shadow of my fears,
> That in my nothingness may blaze your light.
> O Joy! O Immanence!

I slept on a mat. Through the night, I pursued my dream, that held me as though in bonds. I lived in the joyfulness of my solitude and nakedness, that I might the more swiftly welcome into myself the accustomed guest, so fully desired. This was for me a joy unspeakable and new, so new that as yet I didn't know its name, and had no words to describe it. But are there words to describe it -- to enclose it without killing it? The Bible was always with me, and my meditations on it left me as though bleeding with desire and love. I wasn't content with just reading it: I sang on awaking, along my ways, about the house, and as I went to bed. Aristotle wrote that, to devote oneself to music, one must be drunk, or mad, or much in need of entertainment. Undoubtedly, I must

have been both drunk and mad at the same time, to fill
my days and nights with the chanting of the Bible. It
is a lasting mystery to me that Aristotle didn't
discover the power that music has for expressing the
realities of man and of the world. My discovery of
Bach had meant much more to me than a multitude of
books read and studied. His concertos, oratorios,
Passions, and his Mass in B-Minor had contributed as
richly to my interior life as, from now on, would the
Bible. I became conscious of a harmony beyond that of
human voices, stark and forceful in its manifestation
of love.

To the study of Hebrew

But it wasn't enough to love and to sing. At
nineteen, I was on the point of obtaining my
licentiate's degree in law. My conversion to the God
of Israel led to a definite step that decided my
future. On April 22, 1937, I wrote to Grand Rabbi
Maurice Liber, Director of the Rabbinical School of
France, to ask about the conditions for admission to
his school, and the content and duration of the
studies pursued there. On the second of May I took my
first lesson in Hebrew since the celebration of my Bar
Mitzvah. I had found again, on the Rue Vauquelin, a
classmate of the school at Oran, Andrè Zaoui, with
whom I had established a firm friendship before his
departure for Paris to enter upon his rabbinical
studies. He undertook the task of helping me catch up
with my neglected Hebrew studies, and gain the
understanding I needed in order to recover the
patrimony that had been bequeathed to me by my
ancestors. At the Rabbinical School, despite the
filth of the walls, (assuredly, seminaries of all
religions are alike) and the informal sociability with
which studies were conducted, I found competent
instructors to initiate me in Biblical and Talmudic
studies. It was there that I had the privilege of
becoming the pupil, and then the friend, of Georges
Vajda, who was, from that time on, the soundest
teacher and counselor in the new direction I had thus
chosen for my life. Transplanted into the garden of
French culture, I had chosen to return to my native
Jewish heritage, ravaged by the Nazi savagery. I had
to go about it quickly, to regain lost ground. I
managed it, through a combination of obstinacy and
enthusiasm. In the urgency of the perils surrounding
us, a certain amount of asceticism had become a

constant in my life. Beyond time and space: it was there that the better part of me aspired to live -- but the actual and tangible never ceased to stimulate me, and sometimes to terrify me.

The wretched state of the world affected me like a fever. I was convinced that the effort needed to remedy the world's distress was beyond the power of man, who had made a hell out of the living liturgies of the Creation. Is it possible to act without lying -- without lying to oneself? Rather than do that, we had to go straight for the goal, and, empty-handed, forthright as a gift, face the gates of Hell, and, if necessary, share the fate of the martyrs. Before God, the insignificance of our beings is evident. Before men, no. I knew myself to be anxious, anguished, ridiculously scrupulous, shuddering before the nightmare through which the warring world was living. Yes, I was worn out, hopelessly fastened to the cross by the nails of the persecutors, the same cross upon which the Roman Empire crucified the peoples who dared resist its law. We were not even offered the choice of submitting to the law of Hitler, since by that law itself we were irremediably condemned. But I, though also nailed on that cross by the weakness and wretchedness of men, and often by the unconsciousness with which they dragged the ball and chain of their slavery to the world, saw plainly that the worst danger was not dying in a concentration camp, but losing one's soul by fleeing from the combat upon which everything was going to depend -- our life or our death.

Intolerance of limits

One prayerful night I wrote on the sand of a beach, "Let the dead bury their dead." I had loosed my moorings to sail on the high seas of the will, knowing that, having determined my direction , I must not, from this time forward, look back. My prayer was that He cause love to increase in us. He -- YHWH, the living God, the changeless Creator of all reality, the God of love, the God who is Love. Often, those who heard me knew nothing at all about Israel, overwhelmed and wounded by its superabundance of love, in its humiliation as a pariah destined for the crematories.

To serve the God who is Life, to devote oneself to the works of life, giving material expression to his will -- in this necessity I saw the manifestation of the free will of God. To go to the very end of one's possibilities, intolerant of any limitation -- to be solid as granite. All that is not God is to me a thorn in the flesh.

The center of my life was consecrated to the study of the Bible and the Talmud. My research on the concept of law in the Bible allowed me to plunge into these texts, to read and reread them tirelessly, to analyze and classify them in order to extract their deepest meanings. My first translations of the Bible date from this period. Having them now before my eyes, I can measure the abyss that separates them from the ones I have just published. However, in the Rabbinical School I had excellent teachers. Some of them seemed to have stepped out, with their long bushy beards, from a chapter of the Bible; or, with their long flapping overcoats, from the Talmud. But, in translating, I was encumbered by the worst habit of classical studies; and at that time I had too scanty an experience of Hebrew to discern the precise bearing of each root, to identify each concept, and to distinguish, in a series of synonyms, the exact nuance of each one of them.

The more I resumed possession of my Hebraic heritage, the more clearly I recognized the rightness of Rainer Maria Rilke's image: he perceived Judaism as a ship loaded with all the splendors of the world, so heavily loaded, indeed, that it could not sail in waters of insufficient density: hence its shipwreck. At the bottom of the sea, the beautiful sunken ship awaited the coming of the divers who would raise it. The things they would bring back to the light of day would dazzle the world. The poets are never wrong: I was going to become one of those divers of whom Rilke spoke, impassioned in my undersea quest, and truly dazzled by all that I was discovering in my beautiful Hebraic ship.

"You're too fond of the Bible," my fellow-student at the Rabbinical School, Oscar Wallach, said to me, in a voice as sharp as his keenly intelligent look. He was to be deported, and to die in a crematory oven, some months after the defeat of France. I had found my way: we must raise the sunken ship or perish in

102

it. I no longer frequented the Rue Soufflot except to do what was necessary to obtain my licentiate, my diplomas of higher studies, and my doctorate in law. It would never have occurred to me that my voyage around the Hebraic sea would carry me so far from the dreams of my boyhood in Témouchent, and from the horizons of the Ile de France. I had found again the living spring of my true culture. The Bible, with its commentaries in Hebrew and in Aramaic, had become my daily reading, the substance of my constant meditation, and the object of my eager curiosity. At the Sorbonne, I was studying Hebrew under Edouard Dhorme: when he called on me he termed me "the lynx-eyed man." But this study for me was more than an intellectual exercise. It was a dive into the unspeakable mystery of being.

The Bible had conquered me, laid me open, pierced me, and it held me. Its verses, read and reread a thousand times, were forever new. At the thousandth reading it would seem to me that I was discovering a text for the first time and I would be astonished as I began to understand it. All lovers of the Bible have this experience, encountering pages they feel they have never before seen, even though, in fact, they know them by heart. In Hebrew, the structure of the language conduces to the formation of an infinity of overtones in each verse. The reading is never finished; a book read is ripe for a new reading, which will give it a new meaning.

My lessons in the Talmud introduced me to a new language, Aramaic, and, above all, to a new approach to the Biblical text, which, though not that of the university professors, was no less rich in meanings. The Bible is here treated as an absolute, on whose fixity the spirit exercises itself like an athlete on the horizontal bars. The intention is to break through the barriers of rational judgment, and go beyond the limits of the individual mind, to free the powers of pure intuition. A verse is analyzed in a thousand different ways, according to precise techniques. Each conclusion is again questioned and refuted endlessly, thesis giving rise to antithesis in an unceasing fugue of arguments drawn from linguistics, from the text and its context, and from the precise import of each word, taken in the multiplicity of senses in which it is used in all the other texts of the Bible. It is a disorganized race, with no other purpose than to exercise each racer for success in another arena, that of life, through harmonizing his relations with God and his neighbor. This way of reading never ceases to be disconcerting to a western mind, accustomed to the rigors of Cartesian logic. It is, no doubt, closer to the cultural and historic context of the Bible than Descartes could ever be. It makes possible an incredible familiarity with a text, taken with all its tones and overtones, like a necessary note in a fantastic symphony, attuned to the infinity of the creation.

The Cabala

The Cabala opened to us another road by which we could get back to our beginnings. Reading it was an introduction to the knowledge of the deep realities of God, whose proper name includes as many letters as the complete text of the Bible, from the first word of Genesis to the last word of Chronicles. I learned to rove among the ten celestial Palaces of the uncreated glory; to withdraw into the seven sanctuaries in which are gathered the supreme realities of the Real, the three firsts that make but one, whose earthly manifestation was the Holy of Holies, that of the Temple of Jerusalem, forever present in our minds.

In order not to be blind to the essence of the real, we had to penetrate those sanctuaries to which Rabbi Shimon bar Yokhai and Rabbi Meir (yes, the Master of the Miracle, Baba's protector) had bequeathed us the keys. To open them and enter in, we must be pure of every fault, transparent in the sight of God and man, clear of any speck of dust, that the light from on high might penetrate us, shine in us, and disclose in us the wisdom and the madness of adoration. For the God of Life wishes the heart, and the heart only opens, and only gives itself, in the mystery of love.

Bible, Talmud, and Cabala were the three languages of the message of Israel. It was this message that I wished to know, in order to understand all about myself and the reason for the horrible dance of death that the Nazis were performing around my Jewish self. Three languages, as dissimilar as possible, but directed solely toward the understanding of the real, and of the infinite fountainhead, YHWH Elohim, the God of Abraham, of Isaac, and of Jacob. Three languages, unbelievably original, worthy of the people appointed to proclaim the God of Life. Nothing in world literature seemed to me to approach in power of evocation what the Bible, the Talmud, and the Cabala displayed to me about creation, about humanity, and, finally, about myself. I was close to the place from which my wellsprings burst forth. My life, with no possibility of question or doubt from this time on, would be entirely devoted to God, and, to the utmost extent of my powers, to the service of Israel.

The power of prayer

I discovered Israel in its Scriptural sources, in its history and in its prayer. In truth, Israel has survived its exiles through the power of its prayer. Its liturgy is the diamond in its crown. The three principal points of this crown are the three daily prayers, those at dawn, those at midday, and those at night, that bring into our lives the very rhythms of the worship formerly offered by our ancestors in the Temple of Jerusalem, from the time of King Solomon, who built it in the year one thousand, to that of Titus, who destroyed it one thousand and seventy years later.

I had learned to pray as a child, with my father. I accompanied him, with my eyes and with my heart, in that endless marathon in which he pursued his private meditation, whenever he had the free time for it, at the liturgically appointed times, of course, but also at any unoccupied moments, between two visits or between two customers. I respected his punctuality, the gravity of his expression and voice when he was thus presenting himself before the creator of heaven and earth: he, Isaac Chouraqui, the son of Saadyah, a dealer in grains during his exile in Témouchent, but a worthy candidate for paradise, where his ancestors, the saints, the upright, are living, in the serene expectation of the resurrection of the dead, a resurrection certain because promised. I admired his tranquillity and the strength that shone forth from him when he bowed in prayer before his God of love, the God of mercy, even after my teachers in the Oran boys' school had made of me a leftist atheist.

I loved the liturgy of Israel because, by its entry into history, it introduced a transcendent dimension. The eighteen benedictions in the daily office mark stages in our long journey from the Creation to the end of the world, from the calling of Abraham to the Messianic redemption. Standing, the face turned toward Jerusalem, from any latitude to which our exiles may have taken us, we dreamed of the return for which we never ceased to hope.

"And to Jerusalem, thy city, return in mercy, and dwell therein as thou hast spoken; rebuild it soon in our days as an everlasting building. Blessed art thou, YHWH, who rebuildest Jerusalem."

We have been repeating these words through two thousand years, several times a day, and experience had never persuaded us to renounce the dream, apparently utopian, of return. I was saying these prayers at a time when thoughtful observers were, quite reasonably, predicting the end of Judaism, and while Hitler was doing his utmost to bring about our physical destruction. Imperturbable, I would turn my face toward Jerusalem, where I had never been, and, quivering in my internal dance, repeated endlessly:

"Blessed art thou, YHWH, who rebuildest Jerusalem."

The commentary in my book of prayers said: "As long as Jerusalem shall lie in ruins, or be in other hands than those of Israel, no laugh may brighten our countenances. We must pray for Jerusalem, since, far from her, in place of joy we have but suffering. Our joy will be complete only when God once more dwells in his city, filled with his children returning to their land, and gathered around the city on the hills of Judea. The core of our prayer is hope for the return of the divine presence in Jerusalem, so that, along with Israel, the world may be saved." I fed thus upon dreams, the while the panzer divisions of Hitler spread out over Europe, and while, like human cattle, the Jews were driven with prods into the maw of the crematories.

In my life, detachment and love became equivalent concepts. The measure of renunciation was not, in my opinion, to be found in the number of scourgings one might give oneself in a self-mortifying ascetic

106

program, or the number of meals one might do without. Taken in this way, ascetism can go astray, and become a subtle form of idolatry. It is glaringly obvious that we must have nothing to do with idols, but attach ourselves to God alone. The power to renounce is at the same time the power to love. I renounce when I love. I renounce my separate "myself" when I love God. If love lives in me, renunciation becomes the measure of my essential freedom. It becomes my rule of life, my natural exercise. Yes, as it is impossible to love without making a choice, it is impossible to make a choice without renunciation.

I had chosen for my doctoral dissertation in law a subject capable of casting light upon two of my centers of interest: The Concept of Law in the Bible. I read and reread all of the Bible, and everything closely or remotely associated with my theme, in order to get together the materials for this study, but I have never published it, in spite of the mass of documents I had gathered toward that end. No doubt what had inspired me to undertake this labor was the desire to get rid of the old self that breathed (badly) in me, in order to make way for the blazing forth of my true self, its reawakening, its release in the liberty of love. To live a contemplative life, but among men and in the world -- a world that must be freed, changed, and brought into a state of peace through the power of profound love. To be holy, to be consecrated, did not mean, in my language, to live shut away behind cloister walls. The true consecration lies behind the shield of love, and there alone!

"Do you tremble?"

Then the first German bullet, fired on the Eastern Front, killed my illusions, shattered our dream. I awoke to discover the horror of the bloodiest of conflicts. Israel lived in me -- and hurt me. Some days before the declaration of war, I had almost broken my skull on a rock in a valley near Aïn-Témouchent in a bicycling accident. My brother-in-law, Jo, found me covered with blood at the bottom of a ravine. It was in a hospital bed that I learned of the beginning of open warfare by the Allies against Nazi Germany. I wanted to die, tormented as I was by the tragedy that we were living through. As in the

years that followed my attack of infantile paralysis,
I kept thinking of suicide. All my being rebelled
against a world that filled me with a hate of hatred.

The press poured out upon us the terrifying totals
of daily calamities -- battles, bombardments, famines
-- that accompanied war. I wrote to one of my
Christian friends, Rolland Simon: "Read the
Apocalypse and tremble. Tremble, for yourself and for
all who are yours, near and far; and for me, and for
each one of us all. Tremble, Rolland, on behalf of
those who speak, and lie; tremble on behalf of those
who keep silent. Yes, here is the judgment, from
which we cannot flee; here is God, before us, whom we
want to drive away. And on account of this, Rolland,
we are all dead. We are dead to reality, dead to the
realm, dead to the call to arms, eternally dead to
glory and dead to justice. And all your words and
doctrines and dogmas, Rolland, do nothing but pile up
on top of our death. Do you realize this? And do you
tremble? Do you tremble?"

With regard to the Nazis all was plain. With
them, there was no room for misunderstanding. We had
to fight against them with the weapons that they had
forced us to take up. And I did it. What caused my
suffering was that those who by vocation should have
fought didn't do it. What art they displayed, in
their speeches, in order to say the opposite of all
that they had been saying about the Nazi terror in
Europe; what a show of flags and portraits of the
Marshal in the churches! What voice was raised to
condemn the war, and, in the war, assassination
planned and carried out in the light of day;
assassination of Jews and other pariahs doomed to
death by Hitlerian insanity? For whom was the Cross?
Where was the witnessing? I would have wished then to
hear one word of love, the call of battered human
brotherhood. The call of the man nailed on the cross,
and not the slop of a latent idolatry, a complacent
boasting insulting to God and to the misery of
mankind. I wanted to see all the Temples open wide,
that their unfettered message might encompass and
enkindle the world. I wanted to see the men of God
spread out over the roads of the world to proclaim
justice, like Amos, or love, like Isaiah.

To the affliction of the world at war was added, in France, that of defeat, of the occupation, and of collaboration and its crimes. For the greatest number, fear and its related meannesses dominated, sometimes even among the Jews. At the time of the deportation of foreign Jews picked up in Paris, I had prepared a letter of protest. I hoped that it would be countersigned by one of the highest Jewish dignitaries in France and sent to Marshal Pétain, but this was never done. The reasons advanced, the fear of compromising legitimate moral interests, paralysed the people in office, whatever group they might belong to. Frontiers seemed to have changed places; there was nothing any more but men with their shadows and their lights. Those who had chosen the Resistance were a tiny minority. So far as I was concerned, after fleeing from Paris at the moment of the downfall, I had gone back to Algeria. The statute concerning Jews withdrew my French citizenship, and expelled me from the bar, at which, as a young lawyer, I had had myself enrolled. On the twenty-ninth of August, 1941, a choice presented itself before me: to leave for England or America to continue the struggle; or to rejoin the ranks of the resistance in Europe. Finally, I chose the second solution, on account of my constitutional inability to run away from danger, to overcome the fascination of risk. Without any feeling of homecoming, then, I left the land of Egypt and its surfeited sojourners, lodged in life as in an armistice, to get involved in the Maquis of France. The idea of taking my place in a society that had brought me down to the rank of pariah revolted me. I had the bearded face, the sorrowful countenance cast in fleshly lava, of a pariah. Bitter, naked, exhausted, humiliated, solitary -- I was like man after man in the despair of our desert, where, with the lost stare of suffering, I must take upon myself the universal curse of death.

BREAKING THE FURROW

To drink the bitter cup

Thus it was that I drank of the bitter cup that had so often been held out by fate to my ancestors. From the time they first established a fatherland, they had had to defend it from the giants that wanted to seize it from them -- Egypt, Mesopotamia, Persia,

Greece. Finally, Rome, to overcome their resistance, perpetrated a veritable genocide; hundreds of thousands of Judeans and Galileans were exterminated by her legions. The survivors, in the ghettos of their exiles, tried, with their bare hands, to salvage the vestiges of their language, of their culture, of their traditions. In history books, I was filled with rage as I read of the persecutions that had fallen to our lot. I was one of the thousands of victims whom Hmelnitski, Hetman of the Cossacks, slaughtered and burned, children split open like fish to be cleaned, massacred on the breasts of their raped mothers; women, disembowelled while still living, and living cats sewed into their stomachs. I was sold as a slave with the Jews of Jerusalem or those of Kiev. I was among those whom the Cossacks of Nemirot threw into the water and pierced with arrows, so that they might enjoy the sight of a river of blood flowing between its banks. I stood beside Samson d'Ostropol, wrapped in my shroud and my prayer shawl, reciting the Psalms while waiting for the bloodthirsty soldiery to come and slaughter me, along with my three hundred brothers who preferred death to apostacy. And I was today among the victims of Hitler's persecution; it was going on before my eyes in the silence, impotent or culpable, of the nations. Idolatry was triumphing everywhere: modern man was adoring Thor in the barracks, Priapus in the whorehouse, Mammon in the stock exchange. Thirty-three centuries of Hebraism and Judaism since Moses, and twenty centuries of Christianity since Jesus, and still the nations were powerless to say "No" effectively to the madness of these idolatries run riot. Powerless. In a situation halfway between free choice and compulsion, unarmed, we lined up before the Nazi herdsmen of the concentration camps and crematory ovens, as if the only possible response to the savagery of Hitler and the indifference of the world were to precipitate ourselves in a body into martyrdom.

In the Resistance

So I sought refuge from despair by taking my place in the ranks of the Resistance. There, the pariahs that we had become recognized one another, not by their religion, but by the intensity of their suffering, the courage of their fighting, and the boldness of their hope. Among us we counted Jews, Christians, Moslems, and freethinkers, ready to offer their lives that freedom might be won and that life might triumph over death, toward which, in the streets of occupied France, we were pressing forward in starving droves.

In the Maquis, the awareness of my freedom became all the more firmly fixed in me. The laws of Vichy had expelled me from the French citizenship that had been granted to my great-grandparents in colonial Algeria. Through five generations we had done everything we could, poor innocents, to persuade ourselves that our forefathers had indeed been the Gauls, and not the Hebrews. In this matter, at least, the mask was off. Our ancestors had been so clearly and conclusively the Hebrews that Hitler, aided by his French collaborators, had mobilized against me all the police forces of Europe, in order to put an end to me as quickly as possible. I could not criticize this project on the grounds of insincerity! Frankness for frankness -- I entered upon the battle openly, under my true name, joining a network, that of the underground O.S.E., that distributed thousands of forged documents of identification to any who wished them. And that there might be no possible hedging about my Jewishness, I had let my beard grow, so black and curly that it looked blue. As for that beard, I had to give it up, in consequence of a great struggle, my comrades having held me down and shaved me. "Go and commit suicide if you want, but do it without endangering all the rest of our network," they told me, scraping away the skin of my cheeks along with my beautiful beard.

I lived through this time of madness in the peace of the depths. I learned my calling as a man through running the risks of secrecy, where I had still to go forward, carrying my human cargo, toward life, and toward death. At night, worn out, I would fall asleep in the darkness of a forest, near a tree, on the bare ground. In the conflagration of the world, I seemed borne up by a sense of wholeness. As night ended and dawn blazed forth, I would be seized again by the same vision of the return, of the liberation, of universal brotherhood, of peace.

In the first days of the war, I had had a dream as clear as a vision. I was entwined with a woman on a cliff like that on which I had often plucked flowering broom, east of Oran. Suddenly the sea, rising in fury, leapt to attack the rampart on top of which we were clinging. It overwhelmed us, but then, as calm returned, it withdrew. We were still there, alive, saved.

It was thus that I went through the war along with Colette. She had given up her career as a virtuoso to follow me in the Maquis, forsaking the Christianity of her childhood the better to unite herself with the witness and the passion of Israel. We were united in the same struggle and with the same understanding, joined in the hope of overcoming the spirit of opposition, and weaving the seamless garment of the coming unity. This was a love that the war and its ravages could never succeed in crushing, because the weight of eternity pressed down too heavily upon its dawning eyes.

In contemplation, my disjoined self, useless and empty, opened itself to the Being whose universality I penetrated in the silence of my prayer, beyond words and creeds, in itself and for itself source of life and salvation. The underground existence, by placing us on the margin of society, bestowed on us, paradoxically, a full liberty. Face to face with death, we were accountable to no one for what we might do with our lives. Before the all-destroying divisions of the enemy we were practically defenseless, but utterly free to bear witness in whatever place seemed best to us. We carried on our warfare on two levels. That of the spirit was not the less important for being less visible. It was not a matter of indifference, as we fully realized, that our prayers were firmly on the side of freedom. Chaumargeais served as a refuge for our comrades in arms. Not far from us the Russian philosopher, Jacob Gordin, allied with the Israelite Scouts of France, led a center of studies that we laughingly called "the School of Prophets!" It seemed strange to see, in the woods of Haute-Loire, bearded freedom fighters passing their nights in the study of their Hebrew Bibles, or the Talmud, or, with Gordin, the Cabala, of which he was a profound student. In fact, study and prayer strengthened us for action and increased our courage. They gave us, in the implacable warfare that was waged against us, a serenity, even a joy, that were not of this world. Through prayer, we kept our grasp on the unity, and the necessity, of the real; prayer was for us a state of being sustained by the thought of our

union with God, creator of all being. Opening
ourselves thus to the harmony of the real, we could
fight the better, and bring relief to the frightful
misery of the people crushed by the war.

The frenzy of the dialogue

The embrace of God is as compelling and terrible
as falling in love. At this time, in the Maquis, I
lived surrounded by the battles of the world, saving
what could be saved, witnessing to all that deserved
witnessing, dragging the cross, both visible and
interior, of all our weaknesses before the unleashed
savagery of the world. I am speaking of the cross
with no thought of that cross that lies so delicately
on your plump bellies, Excellencies. To me, the cross
is still what it was in the time of Jesus, the
"guillotine" of the Romans, the instrument of torture
on which they crucified their slaves in myriads,
through all the nations ruled by their Empire. Among
whom were hundreds of thousands of Jews. Our own
special cross, the cross of the Jews in Hitler's
Empire, was to drift away in the smoke of the
crematories in our concentration camps. This was the
cross each Jew must carry. My anguish was not devoid
of joy -- the joy of feeling myself loved and
supported by the presence of God. Adoration often
brought me to my knees; joy wrung me, kneaded me,
joined me to the infinite in the union of love. God
was present, God was living, source of all life, of
all thought, of all reality -- bio-logical God. Along
my roads I was aware of his real presence... But is
it possible to translate into words the fervor, and
all the kindling frenzy of the dialogue with the
Ineffable, with him whose identity for me, beyond
every named creature, had from now on a name: the God
of Abraham, of Isaac, of Jacob? My whole being
shouted forth his praise. I blessed him for having
given us a love stronger, more implacable, more
unconquerable than death. Despite the horror of the
war, life seemed to me marvelously good and beautiful.

The lessons of the heart

Along my way, I had encountered the best of
friends, the author of an ascetic and mystical
treatise that gave me the grammar of my new language.
Bahya ibn Paqûda lived in Spain in the eleventh
century, perhaps in Saragossa. I undertook the

113

translation of his masterpiece, written in Arabic: The Introduction to the Lessons of the Heart, a guide to the interior life, which gave me, with technical precision, directions along the road I had to take in order to reach the haven of total love. God was no longer a concept devoid of concrete actuality. I recognized him in myself, as both the source and the goal of my life. I valued Bahya for the universality of his thought, whose inspiration was thoroughly Biblical. The Biblical passages that he cited -- some fifteen hundred of them -- forced me, in translating them, to define the philosophical problems and the ways of dealing with them that were to affect my own version of the Scriptures. They constituted an anthology that furnished most meaningful route markers along my new road. From the very first time I took that book up in my hands, and read but a few sentences, I knew that I was as closely linked to that work as an echo to a voice.

At this time, more than ever, we felt the certainty of being, each one of us, condemned to death. Africa had become inaccessible, and Europe transformed into a bloody fortress, an immense slaughterhouse, where the Jews were marching toward death at the head of a troop of fifty million victims. Our enterprise, in the Resistance that had barely begun to get organized, seemed more and more foolish, fantastic, quixotic. After the exhausting day of the Resistant, the young man that I then was passed his free time and his nights in putting down on big sheets of paper the translation of a work of some seven hundred pages, written in Spain, in Arabic, by a Jewish ascetic who had lived eight hundred and sixty years before! When friends expressed their astonishment at the work I had chosen, I would laughingly tell them, "At least something of me will survive." Not far from there, Albert Camus was working on La Peste, while taking his place, despite his poor health, in the labors and the risks of the Resistance.

No intellectual creation can fail to inspire emulation. During long evenings among these visionary mountains we found, all of us together, intimate friends or newly met, reasons for not dying without singing. The constricting activities of the Resistance fitted in comfortably for me with the translation of a long medieval text. The daily tasks

114

allowed the meditation of a timeless thought and even profited by it; and the nightly labor strengthened the fighting spirit and prepared it the better to meet its ordeals. My friend Georges Vajda, beside me to guide and criticize the work, constituted an improvement on the inaccessible dictionaries and encyclopedias he was replacing. I found in Bahya the answer to the calumnies in which we were drenched, and the remedy for the evils we were suffering in this war, which, for us Jews, was at the same time a persecution. By the power of love, he broke through the brazen walls in which I was imprisoned by the fact that I was Jewish. A text almost a thousand years old miraculously became contemporary for me, and sustained me day after day so that I could survive the apocalypse. When the effort of translation had allowed me to overcome the difficulties of an archaic language, it seemed to me that, behind the words of the book, I could hear the voice, and see the smile, of a friend. I felt at home in that interior castle, built to shelter, in this day of the dead, my search for the living God. I held to his ideal of life, and I delighted in his portraits of the lovers of YHWH: men who had realized the fullness of their humanity, authentic witnesses for justice and for love, among those called to enlighten and to save. And I have never ceased to live, since the day I came upon it, by his definition of love, the fullest and the most powerful that I know, in which he includes a leap toward the beloved, the detachment that can endure shocks, the union of the lover with the beloved, and, finally, the light poured forth from their embrace. I hoped never to lose anything of the forward leap, of the detachment, of the union, and of the light of love, caught up as I was in the contemplation of the mystery of God, and absorbed in my thirst for life and for peace. That my book on Bahya, published in 1950, was given a preface by Jacques Maritain, added, in my eyes, the witness of friendship to that of love.

Each day, up to the end of the war, I encountered appalling spectacles, scenes that seemed to have been brought up out of Hell. My meditation fed upon them, enforcing upon me a still greater turning inward; I was torn, as though in childbirth. The ring of steel was closing again. After the massacre of Vercors, the Germans had decided to liquidate the Resistance in the Haute-Loire, through which they made sweep after sweep. An agent of the Gestapo had been sent into the

115

region to arrest me. Being warned, I had barely time
to arrange to be hired as a workman in the chateau of
a silk grower. My work was to feed the silkworms in
immense halls that had been made moderately warm
conservatories. Not a bit of news reached me; the man
who was supposed to recall us to service had been
executed. I decided to go back to Chaumargeais. I
felt that I had come to the brink of a precipice.
What did it matter whether my capture took place here
or there? The sooner the better.

I have heard the impassioned weeping
of a Rachel standing in the dawn
over the bodies of her slaughtered sons.
I have seen rise up, from crematories,
from chimneys over tranquil roofs,
the theories of men, of women, children,
turned into smoke and floating up to heaven--
tranquilly killed by gas
that so might come the cleansing of your sewers,
my German brothers!
It is the blood, the blood, that preys upon my mind;
so many throats cut open,
so many skulls laid bare,
so many butchered bodies,
such horrors and such agonies,
the hungers unappeased, the tears,
the thirst unquenched,
and those that died
that so might come the saving of my lambs.

I wrote these lines at the time when the liberation of
France prevented the definitive suppression of the
Maquis. And this was the end of the beginning. We
underground fighters emerged from our passive and
hidden functions. The nocturnal parachute drops of
arms gave us sufficient strength to demoralize the
enemy, to disorganize his communications and sometimes
to kill him. Our army of ragamuffins would have been
able to win if the strength for it had been left in
us; but we were inwardly exhausted by the years of
war. For me, in particular, the physical strain was
doubled by an extreme internal tension. Hitler had
brought me back to the midst of my own people. The
God whom I had then encountered was a jealous God upon
whom I meditated endlessly.

No more than my ancestors in the Bible did I have
need of a philosophical discourse to confirm to me the
existence of a supreme Intelligence behind the
development of the worlds and of my own life. Rather
than refer to the philosophy of Plato and Aristotle, I
would have sought my proofs in reality and in the new
approach to it by the exact sciences. In every
discipline, cosmogony, biology, physics, this approach
brought reality down to a principle of unity, that
which the Hebrews had discovered by intuition,
initiating in history the most formidable of
revolutions, that of ethical monotheism and of its
basic affirmation: Adonai Elohim, the God of heaven
and earth, is ONE.

The better to know him, I went back to the prayers
and customs of my childhood. My meditation fed, night
and day, on the reading of the Bible and of its great
Hebraic commentaries. Nothing could be more urgent
than the need to penetrate the mystery of God himself,
beyond words, beyond time, beyond the conceptual-
izations of him that we have made for ourselves -- to
penetrate the mystery and to know him, in order to
wring from him the salvation of the world. I could
see clearly that the God spoken of by the rabbis, the
parish priests, the pastors, or the philosophers, was
not necessarily the same as the God proclaimed by the
Prophets and the Apostles, he whom I loved, and from
whom, in our great anguish, I sought for preservation.
On the road with my consignments of Jews to lodge and
to save, my beard blowing in the wind, bare-handed,
longing to know him better and to love him more, I
called upon him. He had become the source and
inspiration of my interior dialogue, of the road that
I was making from my self toward myself, in order to
make myself, in the calmed acceptance of my own
nothingness, one with his word of life. I had become
a wandering Jew. Since the war had cast me into the
Maquis of France, I had changed my quarters at least
thirty times; I was without hearth or home. Jean
Couty has painted the aspect I then had, the
distraught look, haunted and horror-stricken to the
brink of madness, of one awaiting the unveiling of
inevitable catastrophe. Dispossessed of everything,
it seemed to me that I was suspended at a dizzying
height between earth and heaven where everything
conspired to make of me a fleshless being under whom
the earth was slipping away. Physically, the harsh
regime to which I had subjected myself had left me

nothing but skin and bones. My earthly ties seemed to be breaking one after another. The Algeria of my birth had become inaccessible to me since the American landing of November, 1942. After the Arab revolt of 1945 and the terrible repression that crushed it, I could see plainly that that land, where my ancestors had been living for more than five centuries, would soon be forbidden to us. All that remained to us there were our family tombs, and we were not permitted even to visit them for pious meditation. Even France, the well-beloved France of my studies and of my nightly watching, she to whom I owed my language and my culture, had consented that I should be cast out from her bosom, and that I be reduced to the condition of a pariah. On the parvis in front of Notre Dame, in Paris, I contemplated the statue representing the Synagogue, blindfolded, and holding a broken sceptre, by the side of her triumphant sister, the Church. But while western civilization was foundering in the stench of its charnel houses and the ruins of its cities -- wasn't it better to be blind and defeated? A broken egg can't be put together again. Would France, would all the West ever recover their integrity, and the ability to lead the world out of the abyss, or, at least, the wisdom to stop building up both the hostilities and the weapons of death?

Religions -- all religions -- had disappointed, often even betrayed, our hopes, like the Last Things that they proclaimed. Thirty-three centuries of Mosaic religion, two thousand years of Christianity, came to their climax in the bankruptcy of the Second World War. But the atom bomb hadn't finished exploding over Hiroshima when the Americans and the Russians hurled themselves into the most absurd and the most fatal of armament races. Yes, only the folly of God allows us to measure that of the world. I saw the disaster of it in the streets of Paris, through which there began to pour the prisoners of war and the deportees come back from the death camps. I saw those living skeletons with their hunted look come out of their hell as from a tomb. The ingrained savagery of humankind displayed here its hypnotic proofs. We knew what was the barbarity of the armies of Nebuchadnezzar, of Titus, and of Attila; that of Hitler's troops surpassed them in satanic designs and methods. The horrors we found in the smoking ruins of Europe overwhelmed all imagination. How could one take it in without giving way to delirium? The wall

118

against which I was supporting myself, body and soul, was crumbling away. I seemed to be losing the foundations of my very identity. One day I felt as though I had been struck by lightning. I had reached the limit of my resistance. I was delirious for weeks; my body burned continually in the crematories in which so many of my friends had gone up in smoke. Set free, unrestrained, I cried out against all the tortures of that war, denouncing the stupid blindness, the cowardly inaction, that had permitted such crimes. We must have been either cowards or monsters to have tolerated them without dying of despair or of shame. Nothing could wash the blood from our hands. How could we go on living, how survive such degradation? And how would it be possible to forget, to add to our cowardice the further cowardice of acting as though all of this hadn't happened? Despair over my being still alive was stronger in me than the relief of our victory.

But, being alive, I must try to go on living, and work to build again upon our ruins. Where, and how? In my delirium, I hoped for the end of our exile, and our return to Jerusalem, to build there, at last, in defiance of all empires, the kingdom of justice and love for which our ancestors, the Hebrews, had never given up yearning. Nothing but the ecstasy of the realized dream could relieve the despondency caused by what we had just lived through. I felt in my heart that the first duty facing me was that of returning to Jerusalem.

III
THE RETURN

THE DECISION

Rebirth of Israel

The most important decision of my life was that which made me an inhabitant of Jerusalem, a returnee on the land where his ancestors lived twenty centuries ago, and who speaks today the language which, three thousand years ago, was spoken by King David. I have told in what a state of interior emptiness, of anguish, I had been left by the Hitlerian persecution, the collapse of France, our fight in the Maquis, and the massacre of so many of our friends. In so great a suffering, where could we turn? At that time I knew hardly anything of the land of Israel, and I looked upon Zionism with my customary distrust of ideologies. The Zionist movement was born and flourished in Central and Eastern Europe; the Arab countries and Western Europe were still free of its influence. My first contact with it had been rather disappointing. When I was a child, my father had received an envoy from Jerusalem, charged with bringing us the good word. A great public meeting was held in the hall of the Splendid-Cinéma of Aïn-Témouchent, including not only the entire Jewish community, but also the civic notables. Alas, the speaker had more enthusiasm than mastery of the French language; that day ridicule killed in our good town the splendor of Zion. There remained to us, until the end, only our books of prayers to sing its glory.

At the rabbinical school the professors reflected the trends of French Judaism; no one ever spoke to us there of the struggle of the pioneers of the Jewish revival. The interest there was in ritual more than in rite, in the Biblical and exilic past more than in the national future of Israel. The fact that England had been involved in the setting up of the national Jewish homeland in Palestine had been sufficient, in the mood of some people, to make them treat the matter as a foreign movement. It took the Hitlerian catastrophe to change that mood and sensitize the great Jewish communities of the West to the resurrection of Jerusalem. The formation of the State of Israel did not fail to affect me; perhaps I thought there was a way out of the blind alley of our destiny. I had passed the night of the twenty-ninth of

November, 1947, in chanting the Psalms, while awaiting the decision of the United Nations on the question of the rebirth of Zion. One year later, I chose the creation of the State of Israel as the topic of my dissertation for the degree of Doctor of International Public Law. At the same time, under René Cassin, I became Deputy Secretary General, and later Permanent Delegate, of the Universal Israelite Alliance. This was the period during which the survivors of the massacres of the war were devoting themselves to healing the wounds and rebuilding the ruins left by the war. At the Alliance, we busied ourselves as well in developing an academic network through which the young Jews of the Arab countries would prepare themselves for their future. We participated also, with René Cassin, in his struggle for the proclamation and protection of the rights of man. I had become the spokesman for the Central Committee of the Alliance, rousing the spirit of its vast network of friends and former students scattered to the four winds. Our work contributed to the reconstruction of European Judaism, to the physical and moral preservation of the Jewish communities of the Arab countries, and, finally, to the realization of the rebirth of Israel, where, as early as 1870, the Alliance had founded the first agricultural school in the Near East, as well as several schools in which Hebrew began to become once more a living tongue.

Thanks to the Alliance, I was grafted onto the trunk of contemporary Jewish history; my time was parceled out in missions to lands where our work supported schools, and to those in which our friends helped to cover the cost of their operation. In this way I visited, in move after move, most of the countries of the world, taking account of the problems of our times and the gravity of the situation of Israel immediately following the massacres of the war. My responsibilities allowed me considerable freedom for studious retirement, which I devoted to writing. I ceaselessly questioned my Hebraic past in the hope of discovering in it the light that could illumine the future. The alternation of active and contemplative periods became a rule with me, and I discovered how contemplation can sustain action and augment its efficacy.

123

For the Jews, the tragedy was removed from the European concentration camps to the battlefields of the Near East. Even before the fight against the British administration had come to an end, it became necessary to wage war against the Arab armies mobilized to invade the land and destroy the new nation in process of formation. Israel had abruptly ceased to be the abstraction of my prayers or of my metaphysical reveries, and had become a reality that was beginning to enter into my life and nature. I achieved my desire to visit the land in the summer of 1950. To be a descendant of Baba, to come out alive from the underground struggle against Hitler, to take part in the overthrow of his European empire, then to board a ship flying the flag of Israel, arriving, four days later, at Jerusalem, and, by that return, to round the cycle of two thousand years of history -- yes, the Psalmist was right, we thought we were dreaming. The utopia transmitted by our ancestors from generation to generation since the destruction of their fatherland under the blows of the Roman legions -- that utopia entered into history with us; we were conscious of being a generation of the miraculously favored, as we, having so recently and so narrowly escaped Hitler's genocide, passed, living, through the gates of the new Israel.

He who has no plot of earth under his feet is no man, according to Hebrew wisdom. Watching, in the dawn, the outline of the peak of Mount Carmel becoming distinct; discovering my new land, from Dan to Beersheba and to Elath, I became another man. My former contradictions seemed to resolve themselves in the unity of my new vocation. I rediscovered in Israel the countryside of my natal Algeria, the azure of the Mediterranean, the climate, the olive trees and cacti, the broom and jasmine, the sun, above all, whose absence I had deeply felt during my years of Parisian life. I returned to my natural surroundings, to the kind of place in which my ancestors had lived, and in which I myself had been born and had grown up.

A page written by a crusader, eight centuries ago, sums up strangely what we, the new Israelis, experience after having made the decision to come home and take part in the rebirth of Israel. Here is how Foucher de Chartres, then chaplain to Baldwin I, king of Jerusalem, described the adventure of returning to Jerusalem: "We were Westerners; we have become

Easterners. He who was Roman or Frank has here become
Galilean or Judean. He who lived in Reims or Chartres
finds himself a citizen of Tyre or of Antioch. We
have already forgotten the place of our birth; it is
even unknown of many among us. Some among us already
possess, in this country, houses and servants that are
theirs by hereditary right. Others have married wives
who are not their compatriots -- a Syrian, an
Armenian, or even a Saracen who has received the grace
of baptism. One tends his vineyard, another his
fields. They spoke diverse languages, and all are
already achieving an understanding of one another.
The foreigner is now native; the pilgrim has become
resident... Those who were poor in their own land,
God has made rich. Those who used to have but a few
crowns possess here an infinite number of bezants. To
those who had no more than a poor farmhouse, God has
here given a town. Why should he return to the West
who has found the East so propitious?..."

Algeria is burning

For us also, the decision was irrevocable. All
the more so for me, since the successful Algerian
revolution made of my birthplace a forbidden land. On
the eve of independence, there were in Algeria one
hundred and fifty thousand Jews; thereafter, there
remained of these only some hundreds, for the most
part old people unable to emigrate and begin again
under other skies. I had foreseen the risk of such a
turn of events since the beginning of the Algerian
rebellion. Just after the war, I was a judge in the
Kabyle region (east of Algiers), the region most
severely tried by the strict repression that followed
the riots of 1945. I knew what the Arab people were
thinking, and how far the colonials were from
appreciating the desperate nature of their demand for
justice and liberty.

I had a disquieting example of that insensitivity
at a moment when it would have been possible for the
French Government, perhaps to avoid the revolt
completely, but surely to reduce its scope and
consequences by changing the course of governmental
policy.

"Your Honor, may I present Baron William Frary von
Blomberg?" In the lobby of the Hôtel Transatlantique
in Bou Saada, I thus met that strange man, with his

125

great blue eyes, elegant carriage, and, though he was young, a snow-white head of hair. His fiancée had died when he was twenty years old, and his hair had turned white in one night of watching by her body. We quickly became friends, Bill and I, in that oasis, where I was the only man with whom he could talk English. He was on his way back from a mission to the Near East, as publicity man for several societies. One morning, he came early and unexpectedly into my justice of the peace court, where, to wipe out the memory of the war and its scars, I was exercising the functions of a magistrate in the court of appeals of Algiers. He wanted to talk to me in confidence, without risk of our being overheard. It was in a long walk among the dunes of the desert that he told me his story. American by birth, he had been adopted by a family belonging to the Dutch branch of the von Blombergs. He had inherited a noble title and a fortune permitting him, thanks to his own talents, to frequent the courts and governmental circles of the world. At the conclusion of a trip to the Near East, he had been summoned to Cairo, where Abdel Kader had taken refuge, grouping about him the principal instigators of the Arab revolt against the French rule in North Africa. It had devolved upon him to establish the first contacts between Cairo and the Algerian nationalists chosen to unleash the rebellion. He disclosed to me the plan of action decided upon at Cairo; the rebellion would begin in Algeria, where it would have to be bloodiest. It would spread quickly into Tunisia and Morocco, where it would be easier to expel the French. We were in 1947. "There is still time to avoid this war," von Blomberg told me. "It will be as catastrophic for the Arabs as for the French. It would be enough for the French Government to make contact with the organizers of the revolt, and negotiate. They have no great matter at stake; they could come to an agreement at only the slightest cost to either side. I beseech you, act, my dear André!"

How to act, when one is a justice of the peace, whose jurisdiction reaches as far as Bou Saada? My friend left, noticeably tormented by the secret he had confided to me. I met him again several months later in Paris for the session of the General Assembly of the United Nations at which the Universal Declaration of the Rights of Man was to be proclaimed. René Cassin, the father of that Declaration, whose assistant I had become, put von Blomberg in touch with

Robert Schuman, then Minister of Foreign Affairs. Our friend had maintained his Arab contacts. The revolt was being organized. In 1948, it was still possible to avoid it by negotiating. The governmental reaction was a surprise to me, but to no one else; my friend was brusquely dismissed by the officials of the Quai d'Orsai. "Algeria is French, sir, and will remain so forever. No problem." And to convince von Blomberg of the truth of this, a complaint was lodged against him; his "anti-French" activities were denounced to the State Department. Upon his return to the United States, he saw his passport confiscated, and was sternly reprimanded by the FBI for the imprudence of his "anti-American" activities! He had tremendous difficulty in trying to escape the troubles this affair had earned for him, including even an attack in which he barely escaped being killed by a madman.

The revolution had long smoldered before breaking forth with its attendant disastrous consequences. One didn't have to belong to the liberal party to foresee the result; the determination of the Arab masses to win their independence was equaled only by the obstinacy of the colonial authorities in refusing it. Albert Camus, to express his anguish at the conflict, wrote of his feelings about his mother. For us, the Jews, the ordeal was surely even more profound, our commitment being total to each of the two camps. We had lived for centuries among the Arabs, their language was our language, their culture our culture, and their religion had never excited the censure of our theologians. The Prophet of Islam adored the God of Abraham, and the forms of his religion were inspired precisely by those of Judaism. We had our place, and we filled a considerable rôle in the household of Islam. We also had our problems there; who hasn't? We were classed there as dhimmis, as dependents, with a condescension that didn't prevent a fellowship -- in fact, a relationship that was, all things considered, fairly happy. We had Arab friends; they frequented the houses and offices of our relatives. Speaking their language, we were as close to their concerns and hopes as they to ours.

The Hitler persecution had shown us the measure of their faithfulness. The agents of Nazism had tried to transplant their ideology into North Africa; a good pogrom would have finely rewarded their work. Despite their efforts, they didn't find the men needed to

127

organize it. "We don't eat that kind of bread," was the answer given to them by those to whom they had offered subsidies and a free hand to pillage the Jews. When the law concerning Jews dispossessed us of all our goods, and thousands of candidates proposed themselves for the newly created posts of administrators of Jewish property, all were Christians -- not a single Arab was ready to dirty himself in that way. Our friends the colonists accepted in principle the discrimination under which we were suffering, even while bemoaning the excesses of the persecution that was crushing us. When we were excluded from French citizenship, not one voice was raised in protest against that measure. By the law of October 7, 1940, signed by Pétain, and the order of May 14, 1943, for which Giraud's administration of French Africa was responsible, Jews were excluded from the French community. It took a long struggle and the personal intervention of Roosevelt to abrogate those decrees. From the Arab side, during all this period, we heard only assurances, in a tone of evident sincerity: "Be patient; this will pass."

The King of Morocco, Mohammed V, maintained the same attitude toward the Jews. He, and his people following his example, and also the Moslems of Tunisia, acted with courage and dignity, refraining from anything that would aggravate the condition of the Jews in the region, and even helping them whenever they had an opportunity to do so. These are deeds that remain carved deep in our memories, and that none among us are prepared to forget. How could we disassociate ourselves from the deepest and truest aspirations of the Arabs? But our involvement with France had, in our eyes, no less importance. To the Ottoman Empire, which used to hold a nominal sovereignty over Algeria, our ancestors had unanimously preferred France, without too well understanding where their choice would finally lead them. France was going to implant within the walls of our ghettos the new demands of laicized thought. A strange thing, and one that needs understanding: our forefathers, without a shadow of hesitation, were ready to sacrifice to the new gods to the extent of giving up their roots. In a brief time the Jews molded by the French school system had become almost indistinguishable from the Europeans of the Colony. In 1860, ten years before the grant of French nationality, a Jewish pupil, whose father was illiterate in French, carried off at Oran the first prize in rhetoric and in Latin verse. Since our fathers were the Gauls, we certainly needed to demonstrate that we were worthy to be their children. Our integration into the French family had been so rapid and so profound that we had in general lost even the very memory of our origins. The Nazi tempest and our deprivation of French citizenship had not been enough to make us rediscover the understanding of our true nature. Our assimilation had been too complete. We felt that we were the children of that France that had so fully adopted us. How could we have separated ourselves from her? How could we have spat in the spring from which we had drunk, and fired upon those who had educated us? Our position as natural intermediaries between the Arabs and the French became impossible from the moment the war began. The conflict destroyed the legitimacy of our existence, even before its result expelled us from our houses and from our lands. The ambiguity of our position suddenly became paralyzingly clear. Our commitments to both camps were absolute. The political and cultural reasons for our attachment to the French which I have emphasized were made doubly strong by powerful economic motives. In the orbit of French civilization, we were the first among the natives to benefit by the colonial venture. But our bonds to the Arab masses were no less strong. One cannot eliminate with one stroke a common past of several centuries, shared language, modes of thought and feeling, ways of eating and of living. The most powerful link between us was created by the land itself -- a marvelous countryside, vast, rich, beautiful. We all loved it with an equal passion.

Our double allegiance felt deeply in the most remote Jewish quarter and even by the humblest among us, locked us in an inescapable predicament. It was impossible for us to join the side opposed to France without betraying a loyalty, without breaking faith with a gratitude inscribed in the depth of our being. But it was impossible for us to take the side of France openly without seeming, in the eyes of the nationalist rebels, not simply enemies, but traitors. To remain neutral was no longer possible. The hotter the conflict became, the stronger grew the pressure upon the Jews from the two warring camps. On one side were the French, on the other the Arabs, and in the middle were the Jews in a state of perplexity.

Typical of this situation is the case of the Lévy family of Algiers. The father was assassinated by the O. A. S. (Secret Army Organization: a clandestine and violent pro-French movement opposing the Algerian struggle for independence) because he was a sympathizer with the revolutionary F. L. N. (National Liberation Front); and his son was "executed" by the F. L. N. on suspicion of belonging to the O. A. S. The pillage of the Synagogue of Algiers, on December 12, 1960, and the profanation of Jewish cemeteries by rioters brandishing the green and white flag of the Algerian independence movement, were only symptoms of a deeper evil -- warning signs of our imminent expulsion. We had lost all. We left in Algeria only our tombstones. The impasse had become total. Even at the beginning of the revolt, my mother, clear-sighted, had told me: "To escape disaster, we'd have to have a miracle. But that miracle won't happen." The miracle, indeed, didn't happen. It was prevented from happening, no doubt, by the mortal sin of racism, which infected every aspect of the Algerian situation. After the collapse of the West, I witnessed that of Algeria, in which even the memories of my past were engulfed. From one day to the next my Algerian roots, more than three centuries deep, were cut off; the eradication was complete. Our graves are in the cemetery of Aïn-Témouchent, awaiting the hour of the resurrection of the dead. Under the branches of giant cypresses that form a square, four tombstones keep their eternal watch over the graves of my grandparents, buried side by side: grey granite over Saadyah and Myriam Chouraqui; white marble over Abraham Meyer, Baba, and his wife Esther. Grey granite and white marble, shining in the light of that land now inaccessible to me.

CHANGES

Discovery of Israel

Just as it happens in well-plotted stories, while my links to the past were crumbling away in the upheavals of the world war and of the Algerian revolution, I began to experience the impassioned discovery of the land and people of Israel.

130

Yes, the very first look was a thunderbolt. The impulse that urged me toward Israel grew stronger the more I saw of the land. Before each prospect I had a strange feeling that I had been there before; all of it seemed somehow etched in my memory. Before my own eyes I saw the sky and the earth that my ancestors had never ceased to celebrate and sing about, surely because they also carried them within themselves.

Suddenly, the vision became objective, tangible, at once soothing and elating, having an attraction so powerful that it made easy my release from former attachments. It seemed to me that the land was reflected in me, just as I recognized myself in it. It was no longer a matter of abstract ideology, but rather an interaction of earth with earth, so generally shared by Jews returning to their old/new fatherland, and so powerful, that it seemed to hide from them the nature, and the danger, of the realities that we were involving ourselves in. Like Don Quixotes of history, we had found our Dulcinea. Little did it matter to us that she was poor, disgraced, and gravely endangered. We had determined to defend her with such desperation that no power could ever again take her from us. And we were so convinced of our love that we were sure we would be able to make her as beautiful, as free, and as powerful as in our wildest dreams.

I found again in Israel, not only the sunlight of my natal Algeria, but all the savor of Baba's universe. All of a sudden, it was no longer a world of folklore. Jerusalem was not now a stirring myth, but a real city that was trying to arise out of the darkness that had overwhelmed it on account of our exile. There I encountered the figures that had surrounded my childhood, the men clothed in the white burnous, the women, once more wearing the foutas, and with scarves in battle-array on their heads. All of us spoke Hebrew, and nobody was surprised at this. Even Rabbi Meir was there, no longer as a superstitious notion, but as one of those men who, one century after Jesus, lived and died to ensure the survival of Israel after the savage Roman oppression. Of pagan origin, child of a family converted to Judaism, he gave up his original name of Nehorai, and adopted the Hebrew name Meir, meaning "the illuminator," and indeed his genius continues to illuminate us. "Whoever has forgotten one word of the

Torah," he taught, "is considered to have forgotten
his life." His own life was tragic. His master,
Akiba, to whom we owe the introduction to the Song of
Songs in the canon of the Bible, was martyred by the
Romans, as was also his father-in-law, Hanayah. His
sister-in-law was forced into a brothel serving the
Roman legions, from which he had to ransom her. His
wife, Berouiyah, gave him the news of the simultaneous
death of their two children in the form of a fable,
out of which Georges de Porto-Riche has made a moving
poem: someone had left two precious pearls in her
keeping, and now had come to reclaim his property;
must she now give them back to him? From this time
on, Rabbi Meir was present among us. He is buried at
Tiberias, on a height overlooking the lake, and his
people keep lining up to visit his grave and ask him
for miracles, a hope that he never disappoints. He
had made a vow never to lie down, as long as the
Messiah had not come to save his people, and his
disciples had buried him in a standing position. Also
standing, we came to tell him that, if our people were
not yet saved, at least we had returned to the land
from which the Romans had exiled us, and that we still
treasured the hope in which he lived, and had never
betrayed it. No, we had not forgotten a single word
of the Torah, and that is why the land on which we
were coming to life again had not lost its memory of
us.

But, beyond Baba and Rabbi Meir, as basis and
justification of their faith, I discovered in Israel
the stupendous realities of the Bible. The book that
had fed the long patience of our exiles lay before us
as a living land. Leaving Jerusalem, it took only
twenty minutes on the road to find, in Jericho, the
spot at which our ancestors thirty-two years ago
invaded the land to which we were returning to
establish ourselves. Since we couldn't walk on the
Sea of Galilee, we swam in it. At Engedi we tasted of
the vines celebrated in the Song of Songs, and with
our Shulammites, under the waterfalls, we bathed in
pools formed in the rock, surrounded by the burning
desert. At a glance, we could understand the reasons
for situations and strategies, for alliances and wars.
There were present all around us the heroes of the
Bible, whose stories we knew by heart. At midnight, I
could converse in their own language with Abraham and
Melchizedek, ask Moses the reason for his laws, and
David the meaning of his poems. I could question

Isaiah, that prince mad about God, who was the first to dream of universal peace, and Ezekiel, that visionary who believed in the resurrection of the dead. Even Jesus, even Mark and Matthew, even John and Paul were conversing with us along our roads. They were no longer statues, fixed in the shadows of cathedrals, but had become flesh-and-blood beings, glad to talk with us in Hebrew, of course -- didn't they belong to the family? And we had so much to say to one another! As people deported into a universe other than that of the tribe, they must have felt all the more isolated from us by the abyss that had been dug by our theological differences. We found each other again, after two thousand years of the most absurd, the most fatal of quarrels, just as Joseph found his brothers again. We could talk with Jesus and his companions, telling each other what we thought of the world and of what had been happening to us, in intimate conversation, untroubled by those who had as yet understood nothing, either about us or about these, our brothers and companions of ages past. Nothing and nobody was missing from our reunion at the end of time. Even our neighbors had come back to life: The Egypt of the Pharaohs and the Mesopotamia of Nebuchadnezzar were afoot, and again seized by the mad urge to put us back into the grave from which we were desperately trying to get out. These are habits that are manifestly hard to forget, even after two thousand years. But this time, taught by experience, we were stubbornly determined not to let it be done to us.

It must be admitted that our adventure, so long hoped for that it seemed to us miraculous, finally made us a little drunk. The dream had come true; utopia had become history. The entire Bible was welcoming us, its language, its earth, and the fantastic questions it raised about man and his problems. On arrival, we had repeated the sacramental gesture of prostrating ourselves, our foreheads in the dust, to kiss with our lips that soil too dearly loved. An old Moroccan Jewess answered my unspoken question: "If I don't rejoice in the land, how could you expect the land to rejoice in me?" We were face to face, naked, without masks, the land and we, and we were awaiting the birth, out of our union, of the incarnate Word of our salvation. We were the rescued remnant from the crematory ovens, the ghosts returned from the ghettos and the camps of exile, having in our

133

souls an open wound that glowed through our flesh, and in our hearts a hunger and a thirst that nothing could ever appease. As we landed on the promontory of Carmel, our hands reached out toward Asia, hands strong in the assurance that we were restored to life. Since our wanderings through the night had come to an end on our own regained land, we awaited the coming dawn of a new day.

The revolution of the return

"Think with your hands," said Aristotle. My return to Israel would have taught me the truth of that axiom, there, where no catechism or ideology could mask the truth of thoughts, of hearts, and of deeds. What I truly believe, what I _crave_, that is what I accomplish by my thoughts, my speech, my writings, and my deeds.

At the conclusion of the war, I felt disgusted by a certain intellectualism, either theological or atheistic, in which the West, having just drunk to the lees the cup of violence, took pleasure in escaping from the obsessions whose inevitability loomed over it, a kind of mental masturbation that the miseries of the time had made me despise. I wrote:

Be fearless at the gate where chance and strength
    may give you life or death.
In this Jerusalem in flames, keep a clear view of
    all the broken world-- a feat of sanity.
Refuse to see, so long as in yourself you have not
    felt the burning of the light.
Refuse to hear, when every voice is stilled, and
    you yourself have never suffered from too
    long a silence.
Refuse to grasp, so long as to your eyes your body
    has not yet revealed its end.
Avoid illusion, and renounce division.
Know that your voice is not the word, nor are your
    words the order of your words.
Know that all power is in yourself; but from your
    emptying of self will come your name, your
    countenance, your inner light.
Yet keep enough of self-reproach to cut all
    linkage with the shore, so that your voyage
    may not be chimerical.
And be reborn in light.

Go, my Nathanaël, go; accept the parting with no
lying words. Cast off your moorings, and,
unbound, set sail upon the high seas of the
will.

No, our departure was not unreal. We uprooted
ourselves from the West, which was rebuilding its
ruins without accomplishing the resolution of its
contradictions, while my French Algeria was going up
in flames like a house of cards. More than a
departure, actually -- for us it was a revolution,
probably the most complete revolution of our time,
since it brought us back to our beginnings, to our
very point of departure.

This was a revolution that took place, not in
words, but in deeds. We didn't go in for speeches,
programs, meetings, and demonstrations. We weren't
going out in the streets to thrash some cops or some
bourgeois, nor to set fire to the Stock Exchange, the
barracks, or a whorehouse. No, nothing like that. We
simply put our affairs in order, liquidated our
assets, and foolishly packed our bags. We just
boarded a ship or plane with our emigrant bundle. And
so we said goodbye to our exiles, to our persecutors,
to our inquisitors, and to our warders. To our
friends, we said au revoir. But it would no longer be
we whom they would see again, because the man whom
they had known, the Jew of the Diaspora, was dead;
forever, from the moment he had opted for the return.
Take a look at the last moments of his stay in the
land of his exile. He will never see it again in the
same way. He has been stripped of the skin of the old
Jew, like a molting snake, like a caterpillar turning
into a butterfly. As for the old skin, he has left it
on the quay of his embarkment, or on the runway, near
the gangway on which he sets a foot that no longer
trembles at taking a final departure. He is returning
to the land of his ancestors. This is his revolution,
which it has taken two thousand years to bring about,
but only two days to decide upon. This story took a
long time in the preparation, but, once everything was
planned and determined, there was nothing much to it.
A memory, since it is done, since all is done. By
putting his foot on the gangway of the ship that is
taking him back to the land of his ancestors, this
little fellow, this survivor of the death camps, or of
the ghettos, or of the greyness of the great cities,
or of the drudgery of the towns, is truly the greatest

revolutionary in history. He has thrown off the yoke of slavery. He has won a victory over time, and over the enslavements of all the empires -- of Pharaoh, of Nebuchadnezzar, of Titus and of Hadrian, and of Hitler. And the others who have dreamed of wiping us out, of destroying us, of effacing our being and our memory so that not a trace would remain. This little fellow of a Jew has beaten them all with his bare hands. Without weapons, without an army, without a nation, without territory, without an inch of earth on which to set the sole of his foot. And for a very, very long time all alone, without a soul to have pity on him, to make contact with him, to understand him, to console him. He has traveled through thousands of years keeping on his separate way with his God. It was simple; there was nothing left for him but to cling to God. No credit to him, after all, since he had no other choice. God stuck to him as the rock to the limpet. Thus he had only to let it be done to him. By God. And by Hitler: line up before the gate of the concentration camp. Say, "Excuse me," and also, "Thank you": excuse me for the trouble, and thank you for finishing with it by letting yourself be roasted in the maw of the crematory oven. Living, conscious, and happy after all; what a horror to think that one might have been in the place of that poor wretch who can find nothing better to do than to make living human beings, by the millions, go into gas chambers and crematories, just for the pleasure of seeing them go up in smoke. One must really be lacking in imagination to toil away for the sake of such an entertainment! He's not funny, the God of the Hebrews: I'd really like to meet him. But he's not such a fool as the gods of all the empires, those personified disasters, those vampires. Admit it, my warders; realize it, my poor butchers.

Let's leave it, forget it, get on, since you are no longer barring the way. That's new for me -- a way unbarred. I go where I wish; no one stops me for it, and I can go right on to the end, even if I know that there is no longer any end to my new way. No one turns me aside by force, asking me: "Kindly stand while we tie you to this stake," or, "Please dwindle into a heap of ashes in this crematory." This is a greater miracle than the parting of the Red Sea, on the word of the sworn expert on miracles that, in fact, I am. Yes, I am standing, my bundle on my shoulder, my leather thongs on my lifted forehead and

my fleshless arm -- I, the conqueror. I am free to go
to Jerusalem, of which I have been dreaming for
thousands of years. I am going to Jerusalem; I am
there; I, the conqueror, bare-handed, of all the
empires. But will I know how to conquer myself, I,
the conqueror of God?

I sang then of the long march of the renascent
people toward the hill of the springtime of the
nations:

Seas tranquil for the host of ships well-armed
As they return, the people of the lovers,
O Memory,
Inscribed upon the Book salt-foaming, seas
Lifted to new heavens of the Prince returned
And the long marching of his people
On beyond
The frontiers and the races and the creeds,
Nations and cities of the earth, a people
On beyond
That which the eye can see, the ear can hear,
Hand grasp, foot tread, and the mouth name,
Beyond attachments and beyond all limits,
Beyond all thought, and all that is created,
O march beyond the desert, O place without a name,
O city crowned with silence, O archangelic Eye.

I had gone so long without singing that my poem
choked itself in my throat. It was as though I were
spitting blood. You understand? I had stopped
singing since Daniel burned in his furnace, and since
Jesus suffered on his cross. There's no singing in
front of a stake -- and, Christians, not a word can be
uttered at the foot of the cross on which the Jew is
agonizing.

Brought back to life

Don't listen for his death rattle -- not yet -- I
still have something very important to tell you. I
haven't endured two thousand years in my jails for the
pleasure of it. If I had held my own, at any price,
it wasn't for nothing. I am a Jew, after all. I am
going to tell you my secret. I speak Hebrew, the
language of the Bible, that Nebuchadnezzar and Titus
tried to stifle. They died happy because they
believed they had succeeded in putting out the fire of
its message. They would have succeeded, if I had not

137

stolen that last treasure to hide it under the ashes
of my corpses, ashes so thickly spread that no one, or
almost no one, had discovered it, and so well tended
that it has never been extinguished. Coming back to
Jerusalem, there I found my language again. This,
also, is an event unprecedented in history. A
language born in the first half of the second
millenium before the Christian era, and living through
Biblical times before being assassinated in the Iron
Age. This language, the key to the treasure, I had
hidden along with the treasure itself under the
thickly spread ashes of my corpses, since, without it
-- no treasure, no sacred fire. Nothing! The world
would be a desert. You will have understood this when
you realize what the Bible means to us. Behold, the
Bible also has reawakened from its sleep, and has
arisen. It has begun, not only to speak to us, but
also to make us speak, us Jews. But now (pay
attention, gentlemen!) this is no longer the same
thing. When you hear Hebrew spoken, take note that
this is an instance of a language restored to life and
brought back from afar. It is as astounding as though
from your window, under your very eyes, you were to
see, strolling down the middle of your street, a
fossil! Like us, it is a survivor of a vanished age.
This would be astonishing even if it were not the
language of the Bible, a sacred language. I said to
myself: "If they knew neither what the Bible is, nor
what Hebrew is, how would they know, Nathanaël, what
is the sacred fire?"

O Prince, Messiah, you who have come back
To celebrate the feast day of the King;
The Judgment Day; the emptied sepulchres;
The leaping forth, cinctured and resolute,
With graveclothes dripping from the fingertips
Of arms, athletic, bound with leather thongs;
The passing beyond fears and limitations,
And hates, and every kind of misery,
In hawk flight piercing through the sky of idols,
All dead and toppled from their ivory thrones
While border walls and weapons burn to ash!
O Prince, my Prince, so present and so real,
Desired returner to our hopeful eyes!
White horseman, with your bright, salt-foaming blade!
O heavenly spark, the taking on of flesh
Upon that day when all the dead arise!
And then that rush of peoples toward the hill
Of resurrection and of restoration;

O Prince of victory, so your men-at-arms
Assail the lofty forges of our hells
And grapple from our hands the bombs of death;
To go to war against the war of men;
To transfix hate upon forsaken crosses;
To fling us, naked now, onto the scales
Under the just eye of the archangel,
O Prince, and into your eternities.

"The real is the concrete," said Lenin, who, however, wasn't Jewish. As for me, I am the revolution, not because I want to be, but because I am, having simply come home, to Jerusalem. I have closed the ring; I have returned to my point of departure after two thousand years of wandering and not a few vexations. In changing continents, I have found my own land again -- in a very bad state, surely. But, after all, my land and I always understand one another. She doesn't lie, not she! Moreover, she recognized me at first glance. She saw my bashfulness, and began to talk to me, as a wife to a husband, placing herself in the best position to be tilled and made fruitful. It's just fantastic what she pours out for me, my land, since I've come back to her! Grapefruit, and the best milch cows in the world; eggs and fruit and milk and honey. You want it? There it is, until you hardly know what to do with it all. A land that was called desert, sterile! But that isn't all; at every step she tells me secrets that she has jealously guarded since the day I was driven away from her. As I pass by, she opens her hand and holds out to me all sorts of marvels: living remembrances of the past of my patriarchs, judges, kings, and prophets, and even of Jesus and his Apostles. Hey there, my Christian friends, doesn't that tell you something? When I am neither diligent enough, nor close enough, she makes use of a goat to disclose a cave where my ancestors had placed the fabulous treasure of the Dead Sea Scrolls. At every blow of the pick she tells me something else; she uncovers my ear to whisper wonderful things into it. Here I stand, firmly planted upon her; she is like a woman at my feet, loving, submissive, trembling with love at the hearthfire of our reunion. My strength drawn from her, I know myself as founder and charter member of the revolution that is bringing the new age.

Here we are, then, you my land, you my language, and you my people, brought back to life, reawakened, arisen, and standing, from this time forward, upon the hills of Zion. When a dead person is brought back to life, he doesn't smell good when he lifts the lid of his coffin and comes out of his grave -- that's well known. He stinks, he reeks. People rush away from infection, and also because they are afraid. Have you considered where they, the dead, would take us, if they came back to life?

At the time of burial, people make quite a show: they put on mourning, they sniff, they weep, they grasp each other's hands and pat each other on the back. But, deep down, they are quite comfortable.--To begin with, it's he who's dead. Not we. Not Yet, anyway! And then, there's the estate. That counts. That can, in fact, be counted. We'll be able to divide it up, and enjoy it, in the place of that poor fellow, who, instead of devouring the estate, has himself become the food of worms deep underground. It's queer, isn't it? And the young widow is going to be able to do what she wants with her lover, without having to account to anyone. And the house and lot -- the next-door neighbor is going to get it all for a song, because the heirs will be quarreling like wolves around a carcase.

Now imagine the unthinkable: the dead man comes forth from his grave. Well, that stops the laughing! No more inheriting, dividing, joking. She must disgorge, that widow who has found perfect love with her new husband, who went to bed with her the very night of the burial. And the neighbor, who has already invested enormous sums in his new property. And the nephews, who have fraudulently possessed themselves of the portfolio that was in the safe whose key they had stolen -- however, nobody had seen them! Everything would have gone so well, if it hadn't been for that accident, his resurrection!

When this happens to a whole people, that's no longer an accident, it's a cheat and a scandal. A whole people? But what am I saying? It's happening to the Jewish people -- you hear me? To Israel. I'm astounded, sir! This is no longer to be thought of as an accident, but as an earthquake; not simply a cheat, but a conspiracy, undoubtedly engineered by the Devil himself. Everything has changed in the world since

140

the revived rule in Jerusalem. Only the blind could fail to see it. And another thing! The last time a resurrection occurred in Jerusalem, it took four centuries for the nations to notice and understand what had happened. This time, it is an entire people that has risen from the dead; this makes a lot of bustle and bother. At first, nobody understands what has happened. Then they cover their eyes, stop up their ears, and hold their noses, so as not to see, or hear, or smell, for fear of the consequences. But they end, or will end, by giving in to the evidence: earthquake or not, conspiracy or scandal, this risen body is indeed living. They have to learn to get along with that fact, since there's no choice. This is a bother to the Church, which has been teaching for at least fifteen centuries that she is heir to the Hebrews -- she, the New Israel. Inheriting is from the dead. If one has obtained the estate of someone still alive, one makes arrangements so that he will be as harmless as a corpse. One files down his teeth and nails, and, if he cries out, one locks him up. Isn't that what was done? Thirty years after its birth, the Vatican still hasn't recognized the State of Israel. So far as the Arab nations are concerned, there is no fault to be found with their kings and dictators; they have done everything they could, for thirty years, first, to prevent the resurrection, and then, when that had been achieved, to smash down the risen one and make him go back into his grave. Public order must be preserved, mustn't it?

None of this worked. When you've waited two thousand years to climb up out of the hole in which you've been buried, it's wonderful how much energy you exert to keep from going back into it! The Arab armies have learned this to their cost in the battles of four wars. The last of these, that of Yom Kippur, came close to being fatal to us. We were all in the synagogues, fasting and praying for our own pardon and that of the world, and that we might remove our masks and show our true faces for God and our brothers to see, without any lie or pretense, just as we are, face to face. I was bowed down, my forehead to the ground, praying for the peace of the world in the synagogue Yohanan ben Zakaï, not far from the Wailing Wall, when someone came to tell me that the Arab armies had invaded Israel and that we were done for, since we were all on our knees in the synagogues praying for our own pardon and that of the world.

141

At first, and even to the very end of that Day of
Atonement, I acted like the government and like that
famous general staff of the armies of Israel whose
genius struck the crowds with admiration: I just
didn't believe it until the conclusion of the fast.
By nightfall there were already thousands of dead on
the sacrificial altar of that dismal day. Then, I
think for the first time in my life, I was really
afraid. For sixty hours we had been skirting the
worst disaster of our disastrous history. The Arab
tanks, heading for Jerusalem, Tel-Aviv and Haifa,
might have encountered no resistance, and, occupying
several strategic points, they would have been able,
almost without a blow having been struck on either
side, to give the order to put us to death.

All at once, the risen one, a knife between his
teeth, swore that he wouldn't be caught that way
again. Since it has been rumored that Israel has the
atom bomb, her neighbors, grown wiser, have begun to
talk of peace. And peace is marching on, despite the
problems, and despite those who exploit the problems.

The enthusiasm of the departure

Jerusalem and her people were the real reasons for
my perturbation, and then for my wish to cast off my
Parisian moorings and come to live among the hills of
Zion. Each of my trips to Israel sharpened my
resolution to share fully in the destiny of my people.
But a decision reached is not quite the same as a
decision carried out. In my Parisian life, I was
involved in the work I was carrying on along with René
Cassin for the Universal Israelite Alliance, as well
as in my work as a writer and a translator. In the
grotto of Sainte-Baume, overlooking one of the most
beautiful countrysides in France, I had begun the
translation of the Psalms. The hermit near whom I was
living, Father Ceslas Rzewuski, has told in his
autobiography, A Travers l'Invisible Cristal, of the
spiritual adventure that led him from the court of the
Czars to that hermitage, of which he was the
"starets." I had completed my "stairway" up to Israel
along the ways of recent trips to the Sahara and then
to America. In the company of my host, one of the
most authentically spiritual people it has been given
me to know, my meditation on the Bible permitted me,

142

also, to pass through the invisible crystal. Preparing myself for the future task, I wrote in my Cantique pour Nathanaël:

Freed from a heavy weight, I now can sing of
    liberty.

    I entered into dialogue among the comets
    with a disembodied sage
    who was clinging to their tails.

He heard me and let them all go, to fly the
    better.

    We were both drunk with the same drunkenness
    sampling the honey of the heavens.

    Our wills, all sharpened and made one,
    were whittled down
    to nothingness.

The sun consumed us in its frenzied fires,
and we, consumed, were singing through its pitch-black night.

    Our wills,
    in truth
    made one, were whittled down

    to the perfection
    of nothingness.

And we were singing in the pitch-black night.

    In the twilight of a grotto, I grasped for the first time the nature of a prayer lived in the complete abandonment of self, with no resistance or struggle, with no effort of the will except the desire for love and unity, just as described by Bahya, in the light of the heart, I understood those who, Jews or Christians, like my fathers, or like the host who was welcoming me, had consecrated their lives to following this way, the sole road that can lead toward the light of the ultimate liberations. It felt good to live at that height, where prayer stripped the fat off the heart, and made praise deeper and more beautiful. Still trembling from my memories of the war, I regained my inner peace and my zest for living.

It was Annette, a crystal goblet, who did what was needed to bring what I was into accord with what I believed. Lovers as we were, first of Israel, and then of one another, it was clear that we were to establish our family in Jerusalem, where, indeed, we did marry, and where we have had five children. It was since we have revived our roots that we have been able to rediscover our wellsprings and our song.

The full shock of my change came upon me in the streets of Jerusalem, town of strife and challenge, city of utopia. Not just a town, but a symphony, in which I could hear the music of the universe as though I were at its very center. There I could read the history of humanity, written on its stones. In its streets, Jews hailing from more than a hundred countries would encounter Arabs of all the races and rites of Islam, and Christians belonging to some thirty-three distinct denominations. The city was a microcosm, in which the countenance of the world was re-forming itself around the sources of its Biblical inspiration.

The traces of the war of 1948 had not been effaced. The streets were strewn with debris, and a bloody battleground divided the city in two, separating Jerusalem from Jerusalem. This was the time of the great flood of immigrants, survivors of the European concentration camps and Jews coming from the oriental countries and from North Africa. These had greeted the creation of the State of Israel as an event more Messianic than political: they were coming home because God wished it. His promise had been fulfilled; they had but to await the miracles of the end of time, those similarly promised from all eternity. But if this was the mystic exaltation stemming from two millennia of prayers and fidelity, the reality turned out to be quite different. The Jews who had come from under-developed lands arrived unprovided with anything, burdened with large families, ignorant of the languages and customs of the society they were entering, and sundered from their leaders and teachers. Those leaders and teachers had preferred the present welcome and future opportunities offered to them by France and the wealthy lands to the uncertainties and difficulties of life in Israel. My poor Jews from North Africa soon came up against the incomprehension, and then the resentment, of many of their new compatriots. The conflict, it must be

144

admitted with sadness, was profound. To the disparities of languages of origin, of mentalities, and even of physical make-up, was added another obstacle: the new arrivals were "Arab Jews." They came, in fact, from Arab lands; spoke, ate, and were dressed like Arabs, while embattled Israel was withstanding a siege carried on by the Arab world into which it had come. They found it hard to recognize the realization of their Messianic dreams in the harsh reality that awaited them. The land had nothing for them, and the food rationing aggravated the severity of their unemployment. The new immigrants were directed, from the moment of their arrival, to the frontiers and the most arid areas of planned settlement. No Messiah! Instead, there was a bureaucracy. They understood neither its workings nor its necessity, and it was a creature strange to their Mediterranean or Oriental way of life, against which they kept dashing themselves in vain. They felt abandoned by everybody, victims of a veritable persecution, when they found themselves relegated, despite all their efforts, to the lowest rung of the social ladder. Wasn't this on account of a frightful discrimination, a racism that dare not declare itself?

In fact, the encounter of immigrants coming about half-and-half from the two parts of the world, the rich and the underdeveloped, concentrated in this one country the central problem of the twentieth century. Israel, reflecting the demographic and social structures of the modern world, found dumped in her lap the burdensome privilege of seeking to resolve, on her own account, one of the most serious problems of our time, and thus to play, in this additional way, the part of the pioneer. But, meanwhile, suffering and disappointment were to be seen in the faces of these men, whom I knew well from having become their historian, and whom I loved. No, it wasn't possible for me not to associate myself closely with their lot. They weighed heavily in my decision to come to live in this land, which I had been visiting each year ever since I had discovered it. The war of 1956, unhappy as were its causes, conduct, and consequences, allowed me to participate in the ordeal that affected the whole land in which I then found myself. I felt that the people, instead of celebrating the victory of their lightning war, were taking it soberly, understanding thoroughly that, though that particular battle was over, the war itself was continuing, and,

145

with it, the attendant strains and privations. The dead had to be buried, the wounded cared for, the ruins rebuilt... and a new war had to be prepared for, since no peace treaty had been signed.

One certainty was borne in upon me, that Israel was the adventure of the century, and that I had no right to forego that adventure and fail in my life's mission. Everything inclined me to go to Israel, including David Ben Gurion, whom I met for the first time two days before the Sinai campaign. With his forceful head, his ruddy complexion, and his aureole of white hair, he was then at the height of his powers. One felt in him a powerful will that nothing could deflect, once he had chosen a goal. His enemies condemned his entire policy, domestic and foreign, but without his fearlessness, would the State of Israel ever have been born? Certainly, I had to bring my life into harmony with my convictions. The small country-seat that I was then living in, near Paris, at Coupvray, the sober beauty of its architecture, and the peace and quiet of its park and its orchard seemed insupportable to me when I thought of the destitution of my people. The comfort of my life clashed with the dangers of theirs.

I also saw clearly that only in Israel could I fully find myself. Only there could I rebuild myself, by taking part in her rebuilding. "Since the fourteenth of May, 1948, the date when return was freely offered to all the survivors of our exiles, it has no longer been possible to remain a Jew of the Exile without verging on schizophrenia," declared Ben Gurion. Believers were continuing to pray in the synagogues for something already achieved. Instead of continuing to beseech God to gather them back in Israel, why didn't they present themselves at the nearest travel agency to buy an easily obtainable ticket to Jerusalem? For the Zionists, the contradiction is still more obvious, since they are striving for an object already realized. They proclaim that goal, without resolving to attain it personally, so long as they remain settled anywhere other than in the land of Israel.

The arguments they present to justify their still belonging to the Diaspora are respectable; everyone is free to choose his own path. But their problem remains: they recognize the contradiction between the

146

ideologies, religious or political, and the facts.
This contradiction explains the spiritual weakness of
the Judaism of the Exile. A message can be preached
only to the extent that it is also lived. As I see
it, the exiled Judaism, as well as traditional
Zionism, have been ruined by their own success. They
have no meaning any more, since their end has been
attained by the creation of the State of Israel. I
refused to keep on living on the banks of a river
whose waters, diverted, were flowing elsewhere.
Certainly, I had to go as soon as possible. René
Cassin, followed by the Central Committee of the
Alliance, gave me the green light to go. We bought a
tent, and a sail boat, Annette not forgetting her
guitar, and we settled outselves in Jerusalem. A new
life began for us.

GOD IS DEAD

We have killed him

"Stop the world, I want to get off," say the
English. When a Roman soldier asked Hillel to give
him the whole message of the Bible while standing on
one foot, the genial old man answered him: "Don't do
to others what you wouldn't want them to do to you!"
If I had to explain in one sentence the reasons for my
fear in confronting our times, I should say that I was
afraid because God is dead. And if he is dead, it is
because we have killed him. All of us have seized
control of our world, and have laid siege to God on
all sides. By tried and tested methods, subtle and
efficacious, we have done all that was necessary to
expunge his credibility, and sometimes even the memory
of his existence, from the spirit of man. The God of
the Bible claimed to overcome the idols of the
mythologies of antiquity. He had, as his prophets
have told us, good reasons to desire that they be
defeated and he reign alone. Four thousand years
after Abraham, we have a global vision of humanity,
and we perceive the fact with the utmost clarity: the
truly defeated in history is the God of life, of
justice, and of love -- the God of Sinai.

After three thousand years of Hebraism and two
thousand of Christianity, we can state confidently
that the vast majority of mankind has not yet emerged
from the stage of primitive thought -- or that it has

sunk back into that stage, even though provided with
the magical powers that modern techniques confer upon
it. Whole continents have been barely touched by the
teachings of the Bible that go beyond the mythological
age of thought. Both Judaism and Christianity have
enclosed themselves in the cultural framework of the
ancient Roman Empire as in a prison, whence there has
escaped their bastard child, the West, now endowed
with sufficient power to destroy three times over all
traces of life on the planet. And in that West,
thought, cut off from its Hebraic and Graeco-Latin
roots, has burnt its gods and invented new idols,
falser and more deadly than the old ones. Marxism
serves as the answer to the questions raised by the
masses of the West, who have thrown off their
traditional teachings, or by the masses of the East
and Far East, fascinated by the powers of technical
civilization. The part of Africa that still resists
historic materialism clings to the God of Islam in
preference to the God of the Christians, who has been
too compromised by his missionaries and witnesses, by
the excesses of colonialism, and who is, to tell the
truth, incomprehensible to minds untrained in the
conceptual structures of Graeco-Latin philosophy. The
God of Islam has an authenticity derived from the
safe-kept memory of the deserts from which he sprang,
aided by the simplicity of a coherent theology,
accessible to everyone.

God has not waited to die in our time -- his death
throes go back to the origins of humanity. It was
difficult for God to take his place in a universe
overpopulated with our idols; still more so in the
adulterous hearts of mankind. "The Way that can be
told of is not an Unvarying Way. The names that can
be named are not unvarying names. It was from the
Nameless that Heaven and Earth sprang." Thus begins
the first chapter of Lao-tzu's The Way. Before Lao-
tzu, the Hebrews believed that before time, and
through all time, there was a self-existing being,
eternal, infinite, complete, and omnipresent. They
knew that being to be Unnamable, and that whatever is
named is not the Unnamable. Hence the name of their
God, YHWH, derived from the root HWH, to be. YHWH is
the Being who has been, who is, and who will be. But
his name, being that of the unfathomable mystery of
being, is unnamed, and unnamable. As his name was
sacred, it was pronounced but once a year, on the day
of Kippur, in the Holy of Holies of the Temple of

148

Jerusalem. Since the destruction of the Temple, this esoteric secret of the Hebrews has been lost, so thoroughly lost that no one knows the pronunciation of the name. For us, therefore, the Unutterable is truly the Unnamable. If an atheist of the spiritual delicacy of a Jacques Monod had understood that the word God hides the mystery of the unnamed and unnamable Being, he would have hesitated to deny his existence in such abrupt terms. By an ironic chance, the ADN in which he sees the principle and source of all life is the most used name of the God of the Hebrews, the ADN, the ADON, or Adonai, the master of all life. For the God of the Hebrews is a bio-logical God, the God of the word of life. (The English equivalent of ADN is DNA, deoxyribonucleic acid.)

His misfortunes began when men took it into their heads to name the Unnamable. The human mind is so constructed that whatever is inexpressible is considered non-existent. It was necessary to give a name to him who had revealed himself to Moses in the burning bush as being the unutterable and unnamable being, YHWH. The Hebrews took, in order to speak of him, the name for the gods of their pagan neighbors, the Elohim. They used this plural word as singular, and combined with it the unpronounceable Tetragram, to form the term YHWH Elohim. But, in so doing, they confounded, in the popular mind, the unique and transcendent God of Sinai with the crowd of idols that encumbered the pagan pantheons. On account of this, he became, linguistically at least, a part of that very family which he wished to destroy, in snatching the nations away from the myths and mythologies that were killing them. All language being unfit for speaking of Him, the prophets borrowed that in most current usage, the language in which the nations spoke of their idols. They were using a keyed language, which always meant, to the initiates, something other than the message conveyed by the written words. Undoubtedly it was impossible to do otherwise -- unless they had remained silent. But the risks of false readings were, and remain, great. Our ancestors, the Hebrews, often strayed in this manner, bringing down upon themselves the vehement censure of the prophets. Thus began the agony of Elohim.

The most subtle misreading, the most profound, and the most difficult to deal with, occurred when the rabbis of Alexandria, probably encouraged by the

149

Ptolemies, undertook to translate the Bible into Greek, around the third and second centuries before the Christian era. To make themselves understood by the Greeks they had to use their language. The translation of the Septuagint was resolutely syncretist, and, since it addressed itself also to Hellenized Jews, was frankly written in the spirit of apologetics. It was necessary to prove to the nations that Moses was at least as versed in philosophy and letters as Plato and Aristotle. The Septuagint translators made their adjustments of meanings all the more light-heartedly since, in their eyes, Plato and Aristotle were disciples of Moses; why be surprised to find, here and there, the same thought expressed in the same language?

The first rash step was to call the God of Sinai, YHWH Elohim, by a name that designated the idols of Olympus, Theos, the Deus of the Latins, the Dieu of the French. God, under the name of Theos or any name formed from that term, was thus born in Alexandria of the cross-breeding of the pagan divinities, undoubtedly astonished to discover in their company the austere and redoubtable Elohim of Sinai. As for him, he must have felt himself, in that company, like a displaced person, snatched out of his natal Asia and the solitude of a transcendent God, to become, under the skies of Europe, just one of the gods of the nations. Let us call to mind that this transplanting took place before the birth of Christianity, when the word Theos designated the idols of the nations, and those alone. The Elohim of the Hebrews must have felt himself in exile just like his people in the linguistic, religious and cultural universe of the Graeco-Latins. There was not a single one of his words that could be translated without being warped, deformed, or even betrayed in the languages of the peoples of the North and of the West. The name could be expressed, but it ceased to be the eternal Name, essentially unutterable. As the crowning disgrace, the Unutterable, the Unnamable YHWH received as his Greek name the designation common to the idols of Olympus, grouped around his most unyielding enemy, Zeus (Theos, Deus, Dieu). Unnamed, he was the master of heaven and earth, source of the ascetic fruitfulness of silence. Named, he became the very nadir of his infinite and unnamable essence. In his western career, his long agony was accompanied by some drying up of the springs of his liberty. Debaptized

150

in the West, YHWH, who had become Theos-Deus-Dieu, survived only under the hardly disguised mask -- splendid, it must be said -- of Zeus.

As long as the Graeco-Latin culture remained alive in all the principal parts of the ancient Roman Empire, the mask provided an illusion. God could satisfy himself and satisfy us, in knowing himself the near relative of Zeus, and designated by the same family name. Moreover, with time, the meaning of Theos, Deus, Dieu, took on a profoundly altered meaning. When the Seventy wrote Theos, they evidently meant Elohim. Christianity, beginning with the Gospels, enlarged the concept of Theos by filling it with the multiple meanings of Elohim, with which the Bible is crammed. All went pretty well while the West took its nourishment from the Graeco-Latin culture, and had not entirely forgotten its Hebreo-Biblical roots. The honest man could accept what was said to him in the name of that God, born of the cross-breeding of Biblical revelation with Greek philosophy. The Jews, guided by their theologians, who had been brought up on Platonism, Aristotelianism, or Neo-Platonism, contented themselves, like the Christians, in openly preaching the syncretism of the two cultures, that of Jerusalem and that of Athens, of which the contemporary West is born.

The technological revolution had, as a secondary effect, the sapping of the living roots of the Hebreo-Biblical culture, wherever they had not already been sterilized by the Counter-Reformation; and, as a still more grievous effect, the discarding of the vestiges, once glorious, of the religious, philosophical, and cultural world of the Graeco-Latins. In one generation, the flower of the Christian community, with the exception of a tiny rear-guard of the faithful, had abandoned the study of Latin and Greek, simultaneously effacing the reflection, previously evident in their culture, of the mental and religious conformation of the Hellenistic world. Since this change, the theologies and catechisms built on those lost foundations have ceased to have the same clarity, the same power of conviction -- sometimes ceasing even to be credible in the world that is arising out of their ruins. The new language, that of science and technology, imposes itself on everyone; passing beyond the limits of the old Roman Empire, in one generation it has become universal, total, autonomous, and consistent, invading and subjecting to its uniform rule even those civilizations the most naturally opposed to its thrust. The forms of Hebrew thought and those of Greek philosophy seem archaic beside the demonstrable certitudes of the technological system. Only a handful of men, brought up, as it were, in the seraglio, comprehend what deep meanings, and what realities, are contained in the name YHWH, and in the surnames, Elohim and Dieu. For the vast majority of men, including the great dechristianized masses of the West, God, like the gods of the empires that adopted him in order the better to reduce him to impotence, is from now on naked, dead -- so say the crowds, deprived of his light and of his love -- dead of having been named, dead of having been imprisoned in a conceptual cage in which his fire is smothered and his strength worn down. And since God, as _Dieu_, is dead, the world is at last free to discover his true countenance and his mystery, that of the Unnamed.

The great schism

To the extent to which the West is separated from its traditional culture, the Bible and Graeco-Latin thought, it seems like a drunken boat, tossed from side to side in a channel whose two borders, the point of departure and the point of arrival, are lost. We live in a world shrunken, by the powers of technology, to the dimensions of a province, but a world which has renounced neither its wars nor its divisions. Linked to the "death of God," the great Judeo-Christian schism seems to me typical, by the misunderstandings that gave it birth, by the gravity of its consequences, and by the salvation that would result from its disappearance.

I have been deeply aware of the gravity of this evil since my childhood in that Algeria, given over to all the devils of racism. I understood the true meaning of the words, "Dirty Jew," when my Christian schoolfellows drove it home with blows from their book-bags on my youthful head; so also I learned the meaning of the swastikas painted by our neighbors on the walls of our houses; and of the walls of our ghetto, almost hermetically sealed off, lest it open only upon the surrounding contempt or hatred. As a youth, I had to face the Nazi persecution, peddled in France by the admirers of the Führer, a race not yet extinct. The reckoning is heavy: six million martyrs, including several hundred thousand children. The explanation for these crimes with which so many Christians satisfy themselves seems to me monstrous -- the Jews, having killed Jesus Christ, are paying the price of their perfidy. "The blood of the God-killers falls upon their own heads," as the catechisms calmly teach, adopting without hesitation the doctrine of collective responsibility, even collectively hereditary responsibility, as justifying punishment for a crime whose circumstances and actual responsibilities they don't give themselves the trouble to elucidate. Christian historians had proclaimed this principle vigorously, before the Second Vatican Council condemned it. A Jew, in the eyes of medieval Christianity, was an object, more than a subject, of rights; to such an extent that in the countries of the greatest Jewish concentration the history of Judeo-Christian relations coincides with the history of anti-Semitism. On either side, people have deliberately chosen either to ignore one another, or to hate. The scandal of this schism is all the greater in that Jews and Christians claim to adore the same God, recognize the same Hebrew Bible, believe in the same values of justice and love, and hope for the same universal salvation. How was this curtain of misunderstanding and hatred able to separate them so disastrously? Between the Church and the Synagogue, enemies and sisters, invective, insult, or disputation -- when open persecution wasn't going on -- took the place of any sort of dialogue. It was a great scandal, in the eyes of the Church, that Israel, conquered, exiled, and powerless, still rejected the God who had come out of her womb, while she, the Christian Church, was attracting a growing number of nations, and expecting the conversion of the universe to the law of love of God incarnate in Jesus Christ. In her triumphal progress she crashed into the stubborn resistance of a handful of exiles, all the more incomprehensible and bothersome since it came from the people of that Bible that gave birth to Jesus, Mary, Joseph, the Apostles, and the primitive Church. It has been necessary to wait three decades after the rebirth of the State of Israel for a progressive wing of the Church to begin to recognize a certain legitimacy in the resistance offered by the Jews to the new religion that had been born of them. Throughout two thousand years this Jewish refusal had been considered by the fathers and theologians of the Church as perfidious, obstinate, deserving of the most

153

severe punishments. They saw the absolute proof of the perfidy of the Jews in the unhappy condition of those people; banished from their land, and condemned to the scorn, if not the persecution, of all nations. In their eyes, such constant adversity was the visible token of a supreme crime and of just divine retribution. These shallow conclusions sometimes fed the furor of the Christian masses, and, devoid as they were of all truth and justice, they provoked the resentment of the Jews. Christianity, in their eyes, appeared in a light that wiped out all its values and virtues, leaving in view only its worst countenance. The consequences of this situation still persist in the feelings of a great many Christians and of a great many Jews, besmirching the purity of their relations, dampening their enthusiasm and enfeebling their witness. A general reconsideration of this whole story, taking into account both history and semantics, must be the groundwork for a reconciliation upon which depend, perhaps the salvation of mankind, and surely the achievement of the final goals of both Israel and the Church. Paul, that pharisee and son of a pharisee, proclaimed it twenty centuries ago: "I further ask, does their stumbling mean that they are forever fallen? Not at all! Rather, by their transgression salvation has come to the Gentiles to stir Israel to envy. But if their transgression and their diminishing have meant riches for the Gentile world, how much more their full number!...

For if their rejection has meant reconciliation for the world, what will their acceptance mean? Nothing less than life from the dead."* These sentences, like the whole of the New Testament, can be fully understood only when taken in the historical and cultural context in which they were written. The Judeo-Christian schism has taken on its tragic dimensions on account of the blotting out, followed by the utter forgetting, of the circumstances that brought it about.

Through twenty centuries, the Jews have acted as though Jesus, of whom they often make themselves a distorted picture, had never existed, and as though the Church, faced with the impossible task of

---

*Romans 11, 11-13, 15. NAB

154

converting the nations of the earth to the God of Abraham, had never done anything but persecute them. On the Christian side, the alienation is no less serious; Christians act as though Jesus, Mary, the Apostles, and the primitive Church had not all been born out of Israel; they forget almost entirely the Hebrew roots of the New Testament; they accuse the Jews of complete responsibility for the death of Christ -- all the Jews, collectively and hereditarily -- and, in order to punish them, devise an elaborate series of restrictions that condemn them to the confinement of the ghettos. This cloistered condition intensified their reaction to their situation as exiles. They have existed through the centuries, obsessed by the determination to survive their exile, cost what it might, and to take back to a re-arising Jerusalem the seeds of their former greatness, preserved by their own efforts, to germinate and flourish again in the hour of return and of salvation. The Christian anti-Judaism permitted and fed the development of the modern anti-Semitism such as we saw triumph in the German National-Socialist movement. In the countries that had the fiercest persecutions, notably in central and eastern Europe, the Jews have so hideous an image of the _goyim that they seal themselves completely into their enclosures. This negative reflection of the racism from which they are suffering serves to uphold and justify among them a sectarian intransigence, and to encourage a dogmatic interpretation of Judaism. In the eyes of these extremists, Judaism alone holds the truth, or, to be precise, alone holds it in its fullness. For some of them, Christians are polytheists, the God of the Moslems is not the God of Abraham, and as for the African and Asiatic religions, they don't even bother to condemn religions so devoid of value and interest. They shy away from reality to such an extent that the problems posed by the modern world, technology, and Marxism are never so much as touched upon. Their one obsession is obedience to the strict Judaism of the ghettos of the exile, in the expectation of the salvation promised to the chosen people.

I have used the word alienation to define the psychology of the extremists of both camps. They have become complete strangers to reality, which they have replaced by the hallucinations that have grown out of their phobias. On the one side are those who harry

155

the Jews, assassins of God and Devils incarnate; on the other, those who see in the Christian only a monster, filled with hatred and thirsting for blood.

For a radical cure of these maladies, the treatment must reach right down to the roots of the soul. I think the great schism between the Church and Israel, by cutting off Christianity from its Hebraic roots and separating the Jews from all the gentile nations, has provoked an interminable series of misfortunes, strewn obstacles along the course of history, warped our vision and impeded the path to salvation. I believe it will be impossible to join harmoniously in the building of the city of men, and to avoid the deadly threats that hang over it, unless we put an end to that schism. For this, the Church must bring back to life its Hebrew roots; find again, and reinstate, that Eastern spring from which it rose, Jerusalem, and, finally, give full recognition to Israel and its newly constituted State. The Jews must understand that by looking back in morbid contemplation at the persecutions from which they have suffered, they risk turning, like Lot's wife, into pillars of salt. They must take into account the religious and political realities of the world into which they have come back to life, and stop judging them in the light of their own phobias, however understandable the reasons for those phobias may be. They must discover the values of the Christian world, and the face of Jesus their brother, whose true name is Ieshua ben Iosseph, and learn to see in the New Testament the flesh of their flesh, a text devised and proclaimed in Hebrew, that has sowed throughout the pagan world the hope of a salvation announced by the prophets of Israel.

In this spirit, the reconciliation of Israel with the gentile nations has sprouted from the blood of the battles of the Resistance. The average Christian who, through the centuries, learned from his catechisms all the evil that must be thought of the "faithless and deicide Jews," has not very often thought of the fact that he was abusing living men. For him, the Jewish people ceased to exist, by right, if not in fact, upon the birth of the new Israel, the Christian Church. It roused itself, all of a sudden, upon the ruins of Europe, holding in its arms some six million corpses, the circumcised or the mothers and daughters of the circumcised, killed because they were Jewish. So great a heap of the dead, even when the crematory chimneys have made them go up in smoke, cannot pass unnoticed.

Christians and Jews fought side by side against the Nazi persecutions and those of their collaborators in the invaded countries of Europe. Christians gave their lives to save Jews; and Jews poured out their blood to snatch Christians from death. The cry of one Jules Isaac, whose wife was put to death along with others of her family in the German concentration camps, because she bore the name Isaac, was heard. Judeo-Christian friendships became an organized movement in many countries of the Western world, beginning in 1945. They sought to reform the Christian teaching concerning the Jews, to arrange that for secular misunderstandings and traditions of hostility there might be substituted respect, friendship, and mutual understanding. We wished, in particular, to work together in full cooperation to abolish the inequities under which the Jews, born victims of persecution, had been suffering for centuries. To accomplish this program, it was necessary to go against a current of thought that had been flowing for sixteen centuries, laying a thick layer of sediment on the spirits of hundreds of millions of Christians, and of non-Christian peoples contaminated by these hostile prejudices and infected by the same hate.

We were going into this fight bare-handed, armed solely with conviction and will. Each one of us, in view of the tragedies of which he had been witness, had sworn to himself never to permit their return. We were assembled, a few of the survivors, to decide upon the ways and means of our action. Some Jews, who saw in this endeavor only a Christian maneuver intended to convert us, looked upon it with suspicion; and some Christians thought they detected in it a Jewish plot to undermine the catechetical foundations of the spiritual edifice of Christianity. We had no money, no publications, no offices -- none of the means that are thought indispensable to success. Nevertheless, in less than twenty years our movement contributed to bringing about a spiritual revolution of universal scope. A short period of time permitted habits of thought, embedded for centuries, to be reabsorbed, to a large extent, among those who had the most influence in the churches. By a sort of capillary attraction,

157

the ideas and hopes of our movement spread out through country after country. Bishops set to work to undertake the revision of catechisms and missals, in order to eliminate all that might be offensive to the Jews. Pope Pius XII, whose voice, many of us felt, had not been raised strongly enough in protest against the Nazi persecution of the Jews, allowed the omission of the term "perfidious," in the prayer for the Jews included in the Easter liturgy.

The World Council of Churches, in its First Assembly, in Amsterdam, Holland, in 1948, issued an appeal to all its member churches "to denounce anti-Semitism, no matter what its origin, as absolutely irreconcilable with the profession and practice of the Christian faith." "Anti-Semitism," this resolution affirmed, "is a sin against God and man." In 1961, in the Third Assembly, in New Delhi, the World Council reiterated this appeal, adding: "The Assembly urges its member churches to do all in their power to resist every form of anti-Semitism." The full texts of these and later, still more vigorous proclamations on the subject are to be found in Helga Croner's compilation, Stepping Stones to Further Jewish-Christian Relations (London, New York, Stimulus Books [1977]). These declarations caused a fundamental modification of the relations of Jewish people with the Christian world. Here were no vain proclamations of principles; these declarations transformed the teaching of theological schools and of catechisms. Christian triumphalism, standing facing the synagogue with its veiled eyes and broken lance, before the cathedral doors, was marching in place, to the advantage of historical truth. Both sides were approaching one another by returning to the limpidity of their springs of origin, beyond the centuries of misunderstandings and mutual recriminations.

The Catholic Church remains to be considered. Pope Pius XII, at the end of his pontificate, probably influenced by Monsignor Tardini, had taken notice of several of the problems that the living presence of Israel presented to the Christian conscience: the problems of Israel undergoing the worst of persecutions, and the problems of the warfare for our national resurrection; against all odds, we had at last won our bi-millennial wager against history.

I had met Pius XII at the beginning of July, 1956. His apparent weightlessness was striking. His countenance ascetic, he seemed to live by the fiery look he turned upon the world, but to be actually already on the road back to that "elsewhere" of the spirit from which he seemed to have issued forth. Monsignor Tardini, in charge of the regular business of the Vatican, well understood that the time had come for taking up the question of the relations between the Church and Israel. In his offices in the Secretariat of State or in the Roman orphanage called Nazareth, to which he devoted himself unstintingly, I had, on several occasions, the opportunity of talking to him about Israel. But his good sense had a peasant solidity: one builds only upon sound foundations. Waiting was still necessary; I heard from his mouth and in the same offices the echo of the words addressed by Pius X to Herzl: "We cannot recognize an Israel which will not recognize Jesus."

The turning point of history must be identified as Monday, June 13, 1960, at the meeting of a great Pope and a historian, John XXIII and Jules Isaac. At the close of their conversation Jules Isaac handed the Pope a final note and a brief that recounted his labors. Then he asked if he might take from the meeting some bit of hope. "You have a right to more than hope," exclaimed John XXIII, and immediately gave the papers to Cardinal Bea, putting him in charge of a commission to deal with the question. It required five years of labor and strife, in the fevered climate created by the Judeo-Arab warfare, for the efforts of this commission to culminate, with Vatican II, in decisions effective throughout the Church. Here, again, a small number of people, filled with the courage of the spirit, succeeded in accomplishing a task that, until recently, had been considered impossible.

"This is just the first step on a long and arduous road," said the pioneer of this spiritual revolution, Cardinal Bea. I think so too, and I see clearly that our reconciliation would remain sterile if it did not draw us back to our sources, to take from them the heroic courage to work together toward the realization of our ultimate ends.

Landmarks

The return to the innocence of our sources is easier said than done. We must all, on both sides, free ourselves of centuries of unhealthy habit, of utterly unjustified myths and mystifications. It will take a long purgatory to put us in a state to purify ourselves and strengthen ourselves to face, together, our true enemies, war, hunger, ignorance, hatred, and fear; and to give to humanity, borne down by these enemies, a chance of survival.

Jews and Christians must relearn together to read the Hebrew Bible, and the New Testament restored to its historic and linguistic context. They will see that these texts should unite them rather than separate them, and should inspire in them an aspiration for salvation, rather than exasperate their rancors and hatreds, those unpardonable crimes against the spirit of unity and love that flows from our common springs. This union of Christianity with Israel will remain only a pious wish so long as Jews and Christians have not clarified the historical and theological disputes that have so seriously divided them.

I have no wish to rehash the persecutions suffered by the Jews wherever the Church has been in control. Jewish history books are filled with examples. It would be self-deception to see in these persecutions only theological motives. The Church and the synagogue, true inimical sisters, have in fact been fighting to take over the spiritual direction of the pagan world. During the earliest period, the primitive church, totally Jewish in its roots, lived according to the eschatalogical faith in Yeshua, the redeeming Messiah. The first Christians, Jews or converts to Judaism for the most part, were not obviously different from the Jews who strove to spread throughout the Empire the teachings of their sects: Pharisees, Essenes, Sadducees, Zealots. Each sect had its rabbis, sometimes even its Messiah to proclaim, and each invoked the God of Abraham, and the Hebrew Bible.

Until the end of the first century, what united the Jews of all schools and the Christians was infinitely more important that what separated them. They worshiped the same God, drew their inspiration

160

from the same Scriptures, were faithful to the Temple of Jerusalem, lived in the same traditions and shared a single hope: the coming of the Kingdom of God, which would put an end to the distress of nations. Within the House of Israel, the separation between the Essenes and the Sadducees, or between the Sadducees and the Pharisees, was more important than the separation between the Pharisees or the Essenes on the one side, and the Christians on the other. In adoring the One God, the Jews and Christians placed themselves beyond the borders of the pagan world that surrounded them, and persecuted them as no better than atheists, because of their rejection of the cult of the idols. Theoretically it made no difference, and in practice, a pagan found it impossible to distinguish a Jew from a Christian; a convert to Judaism, faithful to the teachings of the Pharisaic masters, Hillel and Shammai, from the leaders of the Christian Church, Peter and Paul, disciples of Ieshua ben Iosseph.

The controversy that engaged the zeal of the Pharisees and Christians was no different in principle from that which arrayed the Jewish sects one against the other, each aspiring to take over the spiritual direction of the Jewish people. The battle was desperate, and retreat impossible, so strongly was it felt that Israel's last chance of life hung in the balance, menaced by the crushing power of the occupying Roman Empire. After the destruction of the Temple of Jerusalem and the overthrow of the homeland of the Jews, none survived the great Roman massacres but the Christians and the Pharisees. The fight grew fiercer between these two, the first turning toward the Roman Empire, which they hoped to convert to the God of Abraham and of Jesus, and the second desperately trying to save what could still be saved of the wreck of Israel: its language, its Scriptures, its traditions -- and its hope, the hope of the restoration of the Kingdom of Israel and its capital, Jerusalem.

The first rupture was teleogical in nature: while the Church set before itself the goal of the conversion of the Empire, the Synagogue turned back upon itself in order to preserve the seed that would permit, one day, the resurrection of Israel. Christianity thus separated itself from its Hebraic sources in order to speak, in Greek and Latin, to the pagans of the Empire. In this, it relied on the

161

Jewish communities of the Diaspora, amounting to some eight million faithful, already converted to the God of Abraham by the Jewish preachings, particularly those of the Pharisees. The great rupture became irreparable when the early Catholic Church, apostolic in its spirit and Roman in its direction, converted Constantine to the faith of Christ. Christianity became the official religion of the Roman Empire, an Empire already doubly hated by the Jews, because it was pagan in spirit, and because its legions had burnt the Temple of Jerusalem, killed hundreds of thousands of Jews (six hundred thousand, according to Tacitus) and deported the survivors of this genocide to be sold in the slave markets. For the Jew, the Church thus became identified with the Empire. The conflict, now become irreversible, grew fiercer through the centuries.

To the teleological and political aspects of the confrontation between the Church and the Synagogue, it is necessary also to add the opposition of cultures, which made impossible any sort of dialogue other than the dialogue of attack and defense. The Jews kept on thinking, speaking, and writing in Hebrew and Aramaic. The Christians, forgetting these languages, though they were the languages of Jesus, now spoke no tongue but Greek and Latin. This changeover, from the Semitic East to the Greco-Latin west, intensified the split. Words, even those of the Bible, no longer had the same meaning as in Hebrew when they were heard in Greek or in Latin in the context of the pagan world. I'll give but one example of this -- but a weighty one.

The expression "Son of God" is called in Hebrew "Ben Elohim," and in Greek "Huios (tou) theou." These words are perfectly translated, but they have not, and can never have, the same meaning in Hebrew and in Greek. In Hebrew the word Ben designates the son born of a father, but it has many other meanings. It can also designate a young man or a young animal without any reference to sonship, or even all sorts of objects and qualities: the sons of the bow are arrows; the sons of the prophets are disciples; the sons of the troop are soldiers; the sons of exile are the exiled; and the son of man, a man. One is the son of his age, of his stature, of his qualities or of his faults. The term Ben thus expresses a simple relationship, whose meaning extends throughout the universe of which

162

God is the Creator, the father. To say that a man is the son of God is to affirm a truism admitted by all and taught emphatically by Moses: "You are children of the Lord, your God."*

Translate this expression as precisely as possible into Greek or Latin, and it takes on a profoundly different meaning. Ben Elohim becomes Huios [tou] Theou, or, in Latin, Filius Dei. But these words are published abroad throughout the Empire of Tiberius, where the gods are not creators but procreators; where kings and emperors are gods and venerated as such, and where either word, Huios or Filius, has a meaning precise and exclusive. This is one of the most striking of the cases in which an exact translation, made by a simple transfer from one language into another, causes a profound alteration in the meaning of the words. Jews and Christians have clashed through twenty centuries over the signification of the divine sonship of Jesus. But this is a baseless conflict: the words Huios [tou] Theou could never have the same meaning as Ben Elohim unless we destroy the entire conceptual universe of the Greeks and replace it with that of the Hebrews -- or vice versa. The contention between Jews and Christians about the divinity of Christ thus seems to me meaningless, if one admits the principle of the coexistence of different cultures, and rejects the principle of the predominance of one culture over another -- the system by which the Roman imperialism lived and died. Cervantes compared certain theologians to windmills; I fear that they remain such so long as they do not bring history and semantics to the service of theology. They must not forget that the divine sonship of Jesus is taught as a "mystery," which Thomas Aquinas himself proclaimed only in the guise of analogy.

The ignoring, and then the forgetting, of the historic context has brought about terrific misconceptions about the events that marked the birth and then the triumph of Christianity. The trial of Jesus and the teachings of Paul take on a completely different meaning according to whether or not they are seen in the circumstances in which they occurred. Any

---

*Deuteronomy 14, 1.NAB

sentence we speak takes on a different meaning
according to the occasion on which it is spoken, or
the tone of voice of the speaker. With regard to the
New Testament, we must take into account that it was
proclaimed and then written out in the hostile
atmosphere of the Greco-Latin world, where, since the
fifth century before the Christian era, censorship had
controlled all that was said or written, bringing down
heavy punishments upon authors and scribes who dared
to sully the glory of reigning monarchs, or to
endanger the civic tranquillity. Socrates was
executed in 399 for an offense of opinion. He is
indisputably the foremost philosopher in the Greek
world to pay with his life for the free expression of
his ideas. While Jesus was still an infant, Augustus
reinforced the judicial foundation of repression,
while enlarging its scope and increasing the penalties
of the Lex majestatis. It was not only impiety and
blasphemy, but even simple criticism directed against
the Empire and its gods, that were punished with
death. The authors of the New Testament had to submit
to that law; hence the absence of any criticism
directed against the Empire, its gods and its princes,
whose part in the events narrated is thoroughly
obscured, especially in the account of the trial of
Jesus. Had this precaution not been taken, the
manuscripts of the New Testament would have been
burned, along with their authors and their scribes,
who were more easily discoverable in those days by the
police than, in the present time, the printers of a
seditious book. Hence the style of the Apocalypse,
which allows one to say what he thinks without being
understood by the guardians of the established order.

These considerations explain also the obliteration
of one of the most profound meanings of the symbol of
the Cross. O Crux, spes unica, sing the Christians,
who see in it the symbol of the Christ, of the Savior,
of the Word, of the Second Person of the Holy Trinity,
of the Tree of Life, annunciator and witness of the
glory of the Parousia. Most certainly! All these
meanings are intended. But what remains of the
realities of the cross upon which Jesus was crucified,
precisely as "King of the Jews," that is to say, as
rebel to the Empire and to Tiberius, who was then the
true, the only king of the Jews in that Roman colony,
conquered and subjugated by Pompey in the year 63?
Judea, like the other countries that had fallen under
the domination of Rome -- Spain, Gaul, Greece, the

oriental and African provinces -- paid an extraordinarily high price for the undeniable benefits of the Pax Romana. This price is dramatically illustrated by the cemeteries in which were crammed by myriads all those who showed the slightest inclination to resist the invaders. For hundreds of thousands, even millions of victims among the subjugated peoples, the cross was the punishment reserved for slaves. From this fact came its evocative power, forgotten today, over the masses, the victims of the Roman oppression. The Cross became for them the symbol of the revolt of the Sons of Light against the Kingdom of Darkness, the necessary preliminary and advance courier of the Day of the Lord, when the Messiah, King of Israel, would overthrow the Empire and its idols to establish on earth the Kingdom of God and its true peace, of which the Pax Romana was but a hideous caricature. The conversion of Constantine brought about the paradox of making the Cross, upon which Jesus died as a slave in revolt against his masters, the symbol of that very Empire which, aided by its Judean collaborators, had arrested, summarily judged, and crucified him.

Ecumenism, even when it is broadened by Judeo-Christian friendship, will remain superficial so long as it is not animated by the purity and authenticity of the origins. It would recover its true roots if it were to establish its capital in Jerusalem, cradle of our religions and meeting-place of the continents, where, today, we see the collision of the major movements of the modern world, and the gravest of the world's problems.

All purification, and all pollution, is at first intellectual. The meeting of Christianity with Israel must have a double purpose: it must take both of us back to our wellsprings, and, rejuvenated by them, we must together find the strength to go forward toward our final goals. To wipe out the lingering effects of our past conflicts would be fine, but not enough for the heirs of the Prophets and Apostles, bearers of their message of justice and peace to a world adrift. In order not to betray our vocation, or deprive the world of its last chance of salvation, we must turn our thought and action into new paths, no longer engaging them in sterile religious and sectarian quarrels, but at the formidable level of the problems of our times, menaced by the nations with nuclear

165

suicide. Putting behind us the prison of our ghettos,
we must, with the rest of the universe, live in
dialogue -- if that word, traced to its roots, means
advance-toward-the-Word. This advance of Jews and
Christians toward the truth of their sources seems to
me essential to the renewal of their thought. I have
tried to involve myself in it through my labors as a
translator; they have thrust me forward into the
rediscovery of meanings in the Hebrew Bible and in the
New Testament. I have come to realize that the
deliverance of man involves the liberation of the
word.

To liberate the word

The compulsion to translate seized me when I was a
child in our synagogue of Aïn-Témouchent, where I
tried to penetrate the meaning of the Hebrew Bible and
of our prayers, following them in bilingual editions.
As an adolescent, to translate meant for me to
penetrate the meanings of the ancestral heritage that
my parents were struggling to bequeath to me. Then
came the time of making comparisons between what I
understood the texts to mean and what the translations
said of them. For my guidance, I re-established the
meaning of words and the harmonies of the rhythms as
they resounded in my head, in a radically Frenchified
Hebrew. Thus were born my translations of Bahya Ibn
Paqûda's Duties of the Heart, of the Song of Songs and
of the Psalms. My vocation as a translator would
probably have stopped there if I had not come to
settle in Jerusalem. My project of translating the
Bible could be achieved now that I had under my feet
the earth of the Prophets and of the Apostles, and
that I could converse with the Bible in the language
in which it is written. Now that Hebrew had become
once more my mother tongue, I could see more clearly
the defects of my previous translations; they were
smothered under a cloak of customs, embroidered
through thousands of years, so that the forms and
meanings of the original text could hardly be
recognized. The deeper my roots drove into the soil
of Israel, the more clearly I perceived that it was
necessary to take up again, at the root, all the
perplexities and the theoretical systems of the
translations of the Bible. A revolution was needed,
if, by that term, one understands a return to the
origins. Yes, to liberate man, we must begin by
liberating the word.

The hardest part for me was throwing off the weight of habits. A translator of the Bible cannot avoid the obligation of going to dictionaries to decipher its texts, since Hebrew, before its rebirth in Israel, was spoken by no one. Nobody could check up on the statements of linguists by citing the living language. On account of this, the dictionaries themselves were necessarily compiled on the basis of the translations of, and commentaries on, the Bible. Dictionaries were made out of chunks of translations, and translations out of chunks of dictionaries. This closed circle led to the immobilization of translations. The Bible is translated into some 1,431 languages and dialects, but an analysis of the linguistic structure of these multiple versions shows that all of them reflect the Septuagint and the Vulgate, those imperishable masterpieces. The legendary Seventy translated the Bible a thousand years after Moses, and Saint Jerome five hundred years later, in times when Hebrew was already a dead language, and there were as yet no dictionaries, or lexicons, or any of the methods for the study of texts that are now at our disposal. These declarations can only add to the merits of these gifted translators, whose works certainly rank among the greatest monuments of world culture.

The duty of avoiding the beaten tracks, trodden through so many centuries, and getting back to the beginnings, was made all the more pressing by the fact that the Seventy, whose influence on the Vulgate is obvious, chose a kind of translation resolutely syncretist and propagandist. Undoubtedly, they had no choice but to Hellenize the Bible, in order to open the door to it for the Greek world.

What had to be done, therefore, was to take up the task of translation again from the beginning; to reconsider the sense of each word and of each expression, to recover their original and authentic signification. This scraping off of the encrustations of ages was made possible by the progress of exegetic studies, as well as by archeological and historical research. This method was rendered all the more necessary for a new reading of the New Testament, because its Semitic background and historic context had been obscured by the traditional interpretation of the Greek text. The exact transcription of the names of persons and places tended, all by itself, to restore the text to its native Orient, to "decolonize" the heroes of the Bible. It was necessary, also, to disencumber the Scriptures of all the lingering sequelae of Greek dualism that warped their meaning, and of all the terms either badly translated or altered through usage. Finally, it was necessary to give back to God his true mystery, no longer designating him by a name that, in the times of the Seventy, applied exclusively to the idols of Olympus, but under the ineffable, unpronounceable Tetragrammaton which is used for him in the Hebrew text, YHWH, keeping in mind the ancient saying of the Tao: "The Name that can be named is not the eternal Name. Unnamed, it is the beginning of the heaven and the earth. Named, it is the end."

A Bible without "God," without "soul," without "sin," without "eternity," without "angels," and without "devils"! The turnaround was complete, and perhaps appropriately so, befitting the long wait for a new reading of the texts whose presence among us never ceases to put us to the question and to stir us.

After I had been preparing myself for almost four decades, I had translated the Bible in a relatively brief time. I wish to state here why this quick survey of the Scriptures has so richly nourished me. In the Bible, I recognized with admiration the masterpiece of universal literature, the book most constantly read and meditated by Jews and Christians through the ages and in all nations. I perceived in the universal workings of this book an inexplicable achievement in human communication. Every writer, and every publisher, knows that a book is directed toward a particular public and a particular epoch, and that usually its life is ephemeral, lasting but a few years. Book follows book, and is soon itself replaced. But the Bible has ruled over Israel and Christianity since their beginnings, and has accomplished another miracle in speaking to the people of all countries in their own tongues, without losing its power of communication and inspiration. It speaks to the learned and the simple, to the aged and the young, to the contemporary of Isaiah, of Jesus, or of Mohammed as to the inhabitant of the industrial cities of the atomic age.

This triumph, unparalleled, has been achieved thanks to a technique that has made possible a true miracle of universal communication. I like to think that my ancestors, the Hebrews, were the true inventors of the moving picture. The Bible is essentially a factory producing images in movement. From the first verse of Genesis to the last of the Apocalypse, the text describes images or sets down dialogue with the concision of a film script. Open your Bible and read it; you are a spectator installed before the moving picture of a living speech; thought is expressed through concrete images that succeed one another so rapidly that your senses are suddenly caught up by the rhythm. A film can be seen by anyone who installs himself before the screen upon which it is projected. The pictures are taken in directly by all eyes. So it is with the Bible: everyone is invited to share in this spectacle, which the windows, the statuary, and the paintings of the Middle Ages formerly illustrated.

But for a film to be thus projected, and so persistently admired by hundreds of millions of human beings, it must undoubtedly correspond to the most essential realities of man. Splendor of style, felicity of expression, even the fact that these writings are considered to be divinely inspired, both by the Jews and by the Christians, would not explain their extraordinary success, if they did not live by their own light. Today, this book brings us the stories of men who lived on the western borders of the Asiatic continent in the Bronze Age or the Iron Age. Nevertheless, it remains a book for our own time, through its penetration of the mystery of man, and even for future times, through the ideal end that it proposes for humanity.

I delight in discovering, in the books of the Bible, man, described in all periods, at all levels of consciousness, in all states of being, in all the situations in which he displays his talent for good or evil, his love or his hate, his fears and his hope. Finding man, I find myself again, I recognize myself and fathom the deepest reality. This prodigious human comedy begins in Genesis with the first man and reaches its climax with the coming of the Son of Man in the Apocalypse. From beginning to end it is about the man and the woman, about you and about me.

But, still more, the Bible spells out for me a way of life. For the Bible, we live in a universe that rules out indifference. To live in the light or to rot in the darkness of death; to work for peace or to prepare for war; to love or to hate -- these are not equal weights in the balance. Since the world is broken in half, it is of consequence that we place ourselves on the side of life, not of death; of justice, not of iniquity; of peace, not of war; of creation, not of destruction; of light, not of darkness; and of unity, not of division. Moses, David, and the Prophets and Apostles of Israel set forth a way for us in concrete terms -- a way along which God is the mystery that cannot be named.

From the very first verse of Genesis we are thrown into a universe where the spirit must redeem, regulate, and illuminate the original chaos, where emptiness and desolation reign in the soulless night. In the eighth century before the Christian era a poet of genius, Isaiah, defined the whole Biblical scale of values, with, at the top, the love of life. YHWH is essentially the God of life, the Living God, creator and guardian of the supreme value of life. The God of the Bible is thus a bio-logical God, the God of the word of life. Isaiah, in this matter the interpreter of the whole of Biblical thought, foresees, looking forward from the year 740 before the Christian era, the end of all wars. He is undoubtedly the first man to have conceived this thought, apparently so foreign to human nature: the necessity, and the inevitability, of the abolition of war. Isaiah lived at a time when no one spoke up against the recognized fact: "man is a wolf to man," the strong has the right to master the weak, to enslave him, to exercise the power of life and death over him. This jungle law prevailed also in relations between cities.

The Prophets of Israel were thus the only ones to rise up in opposition to this natural order of things, and they flung their firebrand against all the tyrants and all the empires on earth. The only true God is God the creator and liberator of life. Justice will bring about the end of conflicts between rich and poor and between masters and slaves, bringing the reign of peace on earth, of fraternity, of love. One hope is thus carved deep in the heart of man: in the Day of YHWH all battles will come to an end, all wars, and all hatreds. Isaiah proclaims the end of warfare between classes, between races, between nations. The day will come when mankind will beat their swords into ploughshares, and no one study war any more. In our own time, revolutionary thought has adopted this vision, changing the Day of YHWH to the millennium of the final battle for the liberation of the masses. But Marx, Lenin, or Mao Tse-tung -- didn't they have their sleepless nights because, in the jungles, the lion devours the lambs, and the strong crush the weak? Yes, Isaiah, justice, to prevail, must be absolute. In the Day of YHWH, the lion shall live in peace with the lamb, and a little child shall lead them. The Prophets know that reality has an organic unity; that salvation must be global, or it will not be at all. Also, they announce the change -- not the progress -- of reality. They foresee the arrival of a new man, of a new earth and a new heaven, which will be worthy, at last, of the justice and the beauty of YHWH, the God of life. The Day of the Lord is not only the day of a political revolution, but of a cosmic change that will bring the universe, and man, its hidden flaw, into harmony with creation's law of life, installing throughout creation the reign of justice, fraternity, and peace, in the triumph of limitless and endless love.

The Prophets, because they worship a God of life, who abhors all forms of abortion, know that death is the sole enemy of man and of the universe. So long as death exists, the reign of YHWH, source of all life, will not be total. Death brings with it, everywhere, injustice and war; what matters to me the wickedness of a master, the violence of a tyrant, if in the final accounting we must all be the food of worms in the equality of death?

Isaiah already foresaw the retreat of the empire of death, while awaiting its total defeat. He declared, 2,740 years ago, that human life would be greatly prolonged; that a man dying at the age of one hundred would be mourned as one mourns for a young child. These ideas border upon certainties intrinsically linked to the internal logic of the Biblical monotheism: death is destined to be conquered, to disappear. Its empire is called upon to give way; in the kingdom of YHWH no one will ever die. But, in order that the justice of the God of life be satisfied, the dead must be restored to life and come forth from their graves, thus to be recompensed for the violence suffered in their deaths. These ideas were spread abroad in the time of Daniel. They inspired the doctrine, common to Judaism and Christianity, that prophesied the final defeat of death, its elimination, and also the resurrection of the dead. "Foolishness!" you exclaim reasonably. I think so too, but a foolishness perfectly coherent, and, to tell the truth, inherent in the very reality of the God of the Bible, the God of life, whose triumph will be made total only by the obliteration of the empire of death. It is natural for the mind to protest against such affirmations. "Foolishness!" let us agree. Surely, but no greater foolishness than these assertions:

to speak of justice in a world of wickedness,
of unity where all is separation,
of peace while all the nations arm for war,
of love while man remains the prey of hate.

These fooleries constitute the essential cargo of Biblical monotheism. It is thanks to them that the leaven has been put into the dough. These dreams have contributed to the making of a race of new men, who, refusing to submit to the fatalities of nature or of war, have conceived and realized our humanity's supernatural character, the supernature of the Prophets and Apostles, of the mystics, of the poets, whose contemplations constitute our book of the future, the beacon that lights the path through our night. Planted at the head of our route, the Biblical tree has given us innumerable fruits. Today, more than ever, it points out to us the essential directions that can turn humanity toward the narrow gate of its future.

"I have set before you life and death, the blessing and the curse. Choose life, then, that you... may live..."*

Yesterday, this dilemma placed before Moses could be considered as in the domain of the needs or the gifts of the spirit; each one could choose freely without risking anything other than his own life. The new dimensions of the universe, and the means that

---

*Deuteronomy 30:19.NAB

172

technology has put at the disposition of man, have transformed this option offered on Sinai, more timely now than ever, into a political axiom that determines not only life, but the very survival of humanity. The men of our time will be judges, making their choice of the blessing or the curse, of life or of death, the "death without phrases" of atomic suicide, that the nations are preparing for: or the life so powerful that it will subjugate, even to the extent of eliminating them from our planet, the pollutions of death.

Candid souls sometimes ask me if I have been translating the Bible in a state of ecstasy. I recall those years when I undertook this task, while still a youth, in an oasis of the Sahara, at Ouargla, or later, at the period of my first publications, in the grotto of Sainte-Baume, and finally at the hour of the full realization of the entire work at Jerusalem, on the south slope of the Valley of Gehenna, facing Mount Sion, Mount Olivet, and the esplanade of the Temple, from which shine the gilded Dome of the Rock, and the silvered dome of the Aqsa Mosque, just a few kilometers from Bethlehem. There, sixteen centuries ago, Saint Jerome made a large part of his own translation of the same book. Reflecting on those years, and recalling the hours through which I felt possessed by the presence within me of the word, in that room in the hostelry of Latrun, transformed into a linguistic laboratory, I see clearly that the utterance which I found it my duty to interpret was living in me. To translate is to enter into dialogue, or, in the etymological sense of the word that I mentioned earlier, to advance toward the word, toward the living voice of union and of love. I was living in dialogue with the Hebrew text of the Bible, to try to delve into the meaning of each of its words, and the interpretation of the verses. I entered into dialogue also with the numerous commentaries on these texts, thus getting closer to the sources of the inspiration of Prophets and Apostles in order to say in French the things that they had written or said in Hebrew, in Aramaic, or in Greek. The effort to identify myself with their thought enabled me to make their vision my own, inevitably to see it from the same viewpoint, and then translate from the same central point of thought and feeling. At the completion of my task, the man I had been, filled with this strong wine, sometimes to drunkenness, had become different, simplified, purified, fortified by the ascetic exercise of translating, of creating within himself such a silence that there could ring through it, in all fullness, the voice of truth and love that dwells in that unique book.

When those same candid souls stretch their candor so far as to ask me whether I believe that the Bible was inspired by God himself, as the Prophets declare, and the theologians, both of Judaism and Christianity, maintain, I try, in answering, to keep strictly to the facts. Not to risk offending them, I explain to them in what respects the Bible seems to me to be a book unique in the history of universal literature: in its style, in its thought, in the elevation of its character, in its comprehension of the oneness of reality, in the permanence and universality of its influence, in the originality, contemporaneous in every age, of its view of the world and its knowledge of mankind, and in the forward drive of its ideals and of its vision of the future of humanity. I add that I don't know a single writer who wouldn't be ready to die with delight if, just once in his life, he had the luck or talent to write one page attaining the literary perfection that is evident in every line of that book of genius. And I conclude by saying that, confronted by such a work, to admit that it was inspired by God would be to simplify the explanation of the mystery of its nature, and the universality of its influence.

If God gets into the business of writing books, we poor writers can do nothing but throw up our hands toward heaven and surrender. There could be nothing more astonishing to state than that the Bible is what it is. The mystery, in my view, would begin if I were convinced that the Prophets wrote on their own, without the aid of that all-powerful breath still observable in the Bible thousands of years after its compilation. How could simple men, lost in the Asiatic deserts, speaking an obscure Semitic language, have had the genius to challenge the heavens and the earth, to speak familiarly to God, and to lay down for humanity its law, its language, its scale of values and its goals...? Surely, here the natural would seem supernatural, and the supernatural, natural. whichever side of the question one takes, the Bible preserves its mystery.

The frenzy of the unnamed

I count myself as an inhabitant of the universe of the Bible because I recognize myself in it, and in it alone -- in its frenzy, its passion, its violence, and its poetry. I find myself perpetually placed between the two poles that quicken its internal dynamism: the memory of the past, of that lost Paradise for which we are all homesick; and the prospect of the future, which is the Messianic, the Christ-figure hope for the final destination of humanity. My waiting is nourished and encouraged by the certainties of the past. The present state of the world, the realities of evil, wars and threats of war, are transitory and will pass away like a nightmare that fades in the light of dawn. My certainty is based neither on my reason nor on the statistics it knows, which, as we shall see, distract it, but on what I know, see, and hope of YHWH, source of life, of the unnamed mystery of which my being is a part, and which penetrates it. I await the new heaven, the new earth, and the new man, which will achieve, in a decisive revolution, an absolute of justice and of love. I await the death of the false gods, and I wait for my God, unnamed and real, to throw down that mask of Zeus that separates us from him, having made him unrecognizable to us. I await the reign of peace between men, between races, between nations, between churches; and the end of the warfare between species, when the lions will stop eating the lambs, and the strong the weak; and for, at last, the triumph of life over death, of love over hate, and of union over division. I hope, erect and free, delivered from the slavery of my exile, that my liberation will not prove useless. Having been the most degraded of men, my awakening and my re-arising can be a source of inspiration and of hope for the most abject.

Then the wolf shall be a guest of the lamb,
    and the leopard shall lie down with the
    kid;
The calf and the young lion shall browse together,
    with a little child to guide them.
The cow and the bear shall be neighbors,
    together their young shall rest;
    the lion shall eat hay like the ox.
The baby shall play by the cobra's den,
    and the child lay his hand on the adder's lair.
There shall be no harm or ruin on all my holy mountain;

for the earth shall be filled with
knowledge of the Lord,
as water covers the sea.*

For me, the idyllic vision of Isaiah is not an
inaccessible utopia, a poetic vision, or a dream, but
a daily source of inspiration, and of hope. I expect
the end of all wars, and await the day when the stony
hearts of men will be replaced by hearts of flesh, in
which will be engraved the law of love and of life.
If any one man is erect and free, free to create and
to love, why shouldn't all humanity follow his
example? If any one man knows that death is defeated,
that it is nothing but a passage from life to life,
why are you afraid to die? Why are you still subject
to the yoke and all the pollutions of death?

EMBATTLED BROTHERS

A fratricidal conflict

Vatican Council II, numerous declarations by the
Catholic hierarchy, the positions taken by the World
Council of Churches, and the formal establishment of
friendly relations between the Jewish world and
Christianity have taught us that, since Hitler, people
really want to put an end to "the teaching of hatred."
Not all the world is ready to recognize the State of
Israel, but, at last, we have ceased to be officially
a perfidious people, and deicides.

We feel that we are finally able to breathe, and,
back on our native soil, to live in peace in the shade
of our vines and fig trees. It isn't long since the
Jews of the Arab lands broke loose, fleeing from the
Jewish quarters which they had inhabited for twenty
centuries, abandoning their houses and their
possessions, to set forth on this new exodus from our
score of contemporary Egypts.

Herzl, the inventor of the State of Israel, took a
rose-colored view of our return to the land of the
Bible: Christians accompanying us to the ports of
embarkment singing hymns of gratitude to God for

---

*Isaiah 11, 6-9.NAB

176

permitting this miracle; Arabs welcoming us on our newly-gained shores, and celebrating our reunion with joy and feasting. There was, alas, an abyss between the dream and the reality. After the Nazi ordeal, the Jews had to go to war against the British administration in Palestine, and, from the moment of the proclamation of the State of Israel, against the Arab world arrayed against them in monolithic unison. The reckoning for that conflict was heavy: four wars, tens of thousands dead, hundreds of thousands of refugees, billions of dollars frittered away here and there in an armaments race that has transformed the Near East into a formidable arsenal, richly provided with more means of destruction than would be needed to annihilate, several times over, all the surface of the earth, and all the warring peoples and countries.

Why has this fratricidal conflict gone on for more than half a century? Why, behind the warring countries, do we detect the shadowy presence of the world's great powers? Here, of course, what we have is the confrontation of two ethnic families, the Jewish and the Arab. But he understands nothing of the gravity of the conflict who doesn't see, behind the embattled States, the major economic and strategic interests that war with one another through these intermediaries.

In antiquity this part of the world fell victim to a similar implacable fate. The Roman Empire, in order to keep its eastern provinces, needed full control of the land of the Hebrews. Without that, the Empire would have to relinquish its dreams of conquest of the Far East, and of universal rule. On their side, the Hebrews could not come to terms with the colonizing power that was slowly crushing them, and was, furthermore, pagan and idolatrous. No one could draw back without betrayal. From this confrontation there resulted a war that Flavius Josephus has described as having been the cruellest there had ever been, up to that time, between any nations and cities. The Roman legions wiped Judea off the map, and enslaved the survivors of the terrible massacres that followed the taking of Jerusalem, on the ninth of Ab in the year 70 of the Christian Era.

Today, as in the time of Titus, the Near East constitutes a region whose control cannot be surrendered by the empires that aspire to world

177

domination. It concerns them in the highest degree
for two reasons, equally cogent: strategically, the
Near East commands communications between the Indian
Ocean and the Atlantic, between the West and the Far
East. Whoever holds it, holds the key to the routes,
by land and sea, that are of vital importance in case
of war. Hence the desperate efforts of Soviet Russia
to infiltrate the Arabian peninsula, and Egypt, and
Somalia, and to tighten its hold on Iraq and Syria.
The strategic interest is doubled for the West by the
economic needs that determine the survival of the free
world: eighty percent of the oil consumed by Europe,
and twenty percent of the oil consumed by America,
comes from the oil wells of the Near East. The
embargo declared by the Arab countries in 1973 made
all Europe tremble. It took note that it was not
mistress of its own energy resources. The operation
of its factories, of its automobiles, and of its
economy depended on the goodwill of the oil-producing
countries. Thus for Europe and for the United States
of America there must be a foreign policy involving a
presence in the Near East, whose first concern is
blocking the Soviet penetration. To these two major
factors, the open routes between East and West, and
the oil supply, must be added a third of equal
importance: the sale of arms. The war has made of
both the Arabs and the Israelis eager customers, from
whom any price and any labor may be exacted, for all
the world's merchants of cannons and of death.
Planes, tanks, cannons, rockets, radars, electronic
equipment, bullets and shells -- all are put on the
market and reach the arsenals of the warring nations
at a cost of tens of billions of dollars. It's really
crazy -- sellers and buyers alike are acting in the
confident certainty that they are working for the
happiness of their peoples and of humanity. Those
great international corporations, dealing in oil and
armaments, keep their weather eyes open. Any
alteration in the current situation with regard to
strategic routes, or to the market in oil and arms,
could cause catastrophic consequences in countries
thousands of miles away. A decline in the demand for
arms, or an increase in the price of oil, could bring
about economic and political upheavals of an
incalculable severity.

And from these facts comes another: the armies
stationed in the Near East are covered, watched over,
and spied upon by the fleets and air forces of the

foreign powers, who patrol the seas and the skies in order to safeguard their own interests, rather than for the welfare of the Arabs and the Israelis. These ships and planes carry incredible means of destruction, that, more than once, have barely been restrained from crashing down upon any who ventured to modify the fragile equilibrium of the nations and their governments.

Such are the international ramifications of the Israelo-Arab conflict. As hardly anyone speaks of it, let me give you a few facts that throw a harsh light on the foreign meddling in the region. Churchill accused the British administration of having, during the period of the Mandate, inflamed the hostilities between Arabs and Jews, instead of tempering them. This was following, as usual, the well-known Machiavellian principle of "Divide and conquer." When the English and French had been expelled from the region, Americans and Russians hastened to fill the void they had left. In order that the English might get out the faster, the Russians proposed the creation of the State of Israel, and by their vote made sure that it came to birth. Then, through the instrumentality of the Czechs, they furnished them with their first supply of arms -- the arms that enabled them to survive. What the Russians had in mind was clear enough -- to throw the English out as quickly as possible in order to try to take their place -- but this was what the Americans struggled to resist. There resulted the demarcation of the region in clearly defined zones of influence, with each power striving to take advantage of events to extend its territory. Here are some significant dates:

In 1948 the war was distinguished by two cease-fires imposed by the powers, the first when the Arabs were going to wipe out the Israelis, and the second when the Israelis, armed in great part by the Russians, were getting ready to defeat the Arabs. The same thing happened in 1956; Russians and Americans imposed a cease-fire and Israel's withdrawal, when it became plain that Israel was capable of consolidating politically its military victory. The same scenario was replayed in 1967: the Six-Day War was stopped, on orders from the Russians and the Americans, before a political settlement had been reached. It was still more obvious in 1973: in the first days of the war Israel came close to being defeated by the Arabs; then the Americans established an airlift and provided the army with the means of victory; when that had been won, but before it had flowered into peace, the Russians demanded a cease-fire, and threatened to intervene in order to enforce their demand, throwing into the contest the weight of their armaments. On the twenty-third of October, 1973, the world hung for eight hours on the brink of nuclear war. The United States joined the Russians in ordering the Israeli troops to halt, and then to retreat. All these things are what we have been able to see, but they are just the visible tip of the iceberg. Everything happens as though everybody wanted the continuation of a state intermediate between peace and war, as the only state favorable to the sale of arms, and to the control of the sources of oil and the world's trade routes by the Great Powers. These know perfectly well that the establishment of peace would destroy their footholds in the region, while all-out war would risk overturning the current delicate balances and might result in a global nuclear confrontation.

What weight have the peoples, and the local governments, in this giant global strategy of the empires? It seems that everything works together to make them into the active agents of their own misfortunes. The conflict was born with the arrival of the first European Zionists in Palestine, that province of a decadent Ottoman Empire, where the janissaries hanged or shot everything that moved. And the newly landed moved quite a lot, not always taking into account the geographic and human surroundings in which they were living. The Turks saw in them neither Zionists, nor even Jews, but simply a police problem. Terrifically different mentalities crashed into each other, transforming the plain facts into dreadful monsters. The hostile reactions date from that period, when, for the first time in their long history, Arabs and Jews found themselves facing one another as strangers and as enemies. A case in point is the arrival of David Ben Gurion in Palestine, just come from Plonsk at the age of twenty, expecting to settle in Palestine for ideological reasons that were perfectly incomprehensible to the Turkish police. This zealous young man, built all of a piece, urged on by an indomitable will that had caused him to be arrested twice over by the Russo-Polish police during the revolution of 1905-1906, took a job as an agricultural laborer at Petah Tiqwa, in Lower Galilee (seven miles East of Tel Aviv). His years of apprenticeship, from 1906 to 1910, were to be the most significant time in his life. One day, while he was in an orchard along with two of his fellow laborers, two shots rang out. Two men fell, one to the right and one to the left of David. If the Arab or Turk who fired had put a third bullet in his rifle, probably a relic of the Napoleonic wars, the future founder of the State of Israel would also have been dead.

With hardly any exceptions, the new arrivals spoke no Arabic, and knew absolutely nothing of the uses and customs of the society in which they expected to live. Nor did that society know anything about them. The distance between the groups was immense from the outset, and could only increase as time went on. The Arabs were flabbergasted at encountering this new species of Jew: a kind they had never heard of, and so profoundly different from the Jews of the Arab lands. The newcomers embodied among them an incomprehensible presence, that no one ever took the trouble to explain to them. The British mandate over Palestine, and the establishment of the Jewish National Home, marked the beginnings of an open conflict which certain strategists of colonialism were not unwilling to use in furtherance of their own interests. The clash of mentalities was made harsher by more profound distrust; the Arab kings and potentates of the time saw in these wild youths, in these liberated young women, a threat to their world, an attack upon the legitimacy of their power, that must be crushed in its inception. This is what they tried to do in May, 1948, in launching five armies at once against the Jewish settlements. Each shot fired, and each man fallen on either side, tended to cancel out the goodwill that had been manifested from the beginning by many in both camps.

The conflict was to be exploited by political regimes and by great international interests that never sleep or rest. Ben Gurion was hoping, up to his last day, that Nasser would make peace, but the dictator preferred to use Israel as a phantom enemy in order to stabilize his hold over Eqypt.

The longer this state of things lasted, the deeper grew the abyss, and the harder it became to bring about a reconciliation. Arabs and Israelis saw one another only by way of images deformed by hostile

181

propaganda: imperialist Zionists arrayed against the terrorist slaughterers of the innocent. The little that each side actually knew about the other seemed to give plausible support to these opinions. Our children knew nothing of the Arabs except for their wars or their criminal attacks; their children knew nothing of us but our wars, and our repression of their resistance. Most of the leaders, knowing nothing of the profound values of the two worlds that were confronting each other, didn't believe in peace, and sometimes they even feared it. It must be admitted that the spectacle of Arab peace in Lebanon, on the frontier between Egypt and Libya, or in the Kurdish region of Iraq, is not very edifying.

It's better to stay on one's guard than to take upon oneself the risks of such a peace, say the prudent. Extremists, irredentists of both camps sow insuperable obstacles in the path of peace. In doing so, they are making themselves the effective helpers of their worst enemies, the imperialist powers that are contending, in a tragic confrontation, for control over the warring nations. The governments, finally, even when they see the situation clearly, are neither stable enough nor strong enough to impose the compromises essential to any negotiated peace.

The dramatic and courageous peace initiative opened by Sadat in Jerusalem will be in danger of being stranded on these reefs, if the governments of both camps fail to act with the vision and energy to make possible our much-needed reconciliation.

Make ready for peace

The stumbling-blocks are enormous, and overgrown with ineradicable causes of contention. However, it isn't war that is fated, but peace, little though we have wished it. Because I know well both the Arabs and the Israelis, I have always believed this. I proclaimed it more than ten years ago, in 1968, in my Lettre à un Ami Arabe.

In Jerusalem, I lived through the bloody and costly war of 1956, whose surest result was to snatch away from us any chance of peace in the near future. Jerusalem's city hall constituted a privileged observation post from which I could see the dangers increasing from 1965 on. From the beginning of 1967,

182

the raised hackles of the nations were manifest, especially those of Syria. In Paris, I had contacts with a Syrian VIP in order to entreat him to transmit to his government our desire for peace. The man did that, undoubtedly; a little later I learned that his government had thrown him into prison in Damascus. In April, 1967, things began to get worse. For me, personally, the mysterious gestation that precedes the birth of a book had been completed, sped up by the experience I had had in the city hall of Jerusalem. In an Arab village in Galilee, surrounded by the splendors of spring, I wrote the essence of my Lettre. The editing of my manuscript was interrupted by the tension that preceded the lightning war. Throughout the sixty hours of fighting in Jerusalem, under fire, my book was taking final form, in the streets of a Jerusalem reunified, but strewn with Jewish and Arab corpses, mingling their blood on the stones of that town so disastrously loved. Looking upon them, I swore to myself that I would involve myself to the utmost in the struggle for peace, in order to prevent the return of such horrors. In the grip of this emotion, I brought the book to completion, and it was published immediately. Peace between Israel and the Arabs? "Utopian! a dream! just imaginative speculation!" I heard people saying almost everywhere about that book, which was received sympathetically, but more as a gentle poetic reverie than as a political declaration. Ten years later, utopia was knocking at the door of history, and everyone could see that our survival depended upon its realization. In the meantime, Egypt, Israel, and Syria had paid the costs of a war, that of 1973, as bloody as it was costly, all of whose benefits went to others. Hardly had the combatants laid down their arms and buried their dead when the armaments race resumed its frenzied pace. The Near East became a powder magazine, each day more capable of loosing the cataclysm of the Apocalypse. It was whispered everywhere that Israel had atom bombs. It was clear that a fifth war between Israel and the Arabs would be decisive, in the sense that it would signal the obliteration of the Near East, and that it would inevitably bring about a worldwide economic chaos through the paralysis of the Western economic systems; and, finally, risk involving the two great powers in an atomic confrontation. The more people become aware of these risks, the more do my arguments, which I

183

continually defend all over the world as a pilgrim of peace, win significant and often enthusiastic adherence.

Israelis, Egyptians, Syrians, Jordanians, Lebanese, not to mention my North African friends, have written to tell me that they think as I do. A Moslem writer from Tunisia, Salah Elekhouan, sent me the manuscript of his book, an emotional appeal for peace and a violent attack upon the warmakers, those murderers who are bringing ruin upon their people. Along with this manuscript, he sent a painting that he himself had done, symbolizing the reconciliation of Israel and Ishmael: against a night sky gleam a minaret and the tower of a temple, the whole surmounted by a seven-branched candlestick adorned with the Crescent.   "The Menorah and the Crescent stand for our imminent accord.   Their shadow reaches to and cloaks the shame of fanaticism to atone for the blood spilled by dictators avid for power and lordship."   Salah Elekhouan told the tale of his development.   Like many men of his time, he had been brought up to hate and despise the Jew.   Now his awareness inspired him to emotional appeals for peace: "Understand that the Arab masses are only awaiting an opportunity to declare their deepest wish, to cry out for peace..." he wrote.   His prophecy will be fulfilled when the people of Egypt and of Israel heap glory upon Sadat and Begin because they spoke of peace.

The sympathetic reception my book enjoyed was countered by a general scepticism.   My Arab friend was thought an unknown hero, if not a figment of my imagination.   Public opinion had been molded by propaganda to such an extent, had become so wedded to the certainty that the war between Israel and the Arabs would have no end, that it seemed impossible to conceive, not only the peace that I was proclaiming, but even one simple friendship, between one Arab and one Israeli.   We were, in the universal opinion, condemned to war, in perpetuity.   This theme recurs as a leitmotif in the newspapers, where my critics ask me: "This Arab friend of yours -- does he really exist?"   "Who is going to answer your letter to an Arab friend?"   "Well then, when are we going to see appear, from the pen of an Arab author, a <u>Lettre à un Ami Juif</u>?"

184

Utopia is, etymologically, that which has no place. In this sense, the peace between the Arabs and Israel was indeed _utopian_, because it had not taken place. The primary intention of my _Lettre à un Ami Arabe_ was therefore to give a place to utopia. Once it inhabited a book, it would be possible to extract it from that book so that it might change the course of history.

Arab voices were raised in calls for peace, and our conclusions were united. From that time on, the thoughts that had inspired me have been spreading through both camps. Once they have come to your attention, you can follow them through the innumerable speeches, articles, and books the Near East has inspired in recent years. The more time passed, the more alarming became the massing of armaments poised for this conflict, so that even those minds most lacking in imagination could recognize that, all things considered, utopia was preferable to suicide. Then men rose up to try to make this vision enter into history.

The invitation that King Hassan II extended to me at the end of February, 1977, must have constituted an indication of the turn that relations between the Arab States and Israel were about to take. This was the first time that an Arab Head of State received, in broad daylight, a citizen of the State of Israel. In every way this gesture was received as a significant event. The channels of communication between Arabs and Israelis had been frozen ever since the creation of the State of Israel. Neither side knew anything of the other, except as the monster entirely created by hostile propaganda, propaganda that even its inventors came around to believing. The warring states were so thoroughly acclimated to this long war that they had built up around themselves insuperable barriers. The Arabs refused to admit not only Israelis, but even Jewish citizens of other states. As an act of retortion, Israel had made it a punishable offense for its citizens to visit the Arab States at war against it.

This lack of contact between the two worlds facilitated the work of propaganda to such an extent that it seemed impossible to take a calm view of anything. Falsehood extended its reach, and, with the passage of time, was taken for truth even by the most intelligent, and the most peacefully disposed. Papers were written and widely distributed to prove that the hatred between Arabs and Jews was hereditary, and that this hatred would forever prevent any reconciliation. Scholars hastened, one after another, to reinterpret, from this point of view, the history of relations between Arabs and Jews. They would point out the discriminatory nature of the law of _dhimmi_, applying to Jew or Christian in a Moslem city, without making it clear that, at the time when it was established, it constituted a tremendous improvement over the earlier customs, and over the customs in other places. The charter of Omar recognized specific rights belonging to Jews, rights that permitted them, in a condition "humiliated," but not entirely deprived of advantages, to survive, and very often to prosper, in the Moslem city. They pinned down and displayed the persecutions, but without mentioning the fact that the tyrants who organized them acted often with just as much cruelty, if not more, toward their own co-religionists. There is not one example to be found of a good monarch in the Arab world that has persecuted the Jews, as did, for instance, Saint Louis or Ferdinand and Isabella in Christian Europe.

In the government offices, the veil between us grew thicker and thicker. We could no longer see one another face to face, but only as reflected in a mirror so deforming that for those on one side, it let nothing appear of the human and political realities of the other world, from which it was separated by an almost insuperable wall of hostility. I had a close view of this phenomenon in the administration of Ben Gurion, and still more so in the Ministry of Foreign Affairs, in Jerusalem. There were experts, charged with the task of keeping track of Arab affairs, whose competence was indisputable. They read all that was published, knew by heart all the statistics, were up to date on the biographies of all the political personages, had at hand all the papers of the Arab world, and all the radio messages. They knew, not only all that the Arabs were saying, but also all that was being said about them. But, knowing everything, they gave the unhappy impression of understanding nothing, because their knowledge, bookish at best, was deformed by reaching them through the prism of propaganda. Add to this, a fundamental confusion of characters: the Jews from Russia, Poland, or Germany projected upon the Arabs what they knew of the muzhiks or of the country gentlemen, without perceiving how different they were psychologically, and in their ways of thought and speech. If an Arab said a word, that word could be taken to be said forever. The immobility of the Israeli policy since 1967 is explained by the four "Noes" of Khartoum. Since the Arabs had said "No" to all peace with Israel, there was nothing more to do but to entrench ourselves, like them, in negation and waiting. But, if this conclusion was certain, what was still more certain was that we lived under an illusion if we thought that time was working in our favor.

The quasi-immobility of the Israeli bureaucrats greatly hampered minds and hearts. Some experts on the Arab world had been in office since the creation of the State of Israel, and in thirty years everything had changed, except them! Their blindness was all the more hopeless in that they lived, as it were, in a closed vessel, and the errors of each were reinforced by the agreement of the others. Books like my Lettre à un Ami Arabe were not enough to recall them to a truer appreciation of Arab realities. Their opinion was so deeply embedded that they had reached the point of thinking it wasted effort to direct toward the Arab world any written information about the Israeli realities. I have never seen any good leaflet, written in Arabic, to explain to our neighbors the meaning of the Zionist enterprise. Any effort made in this direction was deemed useless from the outset, and doomed to failure.

The tragic mistake of the government and army of Israel, that let themselves be taken by surprise by the attack of Yom Kippur, 1973, grew out of this state of narrow-mindedness. Rare indeed were those who perceived the profound changes that had taken place in the Arab world; that the conditions of 1947 had changed to those of 1973, and then changed again to those of 1977. For the Yom Kippur War was not enough to open their eyes. The efforts of the Arab leaders to open a conversation had not been understood. It was generally thought that what was going on was just more propaganda or political tactics. Neither words nor signs could get through; the old machine just wasn't working any more. Taboos were kept up, and it was still forbidden to enter into any contact with the Arab world. Those who challenged this interdict, like Nahum Goldman, or like the Eliav Group, and sought contact with the Palestinians, were pilloried.* When it happened that American or European Jews visited among the Arabs, and talked to their leaders, took note of the present state of things and brought the facts to the attention of our government, the reaction was always the same: these witnesses were sincerely thought to have fallen victim to enemy propaganda. It was useless to listen to them, our people thought, when they insisted, before 1973, that the Arabs would let loose a war upon us if we kept an unrelenting grasp on all our positions; or again, after 1973, when they said the Arabs wanted peace. All this must be false, since it ran counter to the opinions of our experts!

On the Arab side, the situation could be analyzed similarly, and on that side it was made still worse by the hysterical propaganda, anti-Israel or even anti-Jew, and by the formidable activities of the Palestinian terrorist organizations. As a result, the voices raised on the side of peace, more and more numerous in both camps as a new generation succeeded to the leadership, found it exceedingly difficult to make themselves heard. The movement of worldwide liberality begun by the King of Morocco, and the arrival of Sadat in Jerusalem, opened a new chapter in the lamentable history of our wars, a chapter of direct negotiations between Israel and the Arabs.

Reasons for hope

Nobody was better placed than Hassan II for announcing this good news to the world. His dynasty, the Alaouits, had traditionally been friendly to the Jews. His father, Mohammed V, had had a Jewish nurse named Simha; the milk upon which he grew to manhood was that of a Jewish woman, and, through history, many had been the Jewish wives of the Alaouits. The king had taken great care, at the time of Hitler's victorious progress, to make sure that nothing was done to harm his Jews. The coexistence of Arabs and Jews in Morocco permitted the flowering and preservation of one of the Jewish communities of the Diaspora whose religious traditions, arts, songs,

---

*Encyclopedia Judaica, Vol. 7, p. 723-725. Jerusalem, Keter Pub. Co., 1972.

188

folklore, learning in Hebrew and Aramaic, and observance of the Bible, the Talmud, and the Cabala, are among the richest. Why not rebind our traditional ties of friendship, and renew them, adapting them to the exigencies of the modern world? A Semitic bloc, made up of the combined States of the Near East, would be supported by the mass of the Moslems and by the technical, economic, and financial power of the Jewish communities of the Diaspora. Arabs and Jews, brought together, would constitute a power that, in a few years, could attain a world-wide importance. Such a bloc could reach out, thanks to the support of the Christians, to all who place spiritual values above the values of trade in oil and arms. It would soon enroll the greater part of the nations of Africa and Asia, as well as the common people of Europe and America. Its spiritual and moral force would be bolstered by a power that, demographically, politically, and economically, would easily take the first rank in the world. These ideas obsess me. Only such a bloc might be able to disarm the powers of death, to bring the nuclear arms race to a halt, to prevent the atomic suicide that the nations are preparing for. This prophetic vision, compounded of tangible realities and enthusiastic expectations, was at last snatched out of the realm of pious wishes on the nineteenth of November, 1977, at eight o'clock in the evening. The silver trumpets of the Israeli Guard rang out, and then, in a universal silence, Sadat stepped forth, his face shining with magnanimity and hope. All the people held their breaths. Each of us thought he must be dreaming, as the impossible suddenly entered into history.

"Were you surprised at this event?" I was asked. Well, surprised, perhaps, but certainly not astounded. The really astounding thing, for anyone well acquainted with both Arabs and Jews, is that the waiting took up thirty years -- thirty years of absurd and fratricidal wars, thirty years of bloodshed, suffering, and incalculable destruction.

Shalom, Salaam, Pax! The new message of peace sent forth from Jerusalem was not of itself sufficient to wipe out the causes of the conflict. These continue to exist because ignorance, fear, distrust, sometimes hate, and the lust for power or the desperate will to survive, have not yet given way to confidence and to the determination to turn our backs

189

on the past, and to plan and build for the future. The sellers of arms and oil, the representatives of the great economic and political interests that parcel out the world among themselves, they have not loosed their hold, though today the uranium of Africa fascinates them even more than the oil wells of Arabia.

Pierre Mendès-France was in Jerusalem during the visit of Sadat. For years he had considered me optimistic, not to say naive, for prophesying the improbable reconciliation. "You may well exult," he said to me. "It is you who have been the realist, because, like Ben Gurion, you have believed in the miraculous." Always, one must believe in the miraculous.

To tell the truth, the conflict between the Arabs and Israel had never fully entered into the consciousness of the people at war. It was manufactured by propagandists in the service of the particular interests of monarchs, States, or economic powers, to whose advantage it was to divide the Near East. The people were fighting one another without conviction. The Israelis fought because, if they wished to survive, they had to fight; and the Arabs because they were pushed into it. Even in the fiercest battles I never heard a single cry of hate come from our lips or the lips of the Arab fighters. Never was there a sacrifice more useless and absurd than that of our wars, criminally supported by the warmakers, often fully aware of what they were doing, but sometimes blind or ignorant. Reread the papers of a certain school of journalism over the past thirty years or so -- you will be sickened by a baseness just about unanimous, by their servility in supporting the conflict, in keeping silence about its true scope, and in covering up the real problems by opening their pages only to those who stood to benefit by its perpetuation. Peace was called impossible because of I don't know what hereditary hatred that had long existed between the Arabs and the Jews; no Arab chief would dare brave public opinion by speaking of peace with Israel. The emptiness of such lies was openly displayed when Cairo and Ismailia gave triumphal welcomes to the heroes of peace. A long, and perhaps painful, road must be traveled before the full establishment of peace between Arabs and Israelis, but nobody, from here on, can claim again that it is utopian. Together, they have paid the price of a conflict from which others reaped the benefits. It is inevitable that some day good sense, or, if that fails, the demands of honor or the simple instinct of self-preservation, will overcome the delusions caused by a hatred artificially created and sustained.

My hope for peace is based, apart from the incidents that characterize our present-day conflicts, on the extraordinary parallelism in the history of the Arabs and the Jews, both of whom proclaim that they are descended from Abraham, and both of whom have flourished in the same corner of the world, where, from the remotest antiquity, they have enjoyed close relations, spiritual, intellectual, commercial, and social.

Since the time of King Ahab, the wise men of Israel have recognized, appreciated, and admired the wisdom that rules the lives of the Arab tribes, with whom they have been in constant contact. The kinship between Israel and the Arabs -- regional, sociological, linguistic, and cultural -- grew all the stronger when Mohammed, drawing his inspiration from the Jewish Scriptures and traditions, founded his new religion, Islam. One and the same God, parallel religious traditions, and a moral code inspired by the same spiritual imperatives, gave to the Judaism of the exile and to Islam remarkably similar characteristics. Two peoples, carrying God with them from their beginnings, witnesses and proclaimers of their national God among the nations of the earth, have spoken the same language, the language of the Koran, since the seventh century, worshiped the same God, and lived under the same skies.

The Arabic language inspired the Jews to revive Hebrew. From the eighth century to the fourteenth, Arabs and Jews together enjoyed the golden age of their culture, notably in Spain. It was thanks to them that Europe rediscovered the masterpieces of Greek philosophy, and Arabs and Jews nourished themselves upon these masterpieces in developing their own theological schools of thought.

Beginning in the fourteenth century, the Arabs and the Jews together were driven out of Christian Spain, and together they were present at the formation of that world which stored up against them both the

191

bitter fruits of Western racism: the colonialism that raged throughout the Arab world, and anti-Semitism. This anti-Semitism, at first nominally religious, became atheistic, and its disastrous consequences extended to the pogroms of Rumania and Russia in the nineteenth century, and the vast massacres carried out under the orders of Hitler. While the Jews were dying in the concentration camps, the Arabs were playing out their own drama in their lands, under the domination of colonial powers.

The Arab suffering and the Jewish suffering, results of the same influences, gave rise to simultaneous and parallel intellectual and political movements. Even though these movements were in opposition to each other, they were comparable in nature. For this, indeed, is the paradox in which history has imprisoned the Jews and the Arabs: Arabism and Zionism are born of historic causes operating in the same neighborhood, which, in differing contexts, have brought about results whose transitory conflicts cannot undermine their deep-rooted identity nor their profound interdependence.

Jews and Arabs in contact with the Western civilization and with the Christian world are rising, together, out of their long slumbers, determined to regain their roots and their authenticities, beginning with their languages and their cultures. Arabic and Hebrew, sister languages, became dormant, particularly Hebrew, in different historic contexts and circumstances, but both must equally be roused from their sleep, rehabilitated, and relearned thoroughly, so that they may become once more instruments sufficient for the interpretation of the present-day world and its techniques. Each takes its inspiration from immortal models: one the Bible, the other the Koran. Where else in the world can one find a language that is, like Hebrew and Arabic, at once a sacred language and a living language? In this respect, these two languages are identical, and matched by no other language in the history of humanity.

Grammarians, lexicographers, and linguists must have put forth a prodigious effort in order to create two new languages, capable of dealing with all the modern activities, building on the foundations of traditional languages extinct for centuries, and, in the case of Hebrew, for millennia. These revived languages have set to work to express remarkably parallel ideas. The intellectual reform movement in Islamic lands, called al Nahda, is contemporaneous with, and in many respects similar to, that which, among Jews, is called the Haskalah, or Enlightenment. On both sides, essayists, short-story writers, novelists, and journalists are striving to reawaken the masses benumbed by the humiliations of their long night of colonial rule or exile. Contemporary Arabic literature in Egypt, Lebanon, Syria, the Sudan, Tunisia, Algeria, and Morocco often resembles, in its inspiration, its themes, and its longings the new Hebraic literature. These parallel literatures, in the different stages of their modern development, show remarkable likenesses in their founders, their classics, their poets, and their pioneers. A French archeologist, Jean Perrot, asked a nationalist Arab, who was discovering our land for the first time, what he thought of the Israelis. His spontaneous reply was: "It's frightening how much alike we are." This quip gets to the bottom of things, and perhaps we have to seek one of the roots of the present hostile confrontation in the profound similarity of the customs, cultures, and historic goals of these two peoples -- at once nations, communities, and religions. The stages of their arduous climb toward liberty cover the same decades, and represent outrageous costs for both sides. In their ascent, it was inevitable that they collide, since each was looking only toward Jerusalem. But these two movements are never more complementary than when they clash most violently. Such is the paradox: the Zionist movement progresses fastest when the whip of its Arab enemies lashes hardest. But the reciprocal is equally true: this conflict cements the unity and aids the stabilization of the Arab States, whose history has always progressed in accordance with the vicissitudes of war.

Sadat's journey reawakened hopes that must never be disappointed, lest our peoples be wiped out, and, for all the world, a general nuclear war be let loose. I believe that, strictly speaking, peace will be possible only when the peoples and their governments have matured enough to contemplate the creation of a federation or confederation of the United States of the Near East. On the twenty-ninth of November, 1947, the United Nations announced their decision

193

recommending the creation of a Jewish State and an Arab State in Palestine. The next day, I published my first political article, entitled "The Partition." I recalled the judgment of Solomon, and said that the partition, if carried out, would end in the death of the child, that land so passionately loved. I am sorry that now, thirty years later, there is danger that my pessimistic prophecy may come true, if a new war should break out.

The solution, which could reconcile the legitimate interests of Israel, of Jordan, and of the Palestinians, would be to make, of their reunited territories, a federation in which each ethnic entity would find its national rights recognized and guaranteed. The idea of a monolithic state, Hegelian, Napoleonic, or Prussian, is foreign to the traditions both of Islam and of Israel. It is out of date even in old Europe, which is struggling to efface its ancient and too bloody frontiers. In no way does it serve either the needs of our time or the complexities of the Near East. To unite the disputed territories, but separate the races, the better to assure the protection of their rights -- national, political, religious, linguistic, and cultural -- these are the principles upon which agreement must be reached if we really want to put an end to the conflict. The road to peace is closed because it goes in directions just opposite to what is needed: people think they are to separate the territories, and mix the nationalities, instead of realizing that they must unify the territories, and give the nationalities the opportunity to express themselves through autonomous political and cultural entities. A federation, made up of Israel, Jordan, and Palestine, would be the nucleus of the United States of the Near East. There are plans, precise and detailed, prepared by experts, that open up a choice of possibilities, whose realization, step by step, could be achieved as distrust gave way to the reconciliation of those fraternal enemies, the Children of Ishmael and the Children of Israel.

It is possible to lessen the impact of our oppositions within the framework of two political entities, one Arab, the other Israeli, governed by the above-mentioned confederation, and brought together by political, economic, and cultural agreements of a federal nature. Two freely elected parliaments, that

of Israel and that of Ishmael (the latter composed of
two chambers, one Jordanian, and the other
Palestinian) would promulgate the laws. All the Arabs
in Israel, wherever they might live, would be voters
for, and eligible for election to, the Arab
parliament. All the Israelis, even those settled in
territories with an Arab majority, would belong to
Israel in the same way. Jerusalem, reunited
forevermore, would be the spiritual center of the
reconciled peoples.

I put forth this plan in my Lettre à un Ami Arabe
immediately after the Six-Day War. What then seemed
"utopian" can and must be achieved in our time.
Proposals of this sort inspired the Hussein plan of
1972, and looked to the establishment of a federation
of Jordan, the West Bank of the Jordan, and the Gaza
Strip. In order for Israel to fit itself into this
grouping, the governments, on all sides, would have to
give up the outworn idea of the static sovereignty of
nations, in order to unite, as Europe has done, in
larger groupings. The peoples, exerting pressure on
political stand-patism, could help their leaders to
turn their eyes from a stubborn backward gaze, and
look, instead, toward the future. It will be a future
of glory, and not of death, little as we desire it
now. For all the conferences, all the political
clevernesses, change nothing of the tragic realities
of our conflict, so long as we don't know how to rise
above it, and, ourselves, bring about a just
resolution. The choice before us is that of the
future we wish -- life or death. If we learn to
resist the temptation of nothingness, the pressures of
those who would thrust us into that abyss; if we
determine simply to continue to exist, we must define
the conditions of our survival, Arabs and Israelis,
face to face, as reconciled brothers. This is the
essential -- our determination to resist the vertigo
that attacks us on the brink of death, and to charge
our consciences with the frail chance of survival and
salvation, for ourselves and for the world.

EPILOGUE

FOR A NEW PROPHETIC VISION

FOR A NEW PROPHETIC VISION

If not now, when?

Isaiah commanded his disciples to be the light of
the nations. We all hope that -- but on condition
that it cost us as little as possible. Choose life,
that you may live! I thought of that command of Moses
as I was on my way to the private audience that Paul
VI allowed me on the nineteenth of October, 1977. I
had had the privilege of meeting Pius XII in the last
years of his life, and John XXIII on the very day on
which he received the Balsan Peace Prize in the
Basilica of Saint Peter at one of his last public
appearances. Paul VI received me with simplicity and
warmth, visibly moved at receiving, from the pilgrim
from Jerusalem, the volumes of my translation of the
Bible.

"This must have taken great love...!" he told me,
as he received from my hand the Prophets, and the
first translation of the New Testament ever written by
a Jew -- if we suppose that Matthew, Mark, and John
didn't translate from Hebrew or from Aramaic the
sayings of Jesus. In delivering my Bible to the Pope
I was thinking of the urgent need we all have,
especially the men charged with powers and
responsibilities, to work for peace. I spoke to him
of the situation in the Near East, and of the need for
a spiritual mediation to smooth the way for a peaceful
settlement. From the beginning of the year, and more
particularly since my interview with Hassan II,
appeals had been made to the Vatican Secretariat of
State to break away from its traditional reserve and
support the fraternal dialogue for which Moslems and
Jews were hoping, apart from their religious
differences, so as to strengthen together, united in
heart and mind, the fragile edifice of peace. I
called once more upon the power of spiritual
mediation, to which he held the keys.

The Pope, obviously well aware of the precedents
of which I had spoken to him, told me that he felt
personally responsible for the peace of the Mid-East.

"As for the exercise of spiritual mediation, do
you think the time for that has come?" he asked me.

198

Without hesitation, I replied by quoting an ancient Hebrew saying: "If not now, when?"

Perhaps it's naive to hope that the organized religions can contribute to the recovery of the nations from their madness. But if they don't do it, if they don't rid themselves of the shackles of the past and clear the way to the future, who else can take their place? Who else can cry out that never has our planet, and the human race that inhabits it, been in greater danger of death? Who else can call forth that leap of conscience that would make possible a human mutation without which it is clear that there can be no future but a planetary suicide?

Instead of the new leadership that would make us conscious of the menaces that loom over us, we find a well-nigh universal surrender, even by those whose duty it is to be the guardians of the city. It is an accepted fact that a wind of madness is carrying humanity away to its destruction, and, to keep their consciences clear, people close their eyes to the blinding realities of the coming war, of the hunger that holds in its clutches, over entire continents, an enormous proportion of mankind, and, finally, of death, which, under all its forms, is triumphing in the cancer of our cities and in the atrophy of our consciences.

A new leadership, indeed, must proclaim the resurrection in us of a new man. But, so that the marching song of this new leadership may spring from our lips without hypocrisy, we must first of all unite our wills and our efforts to conquer war, conquer hunger, conquer death. The evidence is easily available and clear to everyone that we are working for the triumph of death in these three fields: the arms race, the hunger in the third world, and the technological cancer. In spite of the warning cries of the most competent commentators, world public opinion remains blind, deaf, and dumb. I know that I am mortal, but I live as though I would never have to die. Civilizations act still more blindly, since they are preparing, with their own hands, the instruments of their own destruction. In the general indifference to the dangers that threaten the survival of the world, there is an admission of powerlessness. Since these problems are beyond my direct responsibilities and my competence, I can do nothing about the matter.

199

Therefore, to concern myself about it would only make
my life more difficult, without benefit to anyone.
This is a surrender of the collective conscience in
the face of a situation whose gravity it is impossible
to exaggerate.

In deadly peril

Let us recall several facts which ought to be
engraved in the minds of all our contemporaries.
Looming in the distance, they dominate all other
problems of our time. The arsenals of the score of
countries that are stocking atomic bombs now possess a
destructive power equivalent to some two million times
that of the bomb that, in 1945, destroyed Hiroshima.
That's a figure that would terrify us if our minds
were able to translate it into imaginable happenings.
But this fact isn't all: each year the nations devote
to their military expenditures a global sum that, in
1977, had reached the level of four hundred billion
dollars. To make this figure clearer, without
anything more than a simple approximation, let us
remark that this sum is equivalent to the gross
national product of an entire continent, South
America. The arms race between the United States and
Soviet Russia has for its goal the possession, by
each, of armaments in ever greater quantities and
better quality.

The most advanced nuclear warhead made in the
United States weighs a hundred kilograms, and has an
explosive power equivalent to two hundred thousand
tons of TNT. The neutron bomb, when it becomes
operational, will magnify these figures to an extent
beyond the comprehension of even the most imaginative
of men. The number of countries producing atomic
bombs never ceases to grow. On the first of January,
1977, there were 173 atomic reactors, with a capacity
of 79,000 megawatts, capable of an annual production
of 16,000 kilograms of plutonium. It takes less than
ten kilograms of plutonium to make an atomic bomb of a
power equivalent to 20,000 tons of TNT. At the end of
1980, some 250 kilograms of plutonium could, all over
the world, go to the making of 25,000 of these bombs.
In 1984, some twenty-eight countries that, as yet,
have no nuclear armament, will probably have a
potential productive capacity of 30,000 kilograms of
plutonium, theoretically enough for the production of
ten atomic bombs of the power of 20,000 tons of TNT

each day. Nuclear technology is spreading rapidly in the third world. Argentina, India, Pakistan, Brazil, Iran, Korea, Mexico, Taiwan, and Egypt have, or will have, at an early date, the ability to make atomic bombs. Cuba, Iraq, and Qaddafi's Libya have announced their intention of entering the atomic bomb race. This will soon be within the reach of any treasury able to pay for ten kilograms of plutonium. The secret of the method of making an atomic bomb has, in fact, become common knowledge. The economic and technical barriers that used to stand in the way of the spread of atomic armaments have virtually ceased to exist. With nuclear warheads that have a striking precision of 350 meters at a distance of 13,000 kilometers (e.g., the American ICBM), it is possible to imagine what a nuclear holocaust would be. In thirty minutes, the time it would take for the missiles to travel from one side of the world to the other, there would be nothing, or next to nothing, left of mankind, and perhaps even of the planet itself.

This would be so horrible, and so absurd, that such an eventuality must be ruled out. "Nobody would ever be mad enough to let loose such a catastrophe!" so I am told by incurable optimists. Thus they demonstrate the truth of the old saying, that the most subtle of the tricks of the Devil is to have convinced man of his non-existence. In this way he is free to go ahead with his deviltries. An attempt is made to convince us that the atomic bomb is perfectly harmless because it will never be exploded. The argument is absurd from any point of view. People don't spend billions of dollars to build up their arsenals without intending some consequences. Atomic war, sooner or later, is bound to happen. It might be unleashed by the insane decision of a Chief of State so sure of his power as to have the illusion that he could destroy, without danger to his own land, the enemy power or powers. If it would take a madman to risk such an attempt, everyone knows that there is no lack of such people among the honorable leaders of peoples and tribes. But it is probable that nobody would ever have to bear the responsibility for the crime; it would be enough that a series of hostile interactions build up to a culmination; or even that there be a simple accident, such as have, several times in the past decade, been barely avoided, to light the fuse for an apocalyptic conflagration. No one can say that

some minor conflict couldn't start the fateful buildup
that would provoke an atomic confrontation between the
great powers. The world just missed being dragged to
destruction in the Cuban missile crisis; and again, on
the 23rd of October, 1973, at the outbreak of the Yom
Kippur War. It is said that an accident is improbable
because an atomic bomb handled under optimum
conditions risks being set off accidentally only once
in a thousand years. Perhaps. But a thousand -- but
ten thousand -- atomic bombs?

During the Nazi persecution, it was said of the
European Jews that the optimists roasted in the
crematories of Hitler, while the pessimists toasted
their flanks on the beaches of California. The state
of stupefaction in which we stand before the atomic
danger seems to me to make everything worse. When we
find ourselves before so deadly a danger, the worst
possible mistake is to take some sort of tranquilizer,
in order to convince ourselves that the situation is
not so serious. Prudence, if not wisdom, should lead
us to gauge the evil that urges the nations into an
arms race -- that wide-spread insanity, utterly
unreasonable, that rushes past all efforts at control
and seems irreversible. Men, in their new kind of
slavery, devote an increasing share of their resources
to the purchase of a more and more obvious insecurity,
at a higher and higher price. It's no longer possible
for anyone to stop in this race, without bringing down
upon all our national and international modes of
living a set of crises, apparently insoluble, and just
as serious as the evils we wish to avoid by disarming.
The disarmament conferences, through more than half a
century, have been happening one after another, and
all just alike. The emptiness of their results is
mainly caused by the fact that nations no longer
control their own investments, increasing still more
the danger of a universal cataclysm. Bertrand Russell
has estimated that, for the next century, the chance
of survival of humanity, menaced by nuclear suicide,
was no better than fifty-fifty. One chance out of two
that the world won't fly off in fragments -- and the
longer it is delayed, the more inevitably the final
crisis looms over us. Since that estimate was made,
the danger has increased still more, and many thinkers
have now reached a point of no return in their
despair. The prudent think that any survival of
humanity into the third millennium, which will begin
in less than a score of years, remains hypothetical.

To conquer hunger

At a world conference on religion and peace, held
at Louvain in August, 1974, I questioned a Buddhist
monk, whose countenance glowed with light: "Do you
believe in the possibility of an atomic war?" He
pondered deeply before replying. "Yes, it will
certainly break out. Its detonator is ready."

"And what is that?"

"The misery of the third world."

Blind to the dangers of nuclear catastrophe, the
West seems to me to be still blinder to the growing
abyss that divides the rich countries of the Northern
Hemisphere from the poor lands of the South and East
of the planet. The traveler accustomed to going all
over the world, when he returns from the regions where
the masses are deprived of even strict necessities,
devotes several days, each time, to getting used once
more to the suffocating riches of the industrial West.
On the one side, people are stifled by too much of
everything, and on the other, they die of a lack of
everything. You don't fully understand the meaning of
a traffic jam in New York or Paris if you haven't
seen, with your own eyes, the crowds dying of
starvation in Asia or Africa. But in this matter,
nothing is more eloquent than the dry statistics. The
commercially developed countries, as of January 1,
1974, counted 780 million inhabitants, having at their
disposal a gross national product of 3,260 million
dollars a year, or an income of 4,180 dollars per
capita. In the under-developed countries and
territories, 1,815 million inhabitants have 558
million dollars for their gross national product, or
an annual income of 310 dollars per capita. The
socialist countries of Eastern Europe are placed
midway in the economic scale, having an average annual
income of 2,000 per capita, while those of Asia have
the lowest average of all, 260 dollars a year per
capita.

At the two extremities of that scale, ranging from
abundance to misery, let us note the American average
of 6,155 dollars, the Swiss of 6,346 dollars, and the
French of 4,851 dollars, contrasted with the 150
dollars of the former East African Community, the 143

dollars of the Haitian, the 135 dollars of the Sudanese, the 74 dollars of the Burundian, and the 73 dollars of the Malian.

You can plug your ears and blindfold your eyes to these figures, that denounce the profound global imbalance of a human race, gathered together in our time on this grain of sand, the earth, in the infinity of space. The situation, that was not felt as an evil before the technical revolution, is insupportable now that the starving beggar of Calcutta has become, thanks to television and the airplane, the neighbor of the billionaire of Paris or of Washington. You can adopt any intellectual attitude you wish in facing this problem, but it is undeniable that it involves the gravest risks to the peace of the world. The class warfare is doubled here, as it is combined with racial hostility, and redoubled in a war between civilizations, spread over the whole planet. The poor constitute two-thirds of the human race. They will never be satisfied with what they have of the revenues of the planet; the disparity is, and will continue to be, more and more seriously exploited politically, to the extent of provoking the worst conflicts between the great powers, that quarrel over their trade with the poor, because the poor are the majority, and because the sources of energy in their countries, seized upon as prey, are necessary for the growth of the industrial nations.

Mastering the technique

The new world that we are entering, walking backward, and blindly, is that of techniques and of technology, that "logos" that is the programmer of our civilization. Many people are busied, in Europe and in America, in analyzing, describing, and explaining this new system for organizing societies. The technical society has been succeeded by the creature sprung from its loins, the "technical system," as Jacques Ellul calls it in describing its characteristics: autonomy, unity, universality, and the summing up. The technical society seems inevitably condemned to a self perpetuating increase of its machines and of its wealth, to a mechanization more and more urged on by the workings of its own machinery, to an unbridled acceleration of the processes of production and of consumption; all set free to proceed on their own, with no goal and no direction other than the profit of the enterprise. Since this is the case with regard to armaments, the machine, originally created to serve man, devotes itself to its own purpose, which is to reproduce endlessly whatever it makes. The machine, whether it is making arms or books, automobiles or preserves, takes such making as its own purpose. This makes part of an economic circuit that cannot be interrupted without increasing the sinister dimensions not only of the particular industries, but of the exploitation of the material world.

In itself, a tool is a tool, whether it be the flint arrowhead or the atomic bomb. In this aspect, it seems exaggerated to assert that the technical system has revolutionized the relation of man with nature, with his labor, with his family, his employer, and his city. In spite of the profound modification of the organization of our several societies, the man of the atomic age and his caveman ancestor resemble each other like two brothers: reading the oldest stories in the Bible, or the literature of the Bronze Age, is enough to convince anyone of that.

What has changed, according to all the evidence, is what results from human activity. A cat and a lion have the same carnivorous instincts, but it is less dangerous to get yourself bitten by a cat than by a lion. The same urge impels the caveman to make a club and the modern technician an atomic bomb, but it is apparent that the consequences of these efforts, identical in purpose, are not at all the same when the tools of death have been made powerful enough to efface all trace of life from the planet. Machines and their products have so proliferated as to change the face of the world. According to the pessimists, they may well annihilate it.

The optimists are more attentive to the positive aspects of technology: man, they perceive, is in our own day infinitely more powerful than all the men who have ever lived since the earliest times, taken all together. While the pessimistic critic sees in all the negative manifestations of the modern world, the after-effects of technological pollution, the optimists emphasize the positive results achieved by science and technology. According to them, paradise is within reach, and it all depends only on us, and on our choice of civilization, to find our paradise once more, and to open up for man, liberated from his prison of time and space, a future of unending progress. While the worshippers of the past see today's societies as dehumanized, enslaved to the demons of the machine, ruled by computers, those sorcerers of our time, whose oracular pronouncements, even in the making of political decisions, tend to take the place of the free exercise of man's judgment, the forward-looking, always without slighting the shadows, joyfully celebrate the present results and the tremendous future possibilities opened to us, from now on, by the technological revolution.

In truth, technology is neither good nor evil: a knife can be used to peel a fruit or to kill a man, a plane to save someone sick or injured, or to destroy a city. Technology can bring life or death, according to the use that is made of it. Instead of pursuing the empty argument between champions of the past and of the future, we must place our emphasis, and concentrate our analytical intellects, on the choice of the civilization that is to dominate our future. For atomic energy, the hunger of the third world, and the risks in which technology has placed us should have, as their principal effect, the opening of our minds and consciences to the crushing responsibility that weighs upon the men of our time, able to save the world or lose it, to open, before us all, the gates of Paradise regained or those of the Apocalypse. For more than three thousand years, the option of Mount Sinai between life and death, between good and evil, between the blessing and the curse, has been understood on the level of personal salvation. This option today is not personal and individual, but global, and, in fact, the survival of humanity depends upon it.

To choose life

To choose life -- this means, today, to opt for utopia. It means to make the utopian view prevail through history; and to reduce, even to nothingness, the zones of darkness still subject to the empire of Death.

My Jewishness, that interior kingdom that I have cherished throughout my wanderings, is but my hope for utopias come true. The Prophets and Apostles of the Bible were right in foretelling a total revolution of

206

society, an absolute changeover of the creation and of man. When I was an adolescent, Marxism charmed me by the precision of its political analyses, and by the generosity of its social ideas. The genius of Marx undoubtedly consisted in his transposing, for an atheistic age, the Biblical dialectic of good and evil, of light and darkness, of God and Satan, into the two dimensions of his analysis of class warfare. The good becomes the proletariat, and the evil, capitalism. Having reduced the scope of the Biblical analysis of reality, he yet kept its messianic fervor. The war between the good and the wicked, the poor and the rich, will reach its climax in the final battle and its millennial culmination, which is a diminished version, on the economic and political scale of the nineteenth century, of the Day of YHWH announced by the Prophets, the day of final changes, whose unbounded effects will reach the entire cosmos. The connection between philosophy and economics that Marx established in 1844, and between history and class warfare, already existed in the dialectic of the Prophets of Israel. The fact that he couched their far-ranging visions in the philosophical language of his time, and dressed them up in a scientific analysis of the economic realities of class warfare, didn't keep him from expressing, in his own way, the messianic ideal of the Bible, which pictures, in the future, that great day when the fall and all its bitter consequences will have been put behind us -- the day of ultimate reconciliations.

The consistent nature of the creative principle of the heavens and the earth, the unnamed God, YHWH, convinced the Prophets that their envisioned utopias would be realized. It is because YHWH <u>is who he is</u> that universal history has a beginning, a direction, and a goal. Despite the cruelty of its unfoldings and backslidings, it is not absurd: it can overwhelm men, and particularly that predestined victim, the poor, but the final victory will nevertheless be won, that of good over evil, of justice over iniquity, of peace over all wars. With open eyes I opt for utopia, even if its realization seems to run smack into a theoretical impossibility. If a miracle means the realization of the impossible, then I believe in the almighty power of the miracle.

The Bible itself is a utopia, living in history, in what it says, in the way it says it, and in its echo, that always resounds in our consciences. The history of the little tribe that wrote it -- writing, from Abraham to Jesus, through some eighteen centuries -- embodies also an apparent impossibility, that of launching the new language of ethical monotheism, which eventually dethroned the idols and the kings of all the cities of antiquity.

Another utopia attained, an impossibility achieved, was the survival of the double genocide that the all-powerful Roman Empire inflicted upon the Hebrews. The first stage of this genocide was the one, lasting through two centuries, from 63 B.C. to 134 A.D., during which the Roman Empire crucified hundreds of thousands of Judeans, in order to leave no memory of Israel and of Jerusalem under the sun. The second stage, a figurative crucifixion, was the utopian survival itself, that took us through two thousand years of patience and suffering, dragging with us, through the misery and humiliation of our exile, the memory of our past grandeur, and the hope of our resurrection. We had to invent hitherto unheard-of techniques, in order to save, not only the seed of our people, but our culture, our faith, our language, and our Scriptures. In doing this, the Hebrew in exile achieved a marvel, a phenomenon unique in human history, passing through the tragedies of two millennia with no weapons but those of faith, hope, and love. The price was only many blows and much spittle in the face, crucifixion on many crosses, and sometimes burning at the stake, or in the crematory ovens of blind inquisitions. What did these things matter? The essential was not to leave the last word to tyranny, not to disappear because the Roman legions had overcome our scattered forces. After all, two thousand years mean little, when a thousand years are as a day in the eyes of eternity.

Baba was one of those heroes of the exile, quixotic in his faith in God and in his saints, and awaiting the realization of the most wild of our utopias, not only our surviving our exile, but returning once more to Jerusalem to rebuild the City of Israel. There, the dream was of full stature, and, in truth, was thought mad even by the boldest of the utopians. The Jews of the exile had none of the materials they needed to oppose the Ottoman Empire, to conquer the British Empire, and to smash the invasion of Arab armies in league against them. All of this was done, however, in time, with patience, and with much blood, courage, and love.

It was necessary also to ensure the rebirth of the Hebrew language. "You don't really expect that, Gentlemen; that has never been done. A man can, in theory at least, be brought back to life, but a dead language, never." And, in fact, Herzl himself died with no faith in the possibility of bringing to life the language and culture of the Hebrews. It is said that one day, in Jerusalem, he met the tubercular teacher, Eliezer Ben Yehudah, who was making a reality of that utopia, building the living language of a new people out of a language that had been dead for some twenty-five centuries. Herzl himself was considered by everyone to be a visionary, because he wanted to create out of nothing a new country for the people of exile; and he looked pityingly upon this poor miserable schoolmaster in a school of the Universal Israelite Alliance, who refused to answer him in German because he had decided to speak only one language, that of his ancestors. But Ben Yehudah's decision was held so firmly, and acted upon so vigorously, that Hebrew has, once again, become the mother-tongue of the children of Israel. An impossibility become reality, utopia become history -- one more time!

Between our desire to return to our own land, to rebuild Jerusalem, to have our city and our nation, and its realization, there lay that infinite distance that separates the dream from the actuality. Herzl, the originator of political Zionism, which was to bring his vision into being, throughout his life was thought a madman by the great ones of this world, and even by his own wife. Up to November 2, 1917, and even up to May 14, 1948, the idea of a Jewish national homeland, and then of a State of Israel, were utopias in which even those who were achieving them couldn't bring themselves to believe. Ben Gurion and the men of his generation, even in their wildest dreams, had never hoped to take part, in their own lives, in the creation of the State of Israel, and in the adventures of the first thirty years of its existence. All in all, these too are realized utopias.

209

Utopian was the arrival of the Jewish exiles,
coming forth under the camera's eye, not now from
Eqypt, like their ancestors under the leadership of
Moses, but from a hundred and two "houses of bondage"
of their Diaspora; utopian was the metamorphosis of
little shop-keepers into warrior-peasants, builders of
towns, conquerors of the desert; utopian was the
birth, out of nothing, of a flourishing agriculture in
a barren land, and of an industry fully competitive in
the world market, and capable of inventing,
manufacturing, and selling everything. In 1948, one
of the principal objections to the creation of the
State of Israel was that the deserts of the Near East
would never be able to sustain their projected
inhabitants: every analysis of the problem wound up
with the same conclusion. Even our own experts who
maintained the opposite opinion, since the political
dispute required it of them, would have been
flabbergasted if they had learned that we would
provide abundant nourishment, thirty years later, for
a population of four or five million inhabitants,
while exporting our fruits, our vegetables, our
flowers, our eggs, and our preserves, to sell on all
the markets of the world, with our rate of increase in
agricultural production the highest in the world. In
this field, our experts are getting ready for the
eighties a number of revolutionary programs that will
push back the frontiers of the impossible, and present
a believable solution to the dramatic problem of
providing an exploding world population with its daily
bread. This is our own special way of praying, and
saying: "Give us this day our daily bread..."

To come together

     To make these utopias come true, we have had to
bring together our wills, forged through two millennia
of exile, and bind them into one, making ourselves
ready to pay the price of our resurrection. This
price has involved much labor and blood, brains and
bravery. But our rebirth has enabled us to redress
some wrongs, without whose correction it would have
been impossible to make our joy complete. For almost
two thousand years, Christianity has looked upon us
as, and has taught that we were, perfidious, deicides,
the assassins of the God tortured and crucified in
Jerusalem under Pontius Pilate. The accusation was
false, and the Christians didn't know that because
they were ignorant of the history of Israel, of our

unfriendly relations with the Roman Empire at the time
Jesus was arrested, summarily judged, and crucified --
because, as a Jew, he constituted a threat to the
public order, the colonial order of an idolatrous
empire that had reduced our people to slavery. A just
man, whom his disciples worshiped as a God, had been
shamefully executed in his capital, occupied by the
Romans. No one can ever tell what have been our
sufferings from the cross, dragged on our shoulders
through nearly twenty centuries. We know that we did
not kill Jesus, and that, in any case, it is insane to
claim that we must be held responsible for that crime
on account of heredity. And we thought we would never
be able to escape from that situation. Think of it!
the Fathers of the Church, the Doctors, the Saints,
the Councils, catechisms and priests and even, it was
believed, the Gospels, condemned "the Synagogue of the
Devil." Even we, who had developed the habit of
believing in utopias, could only with difficulty
imagine ourselves unfastened from the cross to which
we had been nailed for almost two millennia! But
since we were the people of all the utopias, even this
one had to come true: Christians, seeing us all being
crucified by Hitler, took it upon themselves to have
pity upon us, to recognize us as brothers, to console
us and to love us. They then perceived that they
themselves were not entirely without blame for our
Calvary, that they had firmly driven in the nails for
our feet and hands, to immobilize us on our Jewish
cross, as witnesses to the triumph of the Church and
our own perfidy. They thought that they might perhaps
have been wrong, and not understood the true history
of Jesus. In any case, they were ashamed to find
themselves torturing the same body as Hitler. They
released their Jewish prey, stopped speaking of our
"perfidy" in their prayers, and purged their
catechisms of the insults to us that they contained --
not of all of them, as yet, but at last they are
working on it. They have corrected their theological
aim -- the good Pope John XXIII smiled at us and
embraced us, saying to us: "I am Joseph, your
brother!" That was very gratifying. It is indeed
pleasant to be reconciled with one's brothers. After
that, the Council was convened to listen with wonder
to the news that the Jews also were men, that it was
no longer necessary to hurl insults at them, and that
it was even allowed to love them, since, after all,
Jesus also was a Jew, as were his mother, his
Apostles, and his first followers. It follows, then,

211

doesn't it, that these gentlemen, members of the family, could not forever be excluded from the glowing warmth of Christian charity? Vatican II reversed, bravely and radically, centuries of prejudice: this also was, for us, utopia come true, a dream become a part of history.

Then we set ourselves to dreaming all the more vigorously. We thought, if Christians and Jews can be reconciled after a conflict lasting two thousand years, then, truly, we may hope for anything, even to see the wolf and the lamb living together in peace, shepherded by a little child. We find that we must now recognize Jesus as our brother; our historians have reunited the story of his Passion with the passions of our history, and our Biblical scholars have set themselves to study, explain, and translate the Gospels, the Acts, the Epistles, and the Apocalypse, recognizing in them writings of our own tribe, and understanding that the New Testament is not so new as all that, since it says nothing other than what is said in our own Bible. Since we have begun to look one another right in the eyes, without lowering our eyes in shame or in fear, I've told myself that we might be able to get together, to fight, and win, one first but decisive battle, that of faith in God -- for man, for his survival, for his future.

The moment we were reconciled, we were faced with an inescapable dilemma -- in Hamlet's phrase, "to be or not to be." And mankind will be, or will not be. Between the two alternatives lies an infinite chaos, which we all have the power to let loose or to forestall. The stakes are life and death. Should life be the loser in this game, there is a great risk that there may be no one left, at the end of the race, to take note of the result. Since we are the children of Abraham, and since we opt resolutely for life against death, for peace against war, and for love against hate, there must inevitably come for us a day on which we will have to join forces, putting together all that we have, so as not to lose, along with our honor as men, life, peace, and love. Together, we have the power to save the world, since, together, we are both the roots and the tree itself. A tree is nothing without its roots. The roots cannot live without a tree to feed. Together, we can contribute to saving the world from the abyss into which it threatens to dash itself. Jews or Christians, we are committed, and we will be judged, condemned or acquitted, according to whether we win or lose the war we must wage against hate, against war itself, and against hunger, in order to save the world -- really to save it, not just in the drivel of our catechisms and our sermons. If we are not bound to stand fast, and win the wager of life, then nothing will have made sense. All of us together, Jews and Christians, will have been the victims of a monstrous hallucination. Death will be right, in its war against life, and war will be licensed to destroy all peace that is not the peace of nothingness. Moloch will be the conqueror over the God of life in the collapse of the order of creation into the nothingness of the atomic hell. Israel will have had no meaning, nor the Church either, nor socialism/communism, in the overwhelming onrush of universal chaos.

While things are coming into some sort of order in our relations with the Christians, they are completely out of kilter with regard to the Arabs. After centuries of relative peace in our relations -- most of the time without any serious problems, and sometimes even cordial and fruitful -- we find ourselves plunged into a conflict that everyone, with hardly any exceptions, considers insoluble. Four wars, thousands of dead, destruction counted in the billions of dollars, the propaganda wall of hatred, the complete shut-off of communication between the two camps, terrorism unleashed, total incomprehension on each side of the thinking and the reactions on the other -- all this has been aggravated by an international context in which the most powerful interests choose sides in the dispute for the sake of their own selfish advantages.

To conquer death

Despite the very real difficulties that stand in the way of peace, I am determined to hope against all hope. I have been insisting on certain aspects of the history of my people because they never cease to astound me, and to be for me a source of inspiration and hope. If we had the illusion of being a distinct people while we were in the blind alley of our ghettos, now that we have built up our State we recognize ourselves as we are, men, with all the lights and darknesses or humanity, faced with apparently insoluble problems. In many respects, our life is the opposite of what we dreamed it would be during our exile. It is enough to read our daily papers to discover the same impressive list of the crimes of Israel as that set forth and condemned by the Prophets of the Bible: we have our thieves, our swindlers, our drug addicts and drug dealers, our counterfeiters and forgers, and our rapists. Our statesmen are neither more intelligent nor more mediocre than anywhere else; their good intentions are often hampered by their lack of knowledge or of initiative. Their congenital distrusts are explained by the bloody memories of our exiles, and, with regard to the Arabs, by an abysmal ignorance of Arab history, culture, customs, and psychology. I have had the opportunity to observe them first-hand while I was adviser to David Ben Gurion, then when I was Deputy Mayor of Jerusalem, and still more closely during the first two months of the year 1978, when the government and the political parties almost unanimously wished to make me President of the State of Israel. I have always refused the political career into which for more than twenty-five years some of my friends have tried to push me. I see too clearly the limitations and frustrations that the exercise of a public function imposes upon an official, and the minimal nature of real power that he wields, even in the highest offices. My calling is writing -- each of my books is like a bottle flung into the sea. Occasionally it happens that the message is picked up and understood, and that some action results from it. This is what I hope for, in publishing this confession of what I am and of what I believe.

My love of life makes me suffer agonies at the spectacle I must watch, wherever I turn my eyes. The whole order of creation is threatened by our build-up of hostile tensions. Men have found the means of endowing mankind with the weapons needed for a planetary suicide. The Shakespearian question, to be or not to be, for the first time in history, is not a dilemma facing Hamlet alone, but set before all humanity, apparently being dragged by irresistible forces toward the pit of Sheol. The chances of life are perceptibly lighter in the balance, weighed against the formidable powers of death held by the armies and governments subservient to the structures and the contradictions imposed by ruling groups and by economic systems. The capitalistic idealogy is killing itself through its rivalries, and through its

214

inability to resolve, on a world scale, the most important of the problems that affect the future of the planet. The communist regimes are disfigured by the absolutism of the bureaucracies that rule them, taking their inspiration from an elementary caricature of Marxism that Marx himself would be the first to denounce.

The religions seem to me hidebound, powerless, and disfigured by the gulf that separates the ideals they proclaim from their actual deeds. They are fragments of a chain whose two ends have been lost; all of them seem to me to have lost both the understanding of their origins and the sense of the requirements of their ultimate goals. The Church is killing itself with its schisms and its inconsistencies, in a world in which the Greco-Latin culture has collapsed. Islam, equally the prisoner of its past, is suffering the consequences of conquest and colonial rule. It is awaiting the time when its new religious and political elite may finally reach influential positions. The Judaism of the exile seems anachronistic now that the State of Israel has been formed. It perpetuates an ideology and a set of rituals and practices that were necessary to the Jews in our exile. The vast majority of the Jews, especially among the Israeli youth, suffer from the inadequacy of the religious ideologies, whether orthodox, conservative, or liberal, in dealing with the current situation and the crying needs of a people that is dying of spiritual hunger.

Judaism has defined itself through two thousand years within the closed framework of the ghettos. The return has meant the breaking down of the walls that formed that framework. The exiles, atavistic minority groups clustered in their closed cells, where they devoted their substance to preparing the way for the hoped-for redemption, found themselves suddenly masters of their own destiny in their free and sovereign land. Undoubtedly, the coat of exile was too tight at the arm-holes -- the body had grown so much that the old suit didn't fit at all. The orthodox extremists who followed Mea Shearim understood this so well that they enclosed themselves in their quarter, still dressing as their ancestors did in Russia or in Poland in the sixteenth century: a cloak and a big fur cap, a flowing beard and long locks of hair dangling at their temples.

Other religious groups pale beside these wild enthusiasts of prayer. Similarly enclosed within the traditions of the exile, they live without taking note of the new dimensions of the universe, of the land, and of their people. Everywhere, the grey monotone of ritual has replaced the incandescence of religious rites, and the platitudes of sermons have usurped the place of the fires of prophecy. A fundamentalist reading of Judaism, as much as a modernist laicism or nationalist fervor, sometimes borders on racism. By perpetuating itself, it undermines the foundations and enfeebles the fertility of our national resurrection.

Too many sufferings, too many dangers weigh us down, and, through too many centuries, too much Messianic hope has buoyed us up, for us to give up now, and not proclaim in Jerusalem a new Passover of the peoples.

Twice, before now, calls for the saving of the world have resounded in that city. The Prophets, during all the royal period, called upon their people and upon the nations of the world to renounce war, injustice, and hatred. Their appeal was answered by the Assyrians, who overthrew the Kingdom of Israel, and by the Babylonians, who crushed the Kingdom of Judea and carried off the survivors. The same appeal, issuing from the same source, resounded six centuries later, in the voices of Jesus and his Apostles. This time, it was addressed to the Roman Empire. Titus replied by razing Jerusalem to its foundations, slaughtering hundreds of thousands of Judeans, and deporting the survivors of this almost complete genocide.

Do we know how to listen, today, to the same voice, that now calls with greater urgency to a world threatened with death from the poisons it is secreting? Today, the catastrophe to be avoided is more terrible. Compared to it, the Apocalypses described long ago by the visionaries of Israel seem like old wives' tales. The technocrats have succeeded in bringing down the thunderbolt upon the earth, which now it threatens to destroy. Everything has been made ready for the suicide of the end of the world, in which we are all accomplices, letting our countries use our services and our resources to perfect its horror.

The appeal has ceased to have a transient value; it has become an absolute imperative, essentially political, and, in fact, it governs the survival of the human race, as everyone can plainly see. The dilemma faced by Moses on Sinai thirty-three centuries ago bursts upon our consciousness today. No longer is it a pious wish, a beautiful philosophical or religious aspiration. It rises up before mankind with the countenance of fate, and, probably, of misfortune: there stand before us a blessing, and life, or a curse, and death.

"Choose life," ordered Moses, "that you may live." The issue depends solely upon our choice, and our choice must have no other motive, no other goal, than life, threatened in its very sources by our nuclear and biological weapons. This will mean the final extinction of life on earth, or, if we escape that by choosing life, an infinite future of grandeur and glory for humanity.

Man has barely emerged from his prehistoric state. He spent millions of years before mastering fire and the wheel. In 1945, his scientific knowledge, accumulated since his origins, amounted to ten percent of what we know today -- that is to say, ninety percent of the discoveries of science have been made since the end of World War II. Hundreds of thousands of scientists, a greater number than have existed from man's beginnings up to now, are doubling the acquisition of scientific knowledge, in all fields including that of war, every four years. We are thus entering, walking backwards, an unpredictable future, in which each one of us becomes, from day to day, more ignorant, in the midst of a world that wields more and more prodigious powers -- chief among them the power either to wipe out life entirely, or to conquer death.

The call from Jerusalem

The destiny of Jerusalem is, at the same time, peculiarly our own, and also that of the whole world, that of the universal Jerusalem to which are linked all those who have drunk at its springs. The call that it sends forth, for the third time in its four-thousand-year history, is no longer addressed to the pagan hordes of Assurbanipal, of Nebuchadnezzar or of Titus; it is addressed in the first instance to the Jews educated by more than three thousand years of the religious tradition of Moses, to the Christians who for two thousand years have been teaching and studying the message of love and of justice given by Jesus and his Apostles, and to the Moslems who for thirteen centuries have been worshipping the God of Abraham, accepting and spreading his law of life. The peoples of the Far East and of Africa, and the great post-Christian masses of the West, are likewise obsessed by ideals of justice and peace. No longer does anyone teach that man must be a wolf to man, or that war is a good. Everyone, even among those devoid of religion, spirituality, or any ideology, is aware of the prodigious dangers inherent in the present political and military situation. Will the appeal be heard by those very people who profess to believe in it, and who present themselves as its witnesses, its spokesmen, and its missionaries? No world-saving plan, no political speechmaking, even were it uttered before the Assembly of the United Nations by the most powerful of political figures, would have any effect without a great uprising of world consciousness, without a veritable revolt of the masses that are being shoved toward the slaughterhouse.

Despite many piteous cries denouncing the great sewer into which we are being herded, the destined victims of the great massacres that are being prepared are powerless to make their voices heard. The vague plaints and protestations rising here and there are directed only toward secondary phenomena, such as the placing of a new atomic power station, or the method of disposing of atomic wastes. But the essential matters -- the arms race, world hunger, and the technological cancer, rouse no protests. People resign themselves to their inevitability, each of us being conscious of his inability to exorcise their threats. And, indeed, it is not with soft words and pious speeches that we will bring about the revolution that will force the nations to reverse their policies in these three fields, which, among them, engage the whole of their activities and almost all of their investments. The workers of death cannot fail to hear my voice; they will be forced to give way before the clamor of the four billion men whom their industry puts in peril of death.

One narrow way, however, still remains open, that could in fact turn back the present course of world politics, and, swiftly attacking the death and war that are triumphing today, provide a last chance for peace, and for life. Strategically, it is necessary to create a political force that can effectively oppose the will of the nations and make them yield in all that concerns military spending, aid to the Third World, and the harm done by the technological cancer. Such a force, without which all the good arguments and all the good will in the world would be worthless, does not now exist; tragically, the nations are prey to their own fears, and enmeshed in the workings of their economic predestination and their unpardonable politics. The force necessary to divert universal history to a different path must rely upon the will of the peoples, be endowed with tremendous and efficacious tools, and come to birth in a very brief time, before the cataclysm that is impending has had time to destroy everything.

It seems to me that all these conditions could be fulfilled if the Arabs and the Israelis were to reach an accord in Jerusalem, projected capital of the United States of the Near East, and at once the earliest source and the ultimate destination of the forces of peace and justice. It demands no wild imagination to envision what an alteration our reconciliation would bring about in the current disarray of the world. In an earlier chapter I sketched briefly what might be the main lines for a peace settlement between the Arab nations and the State of Israel. Nobody denies, nowadays, that such a settlement might be possible -- it is explicitly desired on both sides, and although, since the arrival of Sadat in Jerusalem, there have been bitter disputes about the price to be paid, no one says that the discussions won't end in a compromise of a federalist kind, acceptable to both Arabs and Israelis.

A new world equilibrium would be born as soon as an accord was reached in Jerusalem. One of the principal markets for the purchase of arms would incline to diminish its military expenditures, and to invest its wealth in the works of peace, which, in one or two generations, would transform the Near East into a center of world civilization, returning it to its vocation as the meeting-place of East and West, at whose crossroads it is placed.

Around the United States of the Near East there would flow, from the very fact of their reconciliation, a political, economic, and moral influence strong enough to make itself felt by any nation whatever. This influence would affect politically the Arab States, the State of Israel, and their friends, especially those of Asia, Africa, and Latin America. In the United Nations, this bloc would swing the votes of a great majority of its 149 members. It would enlist the support of all the small nations of the world, and of many not so small, today held in the silence of impotence on the shores of the Mediterranean, in Latin America, in Africa, and in the Far East.

This gigantic political alliance would be supported by a formidable economic and even military power. Militarily, the arsenals of the Near East today possess one of the most powerful concentrations of arms in the world. Economically, as soon as the alliance was formed, it would have at its disposal the oil and the capital of the Arab states, and the technical power of Israel, and the wealth and power of their friends dispersed throughout the globe, including Soviet Russia. It would be difficult for any government in the world not to take into account the wishes of such a power, which would have, moreover, the support of public opinion everywhere. The spiritual powers, the Churches, which have neither arms to sell nor oil to purchase, would abandon their present cautious reserve to inspire and sustain this third force in its crusade for the preservation of the world.

Those who have been hoping, through the ages, to save the world, and to be the light of the nations, but who have neither saved nor lighted anything, would at last have the opportunity to put their talents to the test other than in the blind alleys of churches, mosques, synagogues, or political meetings. The four hundred thousand or so experts who busy themselves today in perfecting the instruments of death would have as their task, with the aid of hundreds of thousands of specialists in other, more peaceful, disciplines, the job of untangling the inextricable problems of disarmament and of reconversion, with far more serious intent than is displayed in the United Nations debates, or in the grotesque commissions that go by the name of disarmament. Once this major problem was on its way toward a gradual resolution, thanks to the effective will of the third force and the support of public opinion, it would be possible to face, otherwise than just in words, the dramatic realities of world hunger. The third world now receives from the rich nations twenty-eight and a half billion dollars a year, or a fortieth of the annual expenditures of the nations for arms. The problems connected with developing the poorer countries, and reducing the imbalances now prevailing in the world, are at least as complex, inextricable, and apparently insoluble as those of disarmament. The same is true with regard to the efforts now being devoted to the task of enslaving us to technology; efforts which must now be turned toward making technology render real service to peace and the well-being of mankind.

These are colossal enterprises, veritable revolutions involving bringing to the bar of judgment the basic principles of societies and nations, and completely changing the reactions and global relationships of society. This is a crusade that has but a faint chance of success -- and not even that if it does not become the crusade of a central political power, with the nearly unanimous support of the active movers of our societies.

Pessimists, foreseeing the disappearance of the human species within the next fifty years, or perhaps the next hundred, shrug their shoulders when faced with the prospects I have just sketched. They choose the side of despair all the more confidently since they are relying on indisputable facts in thinking that the mad world in which we live deserves, and has earned a hundred times over, the sentence of death that hangs over it. They are quite right, too, in viewing as utopian any program that aims to realize in one generation, and under the worst possible conditions, a revolution that has been vainly hoped for through thousands of years.

Utopian, yes, I admit that, but aren't we living in the century of the realization of the wildest of utopias? Weren't the everyday realities of the world we're living in now considered as utopias through thousands of past years? And now that our planet hangs on the brink of a cataclysm that threatens to blow it to pieces, aren't we going to find the simple courage to assert the rights of life against the

impending cosmic abortion?   There is a way out of our
predicament.   It will be enough if we have hope --
enough for humanity to win that ultimate victory
announced by the Prophets, and to conquer death.   Wish
it, and that will be enough.   It will no longer be a
dream.

Utopia will come to pass

The Bible is open on my table.   Despite war and
rumors of war, behold, my ghosts have vanished away!
The Hebrew letters of the texts I am reading, like
pure flames rising from earth to heaven through the
wild conflagration of my illuminations -- these
letters of the Bible fasten me to the rock of my joy.
Whenever their fire lights up my night, it is as
though I were raised again from among the dead.   To
open my Bible, to read those words that speak to me,
letter after letter, like a murmur from the mouth of
God, brings me back to the immanence of reality.   I
think of the Angel of Isaiah, of the burning coal that
seared the lips of the Prophet, of that fire, of that
blood, and of that solemn undertaking.   Yes, all the
ghosts have fled, the men, the fear, society, death.
In my forgetfulness of self, there rises up the cry of
my joy, the fantastic dance of the fullness of my
love.

The truth of my being is love.   More violent than
the clutch of the world, more compelling and firm than
a rock, it is love that lives and cries out in me.   It
is the calling out of my very being.   I love.

It is in prayer that this love flows out most
freely, wildly, in the abandon of a being that
consents to its surrender, reached after a war of self
against self, through fire and blood.   In my night,
all is at peace.   A damp breeze flows around me, but
my body is still feeling the warmth of my swim in the
azure of the sea.   It is absolutely necessary that the
whole world be held, and perhaps some day submerged,
in the tide of love.   Each prayer crumbles away a bit
of the rock of matter, reduces it to sand and scatters
it.   A day will come -- if we will it, absolutely and
in truth -- a day will come, inevitably and
necessarily, ordained from all eternity, when love
will flow in over all reality, will lift up and carry
away all reality.   Then will the world be drowned in

light, and swallowed up in light, as the sea is swallowed up in the waters. This is a day of YHWH, the Day of YHWH.

"Who is YHWH?"

"Let us say that He is Love. It is a day for Love, the Day of Love. Give him the name of your greatest love, and you will be close to the truth."

Draw tight the meshes of prayer, strengthen the fabric of love, bind yourself to a discipline, and, in the adversities of war, learn to know yourself and to live as a brother among brothers. To write is good, if the motive and goal of the writing is the exaltation of love and its fulfilment. There is no excuse, in the realm of reason, for love to be eternally defeated by the world. It is the name of love that must be cried out and loudly proclaimed, and it is love alone that must absolutely and necessarily be victorious, since it is the origin, the sole reason, and the final end of the world.

There remains some fear that it might seem utopian to envisage a way of escape from the great massacres that are being made ready. In the conferences in which the nations talk about disarmament, precise and plausible proposals are laid out: prevent the arrival on the scene of new nuclear powers; proceed with negotiations for the prohibition of weapons of massive destruction other than nuclear; hold back the production of the classic weapons, and then reconvert the means of production; broaden and strengthen the regional arms control agreements; reinforce the institutions dedicated to the control of armaments; and devote to the development of the third world the funds saved by the reduction of armaments. The intentions paraded by the heads of state are brutally contradicted by the facts. Every year the expenditures for armaments increase in absolute value and in percentage of the gross national product of the nations, while the dollar, with the progress of the techniques of death, becomes every year more murderous.

In fact, war determines the prosperity of the economy, and the arms market may affect the very survival of governments. Many economists and eminent politicians maintain that war, and war alone, fulfills

223

a Malthusian function indispensable for the proper working of society. No longer need we choose, as a half century ago: "Guns or butter!" The manufacture of the bomb, and its economic consequences, are what will guarantee the consumption of butter. Instead of our having to choose between them, it is the combination that has become obligatory. These truths account for the hypocrisy and impotence of the politicians who preach disarmament, while only a thriving arms market keeps them, them and their government, in place.

It's easy to see that a thorough economic revolution must come before any efficacious political move toward disarmament. But this itself would seem to be utopian so long as public opinion blinds itself to the real dangers of the coming war. No effective disarmament will come about without an economic revolution that will permit a profound change in the relations between the well-provided nations and the poor countries. But only a reawakening of the masses condemned by the dreary realities of the modern world could give the impetus necessary for a repudiation of our present inconsistencies, and for an effective search for new directions, capable of creating the conditions needed for the survival and building up of a new man and a new world.

Without a political force that will seize upon the idea in order to make it a real historical fact, peace will remain a dream, to be wiped out by the explosion of the first bomb in our arsenals. But this political force can come into being and work effectively in the hoped-for directions only if it is supported by a spiritual authority devoted to the achievement of the final ends of humanity. This new force could be born in a universal spring forward, despite our unwillingness to renounce the weight of our national and denominational conformisms, and devote ourselves to the building of a new world. We must, in fact, continue to feed upon that past in which our roots are buried, but never give way to the temptation of triumphalism. In a way, the atheists are right to reject the incredible divinity offered to them by theologies still imprisoned in their medieval ghettos, in the language incredibly archaic, feeble, and inadequate of men who are talking of and to a God whom they evidently don't know at all. Their basic error undoubtedly consists in their naming the Unnamable, trying to pin a label on the Ineffable, to reduce to a series of concepts the mystery of being and of life. don't these theologians know that the principle that can be stated is not the principle that has existed forever; that the being that can be named is not the being that always was? There is wisdom in the Bible, where the ineffable God designates himself by the strict tetragram, like a mathematical formula, made up of four unpronounceable consonants, Y H W H. There is wisdom in the Bible that commands: "<u>Thou shalt not take the name of YHWH, thy Lord, in vain</u>."* Isn't this a commandment that only the atheists have had the wisdom to take seriously, they who have the modesty never to speak to him? The faithful continually violate this commandment by speaking very often and indiscriminately about that God whom they have made, by the futility of their babblings, incredible for the great majority of the human race. Unnamed, Ineffable YHWH is Being and Life, he who was, is, and will be; the flowing spring of all creation and of all life, the maker and the womb of reality. What the womb does for the fetus that it receives and vivifies, he does for the whole universe. He enfolds it in its entirety, and in the least of its details. He knows but one value, that of life, and recognizes but one sole enemy, death, with all its pollutions, all its abortions.

It has taken doctors and biologists centuries to discover the oneness of reality, to find out that there is a single principle underlying all manifestations of being and of life. Some among them, paradoxically, have made this a basis for teaching that God doesn't exist. It is A.D.N. that exists, as an effect of pure chance, they say, not God. Poor innocents, who adore YHWH behind their test tubes and microscopes, without being aware of it, as yesterday the sorcerers did behind their fetishes. They say over again in their own language, less accessible, less clear, and surely less beautiful, what the Bible has never ceased to teach us through three thousand years. A.D.N., source of all life: strangely, one of the names of the God of the Bible is correctly written in Hebrew with these three consonants, A.D.N. YHWH is ADN, Adonai, the source and master of all life.

---

*Exodus 20:1.AC

Biologists need not know Hebrew. If they did know it, perhaps they would hesitate to teach so casually that God, the Adonai of all life, doesn't exist.

But, to tell the truth, the problem isn't finding out whether "God" exists or not, nor to choose in what church, synagogue, mosque, or Communist cell he must be worshipped or fought. We are, all of us, embarked on a drunken ship, that of the world, that is in danger of being engulfed along with all of us in the shipwreck toward which the enemies of life are rushing us. Without us men, God, source and creator of all being, of all life, would be powerless to prevent the planetary suicide that the nations, in complicity with death, are preparing. Yes, God needs all of us to save the world.

The revolution must be world-wide, since the danger of death hangs over all of us, though a right of primogeniture in the revolutionary work can be claimed by the heirs of Abraham. Jews, Christians, Moslems -- we must all let the masks fall from our faces, and the dust and plaster from our dwellings, to let in the new light of the great day of our reconciliation and of our salvation. We have an examination of conscience to make, in order to purify ourselves before bathing again in the wellsprings of truth. Let no theologies or liturgies keep us from seeing one another face to face, without masks and without pretense; and, together, to go forward toward the sole end worthy of our ambitions, the salvation of mankind. A new covenant must bind us to one another, all men of good will on the earth, for the world-wide defense of life against all wars, all hungers, all pollutions. Against the technico-industrial covenant, upon which the nations have tacitly agreed for the blind and selfish exploitation of the material resources of the planet, we must forcefully oppose the powers that our spiritual union will unleash. Our combined strength is the only power that can make the nations disarm, and force men to give up their luxuries in order to provide necessities for those who have nothing. We alone can turn toward good those prodigious energies that technology has made available. In themselves, they are neither good nor evil, and if their harmful effects are obvious, this comes, in the first instance, from our absence, our failure. There is no spiritual authority in the world strong enough to make itself heard, and to furnish an axle for the wheels of this drunken universe, in their disorganized and murderous whirling.

The first thing we must do, therefore, is to come out of our respective ghettos in order to meet one another, to open ourselves to one another, to understand one another and to unite our wills, turned at last toward the final goals of our new covenant. Our ambitions must not be less than those of our Prophets and our Apostles. What we wish for we must also achieve: the end of wars between nations, churches, races, classes, and kinds. Our revolutionary spirit must include the highest social aspirations of Marx, Lenin, and Mao Tse-tung, and surpass them through our forceful determination to form a new earth, new heavens, and a new man.

We must assist at the birth of a new world, which must be born, and must be built. Let us be sure of this: our only enemy is death -- and death is, like the pollutions of which it is the source, a reality only in the mind. We must fight to bring down its empire to nothingness. For, grave as are the dangers that threaten us, they are overbalanced by opportunities for life and creation higher than ever before opened before mankind.

These ideas are chimerical only for the short-sighted, who always reject anything beyond the scope of their imaginations. The reconciliation of the peoples of the Near East, brought together in Jerusalem, would make possible the creation of a center around which there could be formed a fruitful union, bringing life and peace. A new hope, that of the small and the humble, proclaiming a new prophecy, would be born of our reconciliation. Utopia must finally come to pass. Upon our forward surge, upon our selflessness, upon our union, upon our enlightment, depend its future, and our own.

Yes, if we wish it, it will not be a dream.

EPILOGUE

FOR THE AMERICAN EDITION, 1984

FOR THE AMERICAN EDITION, 1984

"Utopia will come to pass," I wrote in 1978 near
the end of the French edition of this book. Judging
by the present world situation, this promise would
indeed seem to be a dead letter. The arms race is
continuing at an ever-increasing speed. Though the
atomic bomb may not yet be within the means of all,
yet the arsenals of the world now hold more than forty
thousand of them, representing a destructive power
equivalent to some two million times that of the bomb
that destroyed Hiroshima. The annual expenditures for
new armaments have increased from four hundred
trillion dollars in 1977 to more than double that
number in 1984. We are approaching a thousand
trillions!

In all kinds of arms -- conventional, chemical,
biological, and nuclear -- technical progress
multiplies each day the destructive power obtained at
the same monetary cost.

Not a day passes that some voice is not raised to
warn the people of the world of the dangers that
threaten us -- all too truly, alas, but ineffectively.
Most of the nations of the world (including the State
of Israel, which, sadly, cannot afford to be more
finicky than the others) have become arms merchants,
whose wares range from the simplest to the most
sophisticated. There is no lack of testing grounds:
Afghanistan, Iraq and Iran, Latin America, the Near
East. This last region remains as sensitive as a
neuralgic nerve, its painfulness increasing with the
successive invasions of Lebanon by the Palestinians,
then the Syrians, and then the Israelis. Every day
blood flows on all the battle fronts of the world;
every day there are terrible massacres. And all this
time a greater and greater proportion of the world's
population is suffering the pangs of hunger, even to
starvation. National economies are in crisis, and
unemployment is rife even in the best organized and
the richest societies.

The technological challenge grows each day.
Moreover, nowhere is there a mind prepared to
comprehend its gravity, nor yet to foresee future
developments. We are, as I have said, walking

230

backwards into the future. It will depend upon our wisdom, or upon our folly, whether that future is one of life or of death, of love or of hate.

* * *

For, in the last analysis, it is man alone who is in question. It is he who makes of this planet a hell or a paradise. To the question: "God, what was he doing at Auschwitz?" it is appropriate to reply by another question: "Man, what is he doing in all the charnel houses of the world, both those that are closing down and those that are about to open?" An equally sad question, but turned in another direction.

Or, to put it another way: if, tomorrow, the Messiah were to accomplish all that is prophesied in the Bible; if, really, all the weapons in the world were transformed into plows, wouldn't men, always the same, surely hasten to retransform those plows into weapons, while still beating one another with clubs, until they could once more supply themselves with cannons and bombs?

* * *

A Son of Abraham, that is what I have been all my life long, and most particularly during these decades in the course of which I have, as in an ecstasy, been tirelessly translating the Bible, and writing commentaries on it. The Hebrew characters that I drew laboriously at the age of five to complete the Torah that Rabbi Shelomoh Amar had beautifully transcribed on parchment, as commissioned by Baba, still burn in my spirit and move in a dance of fire. In my native Algeria, the Bible marked the times and seasons, organizing their rhythms: each day, each week, each year. In the West, I have been able to learn in the universities the grammar of the Biblical language. But it is in the East, in Jerusalem, that I have received its keys to life and to peace.

The few Hebrew letters that I inscribed in the Torah of Baba have developed into the seventeen million words since printed in the ten volumes of my Univers de la Bible. The dream of my infancy has become the reality of my maturity. But, from the one to the other, throughout my life, one sole problem has challenged me, agonizingly -- the problem of fathoming the mystery of man.

And it is because I live immersed in this mystery that I do not despair of the future. Despite the forty thousand atomic bombs that threaten to blast out enough of a hole to entomb our planet; despite the hunger and thirst of my brother men; despite their blindness of their folly; despite their violence of their hate -- I keep on hoping.

* * *

If I must assign a motive to this act of faith, I may find reasons in two voyages that I have made recently to that North Africa in which I was born.

The first of these took me, a few months ago, into Algeria. I wanted to see once more the land where I was born, and to show its splendors to one of my sons, before his marriage. It had been more than twenty years since I had seen Aïn-Témouchent. Since I had established my residence in Israel, I had hardly any chance of reëntering that that country whose officials had aligned it with Israel's enemies. But it seemed to me that the time had come for me to go "back home."

I broached this subject to some Algerian friends, one of whom was married to an Israeli woman. Those in authority in Algeria welcomed my proposal sympathetically, and I was thus able to go into the house where I was born, opening the door with the very key my father had given me when I was ten years old, the lock being still unchanged. The occupants of my home, Moslems, welcomed me as warmly as though I were still the proprietor. They had never forgotten the Chouraqui family, were still emotionally moved by our departure, and still more so by my unexpected arrival.

Nearly forty years of anti-Zionist propaganda had failed to weaken the bonds that used to unite Jews and Moslems in that town. In the eyes of my neighbors (who had taken over everything that had belonged to us; nothing but the key remaining in my possession) I was still ould el bled, a native son. It was evident that tomorrow fruitful relationships can be established between us, transcending our political

232

differences. But to those political differences we must indeed find solutions.

* * *

Still more meaningful was my second, and very recent, voyage -- this time to Morocco. On the thirteenth and fourteenth of May, 1984, the Council of the Moroccan Jewish Community held its annual assizes at Rabat. But this event took on an importance far beyond anything that might have been expected to it. A delegation of about forty Israelis -- university professors, parliamentarians and journalists -- was officially received by the national authorities, together with outstanding representatives of Judaism, American, French, Romanian, etc. It was, in effect, a Jewish summit, welcomed by the government of one of the largest and most stable of the Arab nations.

The invitation that the king had extended to me in March, 1977,* was the opening move in the historic process that was to culminate in the Camp David accords. The much larger, and much more open, conference of May, 1984, in Rabat -- will it, perhaps, signal the beginning of a diplomatic process that may bring about the establishment of peace among Israel, Lebanon, and Jordan, thanks to the solving of the very real Palestinian problem? Morocco, through its position as mediator, could well bring about the resumption of negotiations leading toward peace for the Near East.

A plan that might bear fruit would be the creation of an alliance of the children of Abraham: Jews, Christians, and Moslems. These should be brought together for the purpose of making the Abrahamic ideals of justice and peace prevail over the whole earth. Confronted by the national and religious fanaticisms that rage in so many quarters of the earth, the men of peace feel the imperious need to draw together, to bring into a common understanding, if not their conceptions of God, of the world, and of man, at least their needs, their hopes, and also their fears, as they face the all too obvious dangers that loom over us all.

----

*See page 185.

233

Some world assemblies have been tried, such as those that organized the World Conference for Religion and Peace in Tokyo, in New Delhi, in Princeton, and most recently in Nairobi. Men of peace of all the spiritual and geographic varieties to be found on this planet thus brought together their prayers and their efforts to help bring about the birth of a universe delivered from the nightmares of war, of famine, and of hate.

Between the East and the West, we, the children of Abraham, Jews, Christians, and Moslems, constitute a coalition having a spiritual and cultural identity defined by the Hebrew Bible, the New Testament, and the Koran. These books proclaim the same ideals of justice, of peace, and of love. The union of these peoples would constitute an irresistible force if it directed itself toward the realization of the essential Biblical ideal: a new man, living in a universe at last pacified and brotherly.

Jerusalem has, from this perspective, the call to become the seat of a World Parliament of Religions and Cultures, whose object would be to facilitate the relations among men, nations, cultures, and religions, henceforth directed toward the realization of the final ends of humanity.

Everything is ready. The utopia of a victory of life over death can come to pass. The apocalypse has foretold it; death and hell will themselves be thrown into a lake of fire, to perish there, while there will come forth upon earth a new man, under new skies. It is the fitting task of the children of Abraham to hasten the hour of this ultimate deliverance.

André Chouraqui
May 25, 1984